ROGER FEDERER
AND
RAFAEL NADAL

ROGER FEDERER AND RAFAEL NADAL

THE LIVES AND CAREERS OF TWO TENNIS LEGENDS

SEBASTIÁN FEST

TRANSLATED BY
DON McGINNIS AND ZEBBIE WATSON

Skyhorse Publishing

10 9 8 7 6 5 4

Library of Congress Cataloging-in-Publication Data is available on file.

Cover design by Tom Lau
Cover photo credit: AP Images

Print ISBN: 978-1-5107-3071-7
Ebook ISBN: 978-1-5107-3072-4

Printed in the United States of America

To Spain and the Spanish,
who treated me so well.

Contents

Prologue		ix
Chapter 1:	**Towels**	1
Chapter 2:	**Geniuses**	5
Chapter 3:	**Party**	8
Chapter 4:	**Youth**	11
Chapter 5:	**Mystical**	20
Chapter 6:	**Sympathy**	25
Chapter 7:	**Peace and Love**	28
Chapter 8:	**Hurricane**	43
Chapter 9:	**Madrid**	52
Chapter 10:	**Manacor**	71
Chapter 11:	**Toni**	82
Chapter 12:	**Basel**	96
Chapter 13:	**Mirka**	103

Chapter 14: Lille   117

Chapter 15: Shadows   128

Chapter 16: Doping   134

Chapter 17: Laboratory   150

Chapter 18: Plasma   159

Chapter 19: Body   170

Chapter 20: Unrepeatable   183

Chapter 21: Women   193

Chapter 22: Wood   198

Chapter 23: Tears   204

Chapter 24: Argentina   208

Chapter 25: Paris   221

Chapter 26: Nole   224

Chapter 27: Fight   242

Chapter 28: Face to Face   264

Chapter 29: Unbelievable   282

Chapter 30: Eternals   297

Acknowledgments   314

Prologue

"Uh, congratulations; what you did is incredible." That was not, perhaps, my most ingenious nor warmest phrase. I probably could have said something more substantial on that 14th of September in 2010. But it was 1:30 in the morning, I was in the middle row of seats in a white van parked in a dark lot in Queens, New York, and the excitement and tension of the past few hours had taken their toll on my mental agility, as well as on my body. There was so little light in that open-aired parking lot, in the middle of that New York summer night, that had I not climbed into that van with him I simply would have no idea to whom I was talking. I could barely make out his face in the adjacent seat.

Despite having spent the past more than twenty years covering big events, the details of highly competitive sports still move me. In the moment of triumph (or defeat), there is so much light, maybe too much; there are thousands of spectators and dozens, hundreds, or thousands of millions of television viewers. All focused on the star. Before and after, though, that star is alone and shrouded in darkness. And so he was, practically alone. Doubtless in the dark as well.

"Thank you, thank you," was the answer he passed back through the gap in the headrest that guarded the border between us, allowing us to keep a bit of distance.

We opted for silence then, each of us trying to organize the whirlwind that was the past few hours—his without comparison, mine merely journalistic in nature. I took great care to be respectful of a young man fresh from four hours of battle upon the cement, followed by an extensive press conference, and several interviews with the tournament journalists. It all added up to an intensive, nearly ten-hour work day. Because of that, and because it was a barrier that I always impose on myself, I made sure to maintain a not too close proximity to the protagonists. This is an attitude consistent with the philosophy of the medium I was working for at the time, an international news agency.

During that scant minute we spent alone in the van, I was privileged, the envy of practically any man: I was alone with Rafael Nadal, the man who had just conquered the US Open, the one person who could say that he had held aloft the four great trophies, the young man whose legend was now on the same level as Fred Perry, Rod Laver, Donald Budge, Roy Emerson, Andre Agassi, and Roger Federer.

What was I doing there with Nadal? The van was the setting of his last interview of the night, as unusual as it was ideal, because as we were navigating the empty freeway toward a quiet Manhattan, both of us now talkative and reenergized, Nadal gave me one of the best interviews I had ever gotten from him. In order to have a good interview, you need a good interviewer, but you also need a well-disposed interviewee, and Nadal was my perfect counterpart that night. He even offered to neutralize the obstacle that was the headrest on which I had hung my audio recorder.

"You want me to hold that for you?" he offered. "It'll be more comfortable that way." And during the next twenty minutes, while the white van cut through the night's darkness, the man who had just become one of the greatest tennis players of all time held the recorder up to his mouth.

While we talked about wooden rackets, the fear one feels when he is unable to see the bottom of the ocean, and whether it is possible to "hate" tennis, an unusual entourage listened in absolute silence: his father, his girlfriend, his agent, his press secretary, his man at Nike, and his physical therapist.

Finally, we ended up talking about soccer. After all, two months before, Nadal and I had both been at the Soccer City stadium—he as a fan, I was working—where Spain had established itself as the world soccer champion for the first time in the country's history. Argentina, my own country, had surprisingly thrashed Spain 4–1, just days earlier during an exhibition game in Buenos Aires.

"World champions of exhibition games," Nadal laughed good-naturedly, teasing me about Argentina's meaningless victory. The point was well made, especially coming from a man who knows so much about soccer. Two minutes later, the Nadals dropped me off on the corner of Second Avenue and 50th Street in Manhattan, just feet from my hotel.

"Would you mind switching tables so we can put these next to each other and all sit together?" When someone asks you for something so simple and does it that nicely, you always say yes. Especially if that someone is Roger Federer, having just fulfilled one of his dreams.

It was Monday, June 8, 2009, one day after the Swiss tennis star had conquered the French Open, the tournament that had mistreated him so many times in the past. He had finally won the four greats, like Perry, Laver, Budge, Emerson, and Agassi before him—an achievement Nadal would match fifteen months after.

The day after that glorious Sunday, Federer had an encounter with a large group of journalists who wanted to know more, asking questions about the final, the celebration night, and the future. After speaking to the print press, the Swiss man dove into a series of television interviews. I took advantage and set myself up writing at a table at the hotel bar, the only empty one next to a wall outlet—an important detail to keep in mind when one's computer could die at the least opportune moment. At the next table were Mirka Vavrinec, who had married Federer two months before, and the former player Mary Joe Fernández, wife of Tony Godsick, who was Federer's agent.

A while later, I was still immersed in my writing when someone amicably asked for my attention. It was Federer, who could have sent his agent or an assistant or simply delegated the task to one of the waiters in the bar. Most stars would do just that, but during one of his moments of greatest glory he came himself: direct, educated, and very natural.

During these past years, I've been able to interview both Nadal and Federer on several occasions, each alone as well as with a couple of colleagues. But those brief, casual moments in the van or the bar really help to better understand the minds and methods of the duo who set fire to the history of tennis.

I have spoken with both of them in all types of situations. I talked to Federer on a long walk through the Qizhong Stadium tunnel in Shanghai, in the back seat of a Mercedes Benz while we crawled over the endless slopes and through the narrow alleys of Lisbon, and in the gardens and television room of the Dubai Aviation Club. We have shared time in the luxurious Pershing Hall Hotel in Paris as well as just a few feet away from the central Wimbledon court, the stage that has marked his career.

I also traversed half the world in pursuit of Nadal. The New York conversation in the van was only one encounter in a whole series that included a first meeting in a completely empty white room that smelled like fresh paint, in Athens in 2004, alongside his mentor, Carlos Moyá. That younger Nadal still stared at the ground, crushed under the weight of his own shyness. But the Nadal I met in the coffee shop of the Dubai Aviation Club in March of 2008 was completely different. In half a minute and without pause, he came up with his ideal soccer team, comprised of his favorite players at the time. He showed how much he knew after he changed his mind about playing Robinho as his forward and substituted him with someone else: Messi. The Brazilian played for Real Madrid and Messi for Barcelona, which never mattered to Nadal. Although Nadal may have his "hooligan" moments when speaking as a fan, he still understands that soccer has a lot more to it than just colors.

Nadal already seemed more grown up when I talked to him in the club that gave rise to his tennis career in Manacor or in that familiar Porto Cristo restaurant in Majorca. He was in a bad mood, lacking sleep, in the lobby of the Intercontinental Miami hotel; upbeat when with his girlfriend in the cold, gray players' room at Paris-Bercy; relaxed and out in the open in the midst of all the lushness of the Acapulco Princess; and somber and tired at the Monte Carlo Country Club when we talked, out of sight of the Mediterranean.

I have the good luck of being able to speak to Nadal in Spanish, a native tongue we share, and in German to Federer, which is *his* own native tongue. One of the last times I interviewed him, however, in the players' lounge at Wimbledon, the Swiss star proposed a change. "Would you like to speak in German or in English?" I asked him. Without pausing, Federer said, "English, right? More international."

Internationality is an important concept for Federer. Years earlier, in Dubai in 2007, a time when he was the top player in the world, he asked me a question before I started interviewing him: "Where are you from?" It made sense. For the previous few years I had been asking him questions in German during press conferences about the Spanish Nadal or about the Argentinian players. My looks could have convinced him that I was actually German, but my accent and the top-ics of my questions contradicted that impression. So I explained, "I'm Argentinian, but I also have a German passport; I live in Spain, and I work for a German company, even though I write in Spanish." "Wow, very international," Federer had said with a smile, before telling me that he would have liked to have been Lenny Kravitz and played guitar in front of dozens of thousands of people.

In fact, "internationalism" attracted Federer greatly. He came from a country with three official languages, was the son of a South African woman, and married an ex-tennis player of Slovakian origin. During the last years of his career, Federer took particular care to find out all the secret corners and facets of the cities that he had visited over and over again. To accomplish this, he took advantage of his mastery of German, English, and French, because, as he sometimes said himself, the more languages you speak the more you understand the world.

What is certain, though, is that in a way I owe these men a great debt of gratitude. They gave me their time, put up with my questions, and answered each one of them, sometimes with varying degrees of honesty, but (almost) always with kindness. Through my own experience, I know that in sports like soccer, access to superstars of that caliber would not have been as frequent and intimate as that which I had to Federer and Nadal. And they certainly wouldn't have offered to hold the audio recorder.

But we are journalists. If they were to read this book, the two protagonists would find some stories with which they agreed, or that might make them smile or even let loose a guffaw or two, which is what Nadal himself confessed to me at Wimbledon in 2015, "I've been reading a part of your book. I'm having fun." And they would surely find some that bothered them as well or even angered them . . . or perhaps angered their respective social circles, which so often influence the opinions of the stars themselves. There will likely be perspectives that the two wouldn't agree on and situations that they might prefer to forget. This all comes together to create the journalist's conundrum: We're not here to be friends with the subjects of our stories but to relay what it is that they do. We belong to our readers, not to the stars, no matter how nice they may have been to us. And so it must be; we are close enough to feel the heat but also far enough to avoid burning ourselves.

It is in keeping with that, often precarious, balance that this book was written. As Federer said during November of 2005 in Shanghai, when, upon coming to the end of our walk together, a giant Chinese security guard blocked my entrance to the locker rooms, "Come with me." This book contains everything: the good, the not so good, the bright, and some shadows. This is not a meticulous biography, nor is it a recapitulation of matches and final scores. It is what I saw and what I was told, what I know and what I was able to confirm during the long and incomparable decade of Roger Federer and Rafael Nadal.

CHAPTER 1

Towels

LIFE IS SOMETIMES NOT AS hard when one is covered by a towel. When eyes are shut, the back is bowed under the weight of defeat, and tears flow, there is nothing better than the soft, wrinkled, fresh cotton for creating a bubble inside of which the drama may shamelessly spill out.

That is how it was for the Argentinian tennis player Juan Mónaco, on December 2, 2011, as he sat on the bench of an empty locker room in the heart of the La Cartuja soccer stadium in Seville. Hidden under a large towel, Mónaco cried. He cried for maybe ten minutes. As he regained his calm, the Argentinian asked himself how he could have lost in that way.

That week, only thirty-five men on the whole planet were better than he was. That is what the world rankings of the Association of Tennis Professionals (ATP) said. The same ATP that would, months later when he was twenty-seven years old, place him at number ten in the world, a member of an elite group that anyone in any sport or any job in the world would dream of belonging to.

But on that autumn afternoon, Mónaco cried. Losing 6–1, 6–1, and 6–2 in the opening of the finals of the Davis Cup is something to cry about. It doesn't matter if your rival is Rafael Nadal, it doesn't matter if he is one of the best clay-court players in history and he's playing at home. It hurts. A lot.

Mónaco's pride was hurt, he was in debt to his team, and on top of all that he was alone in the locker room. The sport doesn't always wait; Juan Martín del Potro was already in the stadium about to play the next match, and the Argentinian team had to deal with him. And so, Mónaco continued venting his tears and sadness under his towel, getting rid of the anguish that threatened to drown him. Better for no one to see him, better to be alone. Or not. Maybe a bit of consolation wouldn't hurt. A friendly hand.

"I felt someone stroking me head, stroking my head . . . I thought it was the tennis racket stringer or one of the boys. When I lifted my head to look, it was Rafael. He'd asked security at the entrance to the locker room permission to come in and talk to me. He came to ask for my forgiveness."

The towel is key. Sitting on it, or using it as back support. You take it with you to the quarter-finals of the US Open, down the road to the 17th Grand Slam title, and on your way toward becoming even greater in history books. No hard-surfaced bench can get in your way.

Roger Federer goes through a meticulous routine before each match, and that includes sitting on his towel on a chair at the edge of the court. It also includes covering the armrests to make them softer.

His water bottle goes on the ground, to his left, his orange bottle of mineral salts to his right. His racket holder certainly doesn't go on the ground: no, it has its place in another chair to his left. The tennis bag, however, sits on the cement to his right.

Federer began his match ten minutes before midnight. Partway through the first set on one of those typical, humid New York summer early mornings, things are going so well for the Swiss star that Mirka Vavrinec and Severin Lüthi happily allow themselves to be distracted by the screens of their mobile phones—until they have no choice but to raise their eyes. What is happening on that cement rectangle is no longer routine.

Ace.

Ace.

Ace.

Ace.

In four hits, Roger Federer takes the game. Ten meters away, his bench waits for him, meticulously draped in towels so that each switch to a different side is as comfortable as possible, so that nothing disturbs his symphony of tennis.

Lüthi, his coach, smiles with an expression that belies how impressed he is as he looks at the scoreboard. Mirka, Roger's wife, celebrates happily. Robert Federer, on the other hand, who hadn't missed an instant of what his son was doing, gives an encouraging shout without pausing amidst the applause.

Federer tosses the ball to the other side of the net, into his rival's sector. Toward Juan Mónaco. The Argentinian doesn't use towels to cover his chair, and his racket bag is enough to carry everything he needs.

The night was a series of slaps in the face for Mónaco, who just smiled when Federer scored 6–1 and 5–2. It was a quarter to one in the morning when he finally managed to mix a drop shot with a floater to score a magnificent point on his impious rival.

It seemed to take just an instant. Dressed completely in black, down to his hair band, it was clear that Federer had come to bury any hope left for the Argentinian in that match, which ended after one in the morning on September 6, 2011. The final score of 6–1, 6–2, and 6–0 left no doubt.

Once the match was over, and before proceeding to his interview with Brad Gilbert, Federer put a watch on his left wrist; the brand was the company sponsoring him. He had everything under control.

Monaco summed up his experience, "I am able to say that I played against the two greatest players of the game during their prime. Two matches in which I was steamrolled by the difference in skill, and I can even say that I wasn't playing poorly. It could have been much, much worse."

It had been a few years since those two blows and Mónaco—a good friend of Nadal's—was able to see the bright side. Even concerning the four consecutive aces that Federer hurled at him.

"What am I going to do? Nothing. I dealt with it gracefully, and I had fun. When someone plays you perfectly, what are you going to do . . . You can only congratulate them.

"I played against the Federer who possessed such talent, such a perfect tennis technique, with his serve and volley, his slice . . . A few things here and there that Rafael doesn't have. And, on the other hand, I played Rafa, a player who makes you feel like it's impossible to win a point off of him, with such tenacity, euphoria, guts."

"Along two different paths, those two arrive at the same destination. They are brilliant at using their gifts; they exploit them one hundred percent and combine them with skill. That is how they become so formidable."

CHAPTER 2

Geniuses

THE TERRIFYING AND, DESPITE EVERYTHING, fascinating sensation of being razed by two such different and perfect tennis machines is not a feeling monopolized by Juan Mónaco. Dozens of players from all around the world experienced it during a long decade. And not just any players: men of high caliber, men who know what it means to be in the top ten, such men as Richard Gasquet, who possesses a backhand so beautiful that it strikes spectators dumb.

"Oof" is the first reaction of the Frenchman when he hears the question about the two "R"s. It's January 2015, in Melbourne, Australia, and still fresh in Gasquet's mind is what he went through just weeks before in Manacor, having been invited by Nadal to share in a few days of training.

"He ended up broken. Rafa is very, very intense when it comes to training," says Gasquet, and the same thing happened to Mónaco during January in 2015 that saw him arriving in Australia with an injured back after spending several days training with Nadal in Doha.

At that point in his career, Gasquet could have written a doctoral thesis about the two tennis greats. His twenty-eight matches, with twenty-six defeats and only two victories, both against Federer, and nothing but defeats against Nadal in professional games—discounting

any victories when Nadal was still young—make him a definite authority on the matter.

"The two of them are very different. Federer's ball is fast, he leaves
you no time to breathe, hits it the instant it bounces, and gains fractions
of a second that make everything harder for his rival. Nadal's ball, on
the other hand, is very heavy. You see it coming and it throws you back.
You have to be deeply entrenched in order to hold up against it and
return it well. There's no one else who hits it like that."

Whoever was sitting in the Philippe Chatrier on June 5, 2011,
might have understood just how Gasquet was feeling.

The clouds are gray, and a few birds are singing timidly on that
fresh afternoon at the end of the Paris spring. Roland Garros is a setting that presents a cacophony of sounds in which two very different
ones are clearly audible. You just have to close your eyes and listen.
There is a ball that sounds solid, dry, quick, and in a certain way clean.
Full. And another that is a prolonged hum, an agonizing strum of
chords, a parable—the eyes are closed, yes, but the ball takes longer
to fall—and upon ending, closes with a heavy landing. It's one bomb
after another. Nadal is dropping them. On the other side, Federer
responds with missiles.

Neither of them are military men; quite the opposite in fact. But
the metaphor is especially valid for defining their styles of play. There
are variations, yes, but the pattern is basically thus: from Nadal's side
bombs are dropped, and from Federer's sector missiles are returned.

Roland Garros is the least favorable setting for missiles, and the
one in which bombs do the most damage. That's due to the brick dust,
the slowest surface in tennis and the one that allows for the most tactical variations and different strikes. It also seems logical that Nadal´s
bombs would work especially well in a stadium baptized in homage to
a French aviator shot down during World War I.

At the beginning of the rivalry, the French newspaper *Le Monde*
best captured the bipolar battle for worldwide dominion. It did this
using a cartoon strip. In it, Federer appeared dressed in a tailcoat with
a violin on his shoulder. From that instrument flowed sublime notes,

as beautiful as they were harmonious. His smile was animated but soft and disciplined. On the other side of the net, a sort of caveman in a loincloth wielded a club. His left arm looked like a weight lifter´s. His undulating stare was that of a diabolical primate. The violinist asked him as follows:

"What an interesting instrument! Does it make music?"

"No, it destroys."

Throughout the coming years, it became apparent how unfair it was to depict Federer as a violinist and Nadal as a caveman with a club. The violinist was sometimes out of tune, and the caveman didn't achieve his victories only though clubbing.

But during those fascinating first steps of a rivalry unlike any other, such heavy-handedness in their depictions was necessary to show that one side couldn't, at least outwardly, be more different than the other.

CHAPTER 3

Party

"Zamora! Zamoritaaaa!" It's nearly two in the morning on February 27, 2005, and the high society youth of Mexico humiliate themselves unimaginably, desperately twisting and turning, and sweating from pure anxiety. It's nearly two in the morning, and at the entrance to the nightclub, a battle for entry unfolds from a desperation to be included in the party that no one wants to miss tonight.

With his coppery face, his Indian-like features, and his somber presence, Zamora watches all those fair-haired people while hardly moving a muscle. It would be reasonable to think that he is hiding the satisfaction he feels; it makes sense to imagine that he's having fun, causing suffering to all these young men with futures in American universities, these children whose every problem had already been solved at birth. These postadolescents who, were it not for Zamora raising or lowering his thumb to allow passage into the interior of the most popular nightclub in Acapulco, would hardly deign to acknowledge him. To be perfectly clear: Zamora, Zamorita, enjoys every weekend by living life in reverse, the life of an Indian deciding the fate—at least for an evening—of a white man.

Around the corner, a couple of groups hide in dark alcoves and receive constant visits from the gathered youth. You need something to consume on a night that won't end until daytime, in a city where kidnappings, assassinations, and decapitations were standard practice in 2005.

Suddenly, Zamora smiles. A group of ten people squeezes quickly under the rope. They advance quickly, with the step of someone who doesn't doubt that they'll be let in. A well-built young man, with a boyish face and a blue and white-striped shirt two sizes larger than what would be considered fashionable, watches without smiling. This is curious, seeing as the party is for him. It's Rafael Nadal, and the group of friends and acquaintances who have been dragging him around Acapulco for the past couple of hours wants to celebrate his second consecutive title in two weeks. But Nadal is a bit out of place that night on the Mexican Pacific.

A few feet away, a tennis player who will never enter the group of top 50 ranked players fixes her ocean blue gaze on a succession of men. She dances covered in sweat, almost as if she has just climbed out of a pool. She doesn't let any of her marks roam free during that night of celebration, although with Nadal, the timid eighteen-year-old, she doesn't dare try anything. The Spaniard does not seem to have noticed her presence, so she finally throws herself on his coach and rips his shirt open, causing the buttons to pop off.

The Black Eyed Peas start playing, and the crowd gets more excited. Nadal, not so much. Perhaps he prefers instead to think about what he's just done, to remember where he comes from, and where he's going. Or wants to go.

That February in 2005 was key to the career of a man who would change the history of tennis. He was eighteen and had only one title, from Sopot 2004. That victory over his Baltic competitor in the Polish health resort made him realize that he too could win trophies, although it wasn't until seven months later that Nadal really started to become *Nadal*.

The potential of this devastating Nadal had been hinted at during the Davis Cup final in December 2004, against the United States in Seville, but was confirmed three months later in the ATP World Tour: winning two titles in three tournaments in Buenos Aires, Costa do

Sauípe, and Acapulco. Nadal would taste defeat only in the Argentinian capital on a strange Friday night in summer, plagued by mosquitoes. It was at the hands of Gastón Gaudio, who eight months before had won an incredible final at Roland Garros. Gaudio hit dozens of slice backhands to disarm Nadal and win 0–6, 6–0, and 6–1.

After that, Nadal was not to be stopped. He conquered the tournaments in Brazil and Mexico, jumped from 48 to 30 in the worldwide ranking, took Roger Federer to the fifth set in the Miami final, and added his first title in Monte Carlo. He was already in the top ten, seventh worldwide. In July he reached number two, and during the following forty-nine months he never dropped from that vantage point. He would either stay as number two, or he would climb to number one. But everything started during that year in 2005, the season when he won eleven titles, a number that he wouldn't reach again. He was eighteen years old, which might have been his excuse for forgetting his Acapulco championship trophy in a taxi, and he didn't yet know that he was to be the coprotagonist in a totally unique story, that of the "R" years.

CHAPTER 4

Youth

DOES A BALL HAVE POWER? A lot, nearly infinite. A ball, regardless of its size, can teach you how to run, how to get up after a fall, or understand that others are different; but that doesn't make them better or worse. A ball can teach you how to make friends, how to better yourself, how to better understand the world. And how to be happy. A ball can turn a boy into a man, and that's what happened to Rafael Nadal at 4:38 p.m. on June 5, 2005, in Paris, an afternoon overcast with rain clouds. The setting was perfect for his brand of electric tennis, full of energy and urgency, a style of play that dazzled the world during an unforgettable season.

That ball on that afternoon, after an out-of-control drive by the Argentinian Mariano Puerta, provided the point that Nadal needed for a win at Roland Garros. It was the ninth tournament that Nadal would win out of the eleven he accumulated that year, but it was also the most important because it marked the turning point in his career. After that Parisian afternoon, everything seemed possible in Nadal's life. And everything was what happened: he won much more than he had ever dared to dream.

It's true that the left-handed Spaniard had been showing, ever since he was a child, how close he was to greatness. During the Davis

Cup final in 2004, facing the United States in Seville, for example, he achieved two key points. But at that time no one was "pushing" him toward victory from the start. During the weeks leading up to Roland Garros in 2005 they were, because he had already won everything he could on a clay court. It had been years since there was such unanimity in the predictions. And you had to ask yourself, had any eighteen-year-old ever faced the amount of pressure that Nadal was dealing with during those weeks, even though he was nineteen by the final? His birthday, June 3, is in a certain way a predestination: Roland Garros is held during that date, and it would make sense for Nadal to be in Paris, the city in which he would have been born if it hadn't happened in Manacor.

Nadal was already amazing during those days. You need to be made of stern stuff in order to put up with that much pressure, come out unscathed, meet all your expectations, and then continue on as if everything was perfectly normal. This is especially true of Nadal, for whom "normal" is not a word that accurately describes him. Normal doesn't describe a player who jumps up to the rafters in the locker room, motivating himself by screaming "Let's go, Rafa!" Normal doesn't describe a player who wants to win every single point, from the first to the last, and upon being told his list of achievements responds by saying that he still has a lot to learn, and that he still needs to improve.

"I didn't play my best during that match," Nadal recalls eight years afterward in Monte Carlo. "But it was exciting, I felt like I could run for three days straight, just using the adrenaline I felt at the prospect of winning my first Grand Slam."

So much did the young Nadal love to compete that in the first few stretches of his career, he was the "savior" of his uncle's send-off. His uncle, Miguel Angel Nadal, was a memorable defender of Barcelona and, during many years, an integral member of the Spanish soccer team. Nadal formed, along with his uncle, part of the team—a "select" group put together from Spain—that faced off against a combination of stars during July 2005, among them almost all the ones who made up that mythical *dream team* of Barcelona from the '90s. The second half was winding down, the Spanish group was losing, and his uncle would be leaving soccer with a defeat. Rafael couldn't allow this; he cut into the opposing side's territory at an angle, got rid of one opponent with a feint, and launched a left-footed missile that ended up in the net: 1–1, and Nadal showed that, again, he was simply incapable of losing. His soccer skills were put to work off of the field as well. Years later, Real Madrid's president, Florentino Pérez, would follow his advice and hire a player from Mallorca.

Between Zamora in the Acapulco nightclub and Shi-ting, who smiled helpfully in Shanghai, there was a world of distance: ten conquered tournaments and nearly an entire life, if you stop to think about what the year 2005 meant to Rafael Nadal. The season he turned nineteen, on the way to his first title at Roland Garros—a year during which the world took notice, and staggered in an overflow of energy and passion hitherto unknown in tennis.

Shi-ting, in Shanghai, was one of the young hostesses in charge of making sure that anyone entering that ample hall felt completely at home. The hall was larger than a hotel suite, a space that built on itself; you could open every door along the length of a long hallway that twisted and turned through the catacombs of the Qizhong Tennis Center, where the end-of-year Masters was held at the time, an exclusive tournament that gathered the eight best tennis players in the world.

Rafael Nadal must have entered several of those halls on that fresh November afternoon. Unlike Acapulco, where many of the people in the nightclub didn't recognize his face, there was not a person in Shanghai who could not identify him. Especially not on that day, after he had just announced that he couldn't play in the Masters due to a foot injury. It was the culmination of a tragic day for the tournament, after seeing Andre Agassi quit as well. But while the American hurried to quit the tournament almost secretly, Nadal dedicated several hours to a PR marathon, visiting sponsors, talking to the public, and giving out interviews to explain why he wasn't playing. For the Chinese, that level of respect is fundamental. Agassi lost face—and money—in Shanghai; Nadal, on the other hand, made new friends. The man who had started the year at number 50 and finished at number two, the man who conquered eleven tournaments in 2005, had become just that: a *man*. And he would never again be spotted in that striped, out-of-style shirt.

Four months later, in Miami, the fluorescent yellow of Nadal's T-shirt was bright enough in the midday Caribbean sun in March to hurt the eyes. It was a sleeveless shirt, tailored to fit close to the body, as dictated by the latest in tennis fashion. But the man playing did not seem like Nadal; there was one detail that didn't fit: he was losing. Carlos Moyá, his friend, was destroying him with his forehand. And Nadal, uncharacteristically subdued, showed just how hard it was for him to face the player whom he so admired, and who had helped him so much. Nadal lost. Head lowered, drinking a Gatorade, he walked into the press conference room, chilled by an excess of air conditioning, as is the norm for any organized event in the United States.

"For me, it was a match like any other, nothing special. He's my best friend in the circuit," he assured. He avoided talking about the ankle he twisted in the Indian Wells semifinals a week before, but it was apparent that he hadn't been in peak physical condition during the game. He preferred to talk about what lay ahead of him, which he was enthusiastic about, "Now I'm going to get all six of my senses ready for Monte Carlo." Benito Pérez Barbadillo, a Spaniard who at the time worked in the ATP Communications Department and who would eventually become its Chief of Communications and inseparable from Nadal, was shaking with laughter in his seat. "How many?" he asked Nadal to the great enjoyment of the journalists. "Well, how many senses are there?" Nadal asked back. "Five? Even better, I'll add another one, because I'll be needing it this season."

Twenty-four hours later, Nadal was in panic mode. After hours of revelry throughout Miami, until nearly six in the morning, he hadn't had any time to pack his suitcase, and his room was a total mess. Nothing new for him, although in that instance he was scared because he couldn't find his passport anywhere. In fewer than two hours, his plane for Madrid would be leaving, and Pérez Barbadillo was waiting for him in the lobby and becoming desperate as well, for there were still other engagements to fulfill.

Two journalists had appointments scheduled with Nadal and had been waiting for an hour already. One wanted to interview him for *Tennis Magazine*, and the other, from the German press agency DPA, wanted to speak with Nadal about a job that would be new to him: columnist. Nadal would comment on the 2006 FIFA World Cup in Germany for this agency, but first he needed to find that damn passport.

When the document finally showed up, so did the other Nadal. Nervous, timid, and eyes locked on the ground, he wrapped up his conversation about soccer in the lobby, and the tennis interview in the van that took him to the airport. On the way, one more piece of news popped up: *People* magazine had offered to list him in their yearly edition as one of the "fifty most attractive men in the world." But Nadal declined. On one hand, he still felt very young and not much of a man, despite the fact that his title at Roland Garros clearly gave him the necessary status. On the other hand, the image that was being projected of Nadal in those first few years depended on his exuding youth, energy, freshness, which happened to be the ideal contrast to Federer. There would be time enough to appear in *People* later. Young Nadal would never break a racket, would never speak ill of others, would never do anything out of character. Qualities which were, for the most part, genuine, since the education he received from his family had a stronger Prussian influence than a Hispanic one, due to how much they insisted on the value of things, and on the importance of saying "Thank you."

During those years, Nadal was a "thank you" machine, even toward the ball boys during a match, which would have been absolutely unthinkable to the great majority of his colleagues, who hand their towels back without so much as a glance, often with disdain, and who often barely even acknowledge the public. But aside from that education, Nadal and his entourage knew one thing for sure at the time: Fernando Alonso was his direct rival in the world of nonsoccer Spanish sports, and nothing would bring better results than showing himself to be educated, good-natured, and grateful, because at the time the world Formula 1 champion was following a somewhat different path. Nevertheless, one of Nadal's closest relationships is the one he formed, and still has, with the basketball player Pau Gasol.

A month after his loss to Moyá, the Real Club de Tenis clubhouse in Barcelona was hopping. The Catalonian bourgeoisie was enjoying one of its most favorite weeks of the year: the Barcelona Open, a traditional tournament that takes place on brick courts and is played every year at the beginning of the Catalonian city's gleaming spring.

In that clubhouse, similar to so many tennis clubs throughout the world with British roots, there were conversations about tennis and soccer accompanied by *pa amb tomaca* (bread with tomato) and croquettes, all lined up carefully along the bar. One of the fellows remembered an anecdote about Rafa—that's what they called him then—from the previous year when he was meandering through the Barcelona Open with his boyish face. A teenager approached him and shyly asked for an autograph. "I'm Julia," she said, with the implicit suggestion that this was the name he should write next to the signature. Obliging as always, Nadal smiled at the young girl and inclined his head slightly, "Hello, I'm Rafa!" as if Julia needed that clarification in the year 2005.

Twelve months later, in April of 2006, Nadal had realized that everyone knew who he was. He was on the central court facing off against the Finnish Jarkko Nieminen in the quarterfinals. It was an unusual afternoon, because the Spaniard was experiencing one of his few moments of suffering before lesser rivals on the clay court. Nieminen, with a quick arm and quick feet, was beating him 6–4 and 4–1 in the quarter-finals, interrupting the usual pleasure of a sunny day in the Pedralbes neighborhood.

"*Va aquest joc, va aquest joc!*" Nadal repeated to himself, almost possessed, while he paced in circles behind the end line. "Win this game," he was saying in his Catalán with his thick Mallorcan accent from Manacor. "Win this game." Five days before, he had defeated Federer in the Monte Carlo finals, and now he was struggling against a reputation-less player. That, too, is tennis.

"Damn, that guy is really playing!" Nadal commented when he stepped close to the line of journalists. He managed to take the second set, but on the third he was at a disadvantage again, 3–1 low. "He doesn't miss a single fucking ball!" He was getting desperate. On the press bench, some journalist was blaming Mariano Rajoy, leader of the People's Party (PP) who would, years later, become the Spanish Prime Minister. Rajoy was watching the match from his VIP suite. "That guy is bad luck!" he said, combining his nationalistic Catalonian convictions and his leftist views with the supposed destructive power of the conservative Rajoy. Next to him, an Argentinian man was excited about something else. "Vilas's record is going to stand." He would be wrong, because Nadal fought on without rest and took the match point. "*Va aquest joc,*" he muttered again between clenched teeth. And he won the game.

A while later, there was loud laughter. Nadal was once again starring in the production of spontaneity and seduction with which he greased the wheels of the press during his early years. The topic concerned his forty-five consecutive triumphs on clay courts, just one away from the Swedish Björn Borg's record, and eight away from Guillermo Vilas's, from Argentina. But Nadal would rather laugh at himself and tell one of his favorite stories in "broken English."

Unlike his peers on the circuit, such as Guillermo Coria from Argentina, who wouldn't speak English unless he could do it perfectly and, indeed, never did so during his career, Nadal was a kamikaze, a young man to whom the grammar and rules of English were alien, and who talked, talked, and talked in the language of Shakespeare or something similar. If he made a mistake, he smiled, with the result that his dialogues with the press went from one smile to the next.

However, to get to know him better, to understand his obsessions, you had to hear him talk in Spanish. Then he would amaze, because he was constantly bringing up numbers, points, and rankings. Nadal stored in his head all the scores, all the points that had been and would be won and everything that his direct rivals did in their struggle to reach the peak of tennis. He would recite, without looking at a list, all of the tournaments won on clay courts up until that point, analyze the results against his potential rivals for the next day, and bring up again just how unfair tennis could be. "With the points I won in 2005, I would have been number 1 in nearly any other season. The problem is that I have Federer in front of me, who is the best of all time."

Three weeks later, the Mussolinian statues of the Foro Italico looked like they wanted to start clapping. What was being witnessed on the peculiar stage on which the Italian Open was played was a match that would make history. Federer had two match points over Nadal to take the title. But the Spaniard recovered and added another victory. He had just matched Vilas's record of fifty-three consecutive wins on clay, and was once again the indisputable favorite to win the Roland Garros. Federer didn't know it yet, but that afternoon was the closest he would come to conquering Rome, the second most important clay court tennis tournament in the world. It would take him seven years to reach the final again, and on that occasion, with a 6–1 and 6–3, Nadal wouldn't even allow him to imagine victory.

During 2006, everyone wanted to know everything about Rafael Nadal. *"Does he have a girlfriend?"* they asked. Little was known at the time, although it became public knowledge that the young guy was happy at having attracted an ex-classmate from school in Manacor. What he most liked about her—his entourage would say—was that she was never interested in Nadal, the star. In fact, she had become more elusive the more famous he became. But Nadal got what he wanted, proving once again that he would never lose, so entrenched was he in his age of winning everything.

Four weeks later, Nadal was once again writhing in excitement, covering his green shirt in orange dust. He was already the two-time champion of Roland Garros, and again, as in Rome, he was wiping out Federer in a final. It was the best conclusion to two truly perfect weeks during which the Spaniard had enjoyed being in the spotlight of the sporting world. He made his debut on a blog during the Roland Garros tournament. In it, he wrote in detail about what was going through his head and what his days were like during the great tournament. Nadal's blog notably increased the amount of traffic to the ATP's web page and became a regular read for many of the sport's fans. As the years went by, he would lose interest in writing, or even dictating, blogs. Everything became more airtight and commercial.

But in 2006, it was all new and fresh, Nadal was a young man, happy and spontaneous. The day after the festivities in Paris, he would leave for London. He opted for the Eurostar, the train that crossed through a tunnel below the English Channel on its way to London. As many times before, he was late, missed the train, and had to wait two hours for the next one. During that lull, he wrote his first column about Germany 2006 and sent it off using a mini-computer from the train itself. There weren't smartphones or tablets, although there were mobile phones. When his rang, Prince Felipe, the then-heir to the Spanish crown, was on the other end. They spoke at ease for a long time. Nadal allowed himself to make jokes. He had just turned twenty and lived his days with a limitless amount of confidence. He had an angular, olive-skinned face, giant extremities, muscles that seemed ready to burst at a moment's notice, long hair, exaggerated gesticulations, a genuine aston-ishment in reaction to the questions that journalists occasionally asked him, and an unchanging kindness—all things that made the Nadal of those days a peculiar character and which made him an inevitable and welcome star. Vilas's record on clay courts had been smashed to dust. It was Nadal's record now, and the world of tennis asked itself just how far this youth could, or wanted to, go.

CHAPTER 5

Mystical

THERE'S NO NEED FOR FEDERER to say whether or not he feels like the main character in a religious experience; you can see the answer written on his face when he hears the question. "A slight exaggeration," the Swiss star says before laughing openly for a moment.

The *New York Times* published an article on August 20, 2006, by writer and essayist David Foster Wallace, titled "Federer as Religious Experience." A tennis lover, Foster Wallace dissected Federer in his article in a way that had never been done and probably won't be done again.

Two years later, the writer, taken by a bout of depression, committed suicide. Perhaps that's why Federer seems uncomfortable when he hears the question, although he also seems bothered by the memory of some of the other things that Foster Wallace spilled in an article that, regardless of whether you agree or not, is a valuable little account of a phenomenon. "I suppose that in sports we tend to disregard any and all limits, as if we're seeing everything for the first time," Federer said in January 2015 in Australia when the topic was brought up.

Rolling Stone magazine described Foster Wallace as "one of the most important writers of the last fifty years." That man did not have any limits when it came to his admiration for Federer. At the beginning of that famous article, he masterfully described just how he felt when watching him play. "[There] are times, as you watch the young Swiss play, when the jaws drop and eyes protrude and sounds are made that bring spouses in from other rooms to see if you're OK," wrote Foster Wallace, who also described Federer as "human beings' reconciliation with the fact of having a body."

The American felt as much clear admiration for Federer as he lacked in sympathy for Nadal's game. "For reasons that are not well understood, war's codes are safer for most of us than love's. You too may find them so, in which case Spain's mesomorphic and totally martial Rafael Nadal is the man's man for you—he of the sleeveless biceps and Kabuki self-exhortations." According to the writer, the duel couldn't be more uneven and contrasting. "It's the passionate machismo of southern Europe versus the intricate clinical artistry of the north. Apollo and Dionysus. Scalpel and cleaver."

Nadal has never been overheard speaking about that comparison, but Federer himself has made it clear that he does not feel that he is a religious experience nor his historic rival a butcher. He does this with Swiss diplomatic aplomb, of course. "Some pretty incredible pieces have been written about me, about tennis, and about other players. They are interesting to read although sometimes a bit exaggerated. But each individual can judge them as they please."

At that point in his career, Federer was already a legend or even a step above, if such a category exists. There wasn't much left for him to accomplish in tennis, but he kept on, at thirty-three years of age and with four children, fighting at the top, with enough weaponry to defeat anyone. While watching him play, you could only ask, Where did such talent come from? Was he always so . . . perfect?

Roger Federer was born on a Saturday, at half past eight in the morning. Robert, his father, had started a doubles tournament on Friday, and just hours after his son was born, on that same Saturday afternoon, won the finals of that competition.

Enormous feet, seven pounds, fifteen ounces, and twenty-one inches tall. Lynette, his mother, remembers everything. "He could walk at eleven months," she explained in 2011 during a long interview published by *Basler Zeitung*. "It wasn't long before he started to play soccer and catch balls that we threw to him. We would always play with Roger: soccer, ping-pong, and, later, squash. We always had a ball, and if we passed it to him he would pass it right back, while other kids would throw it in multiple directions." Despite his clear motor and coordination skills, Federer's parents clearly stated that they never thought they had given birth to a future Wimbledon champion or a forward like Gerd Müller. Neither could his mother believe how well he spoke French, despite how much he avoided studying and doing chores when he was younger.

It may be obvious, but without Robert and Lynette, there would be no Roger Federer. Lynette and Robert first met each other in Kempton Park in Johannesburg. She, South African, dreamed of someday saving enough to be able to move to the United Kingdom. He, Swiss, was on the extreme southern tip of the Dark Continent to explore the world, gather some money, and return to Europe some years later. She spoke perfect Afrikaans and works in the sales department of Ciba-Geigy. He developed chemical additives for the paper industry, and also worked at Ciba-Geigy.

"Roger had to play sports. If he wasn't moving around, he was unbearable," Lynette recalls. She describes her son during those years as being "impulsive, proud, and a bit of a difficult child at times." During those joyful '70s, Lynette was saving two-thirds of her salary in order to reach her goal of living in London. She had given herself a time limit of no more than three years, but a plane would eventually take her to Basel. An athlete as well, Lynette trained young tennis players, worked with the Basel tennis tournament organization, and developed a preference for golf in her later years. There was a time, between 2003 and 2005, in which Federer's parents managed their son's career, snatching that responsibility away from the powerful IMG. After just two years, control passed to Tony Godsick, who ended up leaving IMG to start a whole new business with Federer: Team 8. Eight is the Swiss player's lucky number.

Lynette took over coordinating jobs at the Roger Federer Foundation, which ranged from answering fan mail to making sure operations went off without a hitch during auctions of Federer memorabilia. Diana, a nurse, is Lynette's daughter, overshadowed by the best tennis player in the world. Lynette knows this and tries to help Diana, two years older than her brother, accept it. "What you're experiencing isn't any different than what happens to me," Lynette once told her daughter. "Lots of people walk up to me to talk, and the only topic is always your brother."

"Calm, balanced, charming," is how the Swiss newspaper *Blick*, the most read in the country, describes the number one's dad, a man who for three years boycotted Wimbledon. Robert had watched his son lose the first round of Wimbledon in 2002 against the Croatian Mario Ančić and didn't return to the players' box on the central field of the All England until 2005, the year in which his son won his third consecutive Wimbledon. Since then, he has set his superstitions aside.

At the age of sixty, Robert remembers well the times when things weren't so simple, "We were always having to manage our finances in order to fund Roger's career." Perhaps this is why he had a serious and frank talk with his son one day, in that manner in which only a father is capable. Roger was fifteen, and he was leaning toward a tennis career despite his great soccer talents. Robert gave him conditions for moving forward. "I'm not going to finance you into your thirties just so you can roam around at 300th place in the rankings." Rotschi—that's what his parents called him—was sure that he could go much farther than even his parents could imagine. Certainty was something he never lacked. "Since he was a kid, he's always done what he wants. I would watch him at the children's and youth tournaments," Robert recalls. Like almost any father, Federer would get excitable and yell instructions and comments to his son. In vain. "He never looked at me. Ever."

What did Roger dream of when he was young? "You always dream about becoming a soccer player and scoring the World Cup-winning goal with a bicycle kick," he recalled during an interview in Dubai, where he installed one of his training bases and where he has a two-thousand-square-foot flat. "Or you dream of a victory in the Wimbledon final, kneeling on the grass, like all your idols did."

The year was 2007, and Federer knew that Nadal would be his successor in more ways than one. Weeks before, he'd had long conversations with the Spaniard during a flight to South Korea on his private plane, and the Swiss had come away with a good feeling. "It's good for us to chat, to talk about the problems on the circuit. I'm happy for him, because he's very young. When I was that old, no one, practically no one, ever approached me to ask my opinions, because my ranking was much worse. He is now in a position of influence and if he, for lack of a better way of saying it, relies on me a little bit, as I'm older and from an almost different generation, that's a good thing. Because decisions made today will affect him more than me, all the changes that are coming for 2009, 2010, 2011. . . . He'll experience those more than I will, because I'll be nearly at the end of my career. And I want to help him, and the circuit should be well structured for when I leave tennis and he continues playing."

Going over that interview will confirm that Federer surpassed his own expectations in regard to his longevity in the circuit, as he saw 2011 as practically the end of his career, although at the time he had already publicly declared his goal of participating in the 2012 London Olympics.

During that February in 2007 in Dubai, Federer wanted Nadal to succeed him. "He's been at number two worldwide for the past eighty weeks. If someone takes my place, it should be him. And in any other situation he would have been number one a long time ago; it's just that, simply put, I played too well, racked up too many points, and was constantly at the Grand Slam tournaments. So if anyone deserves it, it is without a doubt Nadal."

CHAPTER 6

Sympathy

DURING THE MONTHS WHEN NADAL exploded as a tennis star, Federer had taken on a habit: putting on a visored cap and walking with his gaze on the ground. "It's not the best thing, but by now, at tournaments, everyone knows who I am. If I walk with my eyes forward, I can barely move, I would never stop greeting people," he explained in 2007 in Dubai to Bruno Ziauddin, a Swiss writer and journalist.

That omnipresent cap arrived when Federer was on the peak of peaks. Between 2004 and 2007, he won forty-four tournaments, half of the number he would conquer by the end of 2014. Eleven of those were Grand Slams. That four-year magic was the solid basis for his status as a legend.

Federer was fortunate that Nadal was just starting to blow up in 2005 and that it wasn't until 2008 that he won his first Grand Slam outside the clay court of Roland Garros. Five years younger than Federer, the Spaniard was as much an obstacle as he was a boost for the Swiss's career, who enjoyed a couple of years filled with easier rivals than Nadal to really make his career shine. For this reason, within the context of this rivalry, the encounter in October 2005 was curious. Or more than that.

Two sharp, discrete knocks sounded on the door of room 449 of a luxurious hotel in Basel. Nadal opened the door. "Hola, Rafa!"

Federer said. "Eh . . . ! Hi, how are you?" Nadal answered, hardly believing that he was looking at the number-one ranked player. Federer, recovering from an injury and on his first day without crutches, had decided to surprise the man with whom he shared dominion of the tennis world. Nadal had arrived an hour earlier in Basel to dine with the heads of the local tournament, which he would have to quit due to tendinitis in his knees, joints which, together with his left foot, would continue to cause him problems throughout his career. "Roger called me and asked me where Rafa was staying," Vittorio Selmi, the Italian tour manager of the ATP, later explained. "When I gave him the hotel, he didn't pause. 'I'm heading over.'"

Federer is from Basel, which made the encounter easier. This was probably the first milestone in the unusual relationship that the Swiss and Spaniard would develop. These are two men who could have easily hated each other, as was the case with John McEnroe and Jimmy Connors or with the same McEnroe and Ivan Lendl. And maybe it wasn't hatred, but there wasn't a shred of sympathy between Pete Sampras and Andre Agassi. Not to mention Boris Becker, whom the Australian Pat Cash still remembers with rage because of how badly, according to him, he was treated, But what the two "R"s had is incomparable; no rivalry ever had as many Grand Slam matches and finals as they had.

They could have had more than enough reason to dislike one another, or to speak ill of each other, a potential danger which was sensed by some of the people closest to them. Selmi and Benito Pérez Barbadillo weren't innocent in arranging the encounter that left a mark on a nineteen-year-old Nadal and made twenty-four-year-old Federer happy. "Evidently, it was Vittorio who let the details slip; he was friends with us both," Nadal recalled years later. That was the start of an era of peace and love in tennis that would go on for six years.

There had been a prelude to the encounter hours before, just after Nadal had won the Madrid Masters Series on that Sunday night, one of the greatest successes in his career to that point, as it was a victory in a great indoor tournament and on a fast surface. Shortly after that victory, his phone buzzed with the arrival of a text message. "Hey, man! Rafa, good tennis and Madrid. Much happy Rogelio for you." The message had been an absurd, awkwardly worded mixture of Spanish and Italian, but it showed Federer's good intentions and happiness for the success of someone who was considered his main rival. Ever since, Nadal would call Federer "Number One" or "Rogelio," and the Swiss had cheerfully adopted the nickname. Ultimately, they had only matched up three times, two of which were successes for Nadal. Contact was renewed in that hotel room in Basel that Monday night on October 25, 2005. They spoke for no more than twenty minutes, because Nadal had to keep his appointment with the tournament heads. But Federer had time to ask him about his experience in Madrid. "It was hard; I felt lost," said the Spaniard, who had battled through five sets in the final to defeat the Croatian Ivan Ljubičić, who would become Federer's trainer in 2016.

And then they started exchanging information. Federer took off a shoe and showed Nadal his heel, still pretty swollen after having pulled some ligaments about ten days earlier. And there was one unavoidable topic: soccer. Federer once again lamented not having played in the Spanish tournament and postponing that dreamed-of encounter with his soccer idol, Zinedine Zidane, at that time the star of Real Madrid. "Are you going to Shanghai, to the Masters?" Nadal asked. Federer smiled, "I don't know; I'll start running next week, and then I'll start playing."

Time was up. Nadal went to dinner with the tournament leadership, and Federer did the same at the hotel. It was midnight when they crossed paths again, one on his way to bed, the other on his way home. "Good luck," they wished each other. And there is no doubt they had it.

CHAPTER 7

Peace and Love

THE ATP TENNIS CIRCUIT HAD become unbearable for nostalgic John McEnroe and Jimmy Connors fans. The courts looked like a California yoga institute, with the peace and love attitude exuding kindness and generosity. And the guilty parties, of course, were Rafael Nadal and Roger Federer.

It was January 2011, and the onlookers agreed that never in the history of tennis had the number one and number two players gotten along as well as Nadal and Federer. Behind the two leaders, like a happy flock, almost all of the other players were copying the Swiss and Spaniard. "The players see Roger as a total gentleman and Rafa as an extremely likable kid," explained the Croatian Ivan Ljubičić, the ex-president of the ATP Player Council. "Rafa is simply a great guy. And the fact that he plays tennis incredibly well doesn't make him unlikable," he added.

It was hard to find a player who could criticize the attitude of the then-dominant tennis duo. They were around, sure, but they nearly always kept their mouths shut to avoid clashing with the general sense of overwhelming approval of the Swiss and Spanish players. Which was huge considering that, between the two of them, Federer and Nadal had at the time won twenty-one of the previous twenty-three Grand Slam titles. There were more than enough reasons for envy among players, but the two leaders' personalities seemed to nullify them.

It wasn't always so. In fact, what was happening then was a complete novelty. Connors and McEnroe hated each other, and they said so in no uncertain terms during their years of fighting for the top spot. The same thing happened with McEnroe and Lendl. In his era, the German Boris Becker was not very cordial either, and anyone who could remember the intensity of the exhibition during the 2010 Indian Wells could see that Pete Sampras and Andre Agassi were a long ways from liking each other. "I remember when I started playing," said Belgian Kim Clijsters, a former world number one player, "I never saw Agassi on the courts, never saw Sampras; they always trained elsewhere. Federer and Nadal, on the other hand, are always on the courts, they train with other guys, and that's fantastic. There is more respect for them than there was in the past for Sampras and Agassi. And that attitude is also permeating throughout the women's circuit," the Belgian added.

The Zen attitude of Nadal and Federer caught the attention of Connors himself, who prefers his own era, the legendary '70s full of screaming, insults, and excesses. He said so in September 2010, "There were no friendly rivalries in my time, everything was very real. Which isn't to say that this isn't, but it was more than just tennis. It was like Larry Bird and Magic Johnson, Celtics and Lakers, Ali and Frazier. The rivalry today is not even close to how intense it was then." Reactions to Connors's analysis confirm that this former number one doesn't exactly inspire sympathy.

But tennis would have been different without Connors, who won 109 tournaments—more than any other professional in history—and who patented his own unique style. He deserves to be heard, and New York is the ideal place for him to speak. Connors likes Rafael Nadal's type of tennis player. He is much more pro-Nadal than pro-Federer. This isn't surprising; the Spaniard is much closer to his own way of understanding and playing tennis than is the Swiss star.

Connors continues, "Players today have all the odds in their favor: trainers, physical therapists, equipment. . . . They have all the opportunities to play better. And you've got kids working hard, like Nadal, who are willing to do whatever's necessary to become better players. And that's what tennis is all about for me. You set out every day looking for perfection. You don't know whether or not you'll achieve it. But you keep striving for it."

"And enjoying the journey . . . "

"You enjoy everything. Playing here in the US Open is a luxury. Not everyone sees what happens here, the hard work, the training, the sacrifice, and how much of yourself you put in. Every experience in tennis was great for me. My problem was that I couldn't enjoy it all in the moment because I was too busy playing and trying to win. Now it's different. These guys win a tournament and they take three weeks off, they enjoy their victory. You couldn't do that before."

"Does the argument over who is the best of all time make sense to you?"

"The truth is, I don't care. Opinions are like shoes; everyone has a pair. I'd rather not get mixed up in that, I don't care. I don't care if my name ever gets mentioned again or not. That's how I feel."

"[Rod] Laver once said that it doesn't make sense to compare the different tennis eras."

"They could give us the rackets and equipment used today. But, what would happen to these guys of today if you gave them our equipment and rackets from back then? How would they play? Would they hit the same? Could they play the same? So, is it fair? No, no it isn't. I think that if you played well and were big in one era, you would be in any. You would find a way to win. A champion is always a champion, because being a champion entails so much more than hitting the ball. You need more. It's simply just a matter of who has it."

"Why do you like Nadal?"

"I like his routine, the way he handles the job each day. He goes out, plays hard, gives it all he's got. He's ready to stay there and do what's necessary to win. And when it's over, it's over. He leaves, and doesn't talk about what would have happened if . . . "

"Were the '70s more romantic than the current years?"

"Well, I didn't say that, I'd rather not talk about it . . . "

"But now you can watch tennis whenever you want and any of the tournaments, whether online or on TV. Do you think there could be a sort of tennis saturation? In the '70s it was less common to watch matches at home."

"It was. Cable television changed that; tennis is shown a lot, both live and recorded . . . Yes, that was a factor."

"Could too much money also be another?"

"Could there be too much money? I think every generation played for that, to create interest, to attract fans, to get sponsors, and to get television interested in the sport. And now it's finally here, so you can't say there's too much money. Take a player like Nadal, for example; he doesn't care about money. Money comes with victory. It seems like the success of your career is measured by your bank account and not by your wins. So some guys will be in it for the money, and others to be part of a group that transcends time."

"Well, each time the millions that the US Open champion will take home is announced, the audience at the Arthur Ashe Stadium all cheer together."

"It's just that money always breeds interest. The more money, the more interest there is. Because then people think that it's greater, and more important. And it is, these guys that are going out to play for those amounts . . . What I'd like to know is whether they'd play, whether they'd act the same if it was their own money on the line. 'Come on, Johnny Mac, we'll play and I'll lay down a million dollars of my own money. You put down another million.' It's much easier to play for someone else's money. Money is a part of the sport, it's how it's made. And in every sport, the amount of money increases to mind-boggling amounts, but that's what we're all working together for, what we all want; that's why professional tennis emerged, to make a living. And they are making one."

"The fight between Federer and Nadal to accrue the most Grand Slam tournaments is obvious. Is that the most important part of the rivalry or just an aspect?"

"It's just an aspect. Is one of them better than the other, keeping in mind that they take turns winning? Nadal wins two matches, Federer one, then Federer another two, Nadal three . . . The idea behind a rivalry is that the tennis has to be good enough to pique interest each time those rivals face each other. People need to be waiting for them to play and wanting to watch the match. They want to see them, they don't care how often they play; that is a rivalry. If Nadal ends up with twenty-two Grand Slams and Federer twenty-one . . . Who knows? The idea is to go out on the court and play that tennis that really sparks interest. And so far, that's what they're doing."

Two years later, in 2012, the interview continued at the same setting, the Queens concrete.

"Do you still think that today's rivalries are so different from the ones in your time as a player?"

"The kids today play great tennis, but some of the things that happen now wouldn't have been possible in our day."

"Are you talking about so polite, so nice?"

"Yeah, that wouldn't have happened. Tennis is great and all that, but I'm sure that rivalries also need to be too. But that's my opinion. That was my time; I hope that McEnroe looks at me now and says, "I had a tough rivalry with him. And it was real, it was true." The same with Borg, the same with Lendl, the same with [Ilie] Năstase. There weren't hugs in those days, there weren't. I don't know what happened. Is it because they respect each other so much? Of course, I also had lots of respect for the players I faced. I guess it's just a sign of age."

"Is it a matter of personality or more just a difference between eras?"

"I don't know. And luckily, I'm not a part of it all, so I don't feel the need to find out. But it would seem very improbable, if I were playing today, that someone would hug me. That's just how I feel. The same with Mac. It's my feeling, it's the way I see it."

When Cliff Drysdale hears Connors's comments about the excess of smiles and nice words, his reaction is almost physical. He doesn't like a word of what his compatriot says. "I completely disagree. Connors was a different animal, Connors had a rivalry with everyone and with everything. Everyone was his enemy, the circuit was his enemy, the other players were his enemies . . . He looked for enemies."

South African when he was a player, and a naturalized US citizen later, Drysdale is one of the founders of the ATP and a recognized television commentator. He has no doubt that the stars of today and the ones of his time are a different breed; they don't go looking for enemies everywhere. "No, not Federer and Nadal. They're different."

Ivan Lendl was a fundamental protagonist in those years. The topic makes him a little uncomfortable during my chat with him in 2012 next to the Barcelona Tennis Club pool. The Czech American in those days trained the Brit Andy Murray and was the proud father of five daughters, three of them golfers. It's not easy to interview Lendl, to get him to open up, to say what he's thinking. But it's possible.

"Aside from the political differences that they've had lately, Nadal and Federer's relationship was unusually good. How do you see it?"

"I don't know enough about the topic and, either way, it's definitely not my problem. Whether they have problems or are best friends is not something that I worry about."

"Sure, but you've said before, and please correct me if I'm wrong, that you didn't have that kind of relationship with McEnroe or Connors."

"I understand what you're saying, but at the time it was my problem because I was involved. Now it's not. My work is with Andy and no one else. And that's what my focus is."

"Okay, let's talk about the periods of time in which you were involved. Do you think the relationships between you, McEnroe, Connors, Vilas, or whomever could have been better? Were you, maybe, too young and hungry for success?"

"I think if you take any group of people, you'll have some that you get along with well and become friends with, some that you are proper with, but who you don't actively try to be around, and who you simply want to avoid. I'm sure the same thing happens in any group, whether it's school, college, on the golf circuit, or in tennis. It's all the same. There will always be people you like and those you don't. And that's alright."

"But at the time, doubtless, McEnroe, Connors, Borg, or Vilas didn't all inspire the same amount of affection or aversion, right?"

"Like I said, I liked some people more than others."

"Which players did you like more than others?"

"I don't think we have to talk about that. People always ask me why I don't write a book. And I say that if you write a book and want it to be successful, you have to say some negative things. Why?"

"Or nice, positive, interesting things . . ."

"But it'll never be as successful as one in which you write negative things. And I'm not interested in that."

"I understand. Maybe in this case you could just write the book you really want to write. You're in a position to say 'I want to tell this story and not another.'"

"But then no one is interested, unfortunately. Especially in the United States."

"Sell it in Europe."

. . .

"Last year, Pat Cash told me that the '80s were much, much harder than nowadays, that the players were ruthless, aggressive both on the court and off it. Do you feel that way when you think about the '80s? Or were the '80s better than the '70s?"

"I can't comment much on the '70s because I only played two years. It was hard; I had to open my eyes wide to see everything happening around me. So I can really only talk about the '80s and maybe the start of the '90s. I don't know . . . I think that they have the same problems that we had. They ask the Grand Slam tournaments for more money because they think they're making more and don't pay the players enough. And they talk about how to split it fairly among the higher players and the lower ones. The same as thirty years ago, they're still talking about the same things."

• • • •

Pat Cash's appearance is frozen in memory. In 1987, he is a young, twenty-two-year-old Australian who, after winning Wimbledon wearing that black-and-white squared handkerchief on his head, marched up the All England Club platform with his Bruce Springsteen attitude and so much joy that it was spilling out of him. No doubt, it was his happiest moment in the midst of the tough '80s era of tennis. Now, prompting him to look back over his career, I asked him the same kinds of questions I had asked Ivan Lendl.

"How was the circuit with McEnroe, Becker, yourself, and others?"

"We were all fierce competitors. Very different personalities, very different people. Players today are much more calm. We had many of those players who were really ferocious: Jimmy Connors, Ilie Năstase, John McEnroe, and even me. And Boris [Becker] had his attitude, too. Or Lendl. Very aggressive, pretty aggressive outside the court. They yelled, talked loud about how good they were, and all that. Lots of times they talked to the media and didn't exactly say nice things about their rivals. I didn't get that, because I always tried to respect the other players, I always thought it best to beat them on the court."

"Could you expand on that a little? You say they were aggressive. Do you remember a situation that was particularly nasty?"

"No, I don't want to go into specifics."

"But they were aggressive, right? McEnroe was aggressive, Connors was aggressive . . ."

"The way they talked, said things about you, said it to the media. Those things . . ."

"And you win Wimbledon in 1987 and become a bigger rival for them. Do you remember any reaction that wasn't particularly kind after that victory?"

"It wasn't uncommon for the only people to congratulate you to be your Davis Cup colleagues. I had a good relationship with the Swedes, [Stefan] Edberg and [Mats] Wilander, who I loved a lot. I congratulated them, we talked a bit. But I don't think I ever talked to Lendl or Becker, aside from a casual exchange. And they said things about my family."

"They did that?"

"Yeah, Boris did it. He would say that I should take my family on trips, and things like that. That I wasn't giving them a proper life, things like that. And afterwards, journalists would ask me, they'd say, 'Boris said this and this.' I don't know if he said it, but I wasn't inter-ested in spending time with him. Lendl would say all kinds of things, too, but it's fine, it was their personalities. And it's been a long time. I always had a great deal of respect for my opponents, for all of them. Which doesn't mean you want to be around them all the time. I was young, I had a family, I didn't go out much with other players. I had my family and the Australians, that was everything."

"Is everything nowadays less spontaneous than twenty or twenty-five years ago? Connors says that back then things weren't so professional, there wasn't as much marketing and management, so they did what they wanted to."

"That's exactly how it was. I used to play music in the other players' rooms; I would go out with McEnroe, we would play. Some people played guitar, that type of thing."

It was hard to establish which player had more merit in the peaceful duopoly in those first years of the third millennium. Federer, for knowing to accept the fact that during his last seasons a rival five years his junior would prevent him from dominating tennis at will? Or Nadal, for knowing how to fight and win without giving in to arrogance or provocation? Once more, the credit seemed to be split.

When asked this same question, Federer made it clear that the peaceful environment hadn't happened by chance, but that it was a deliberate choice. "I always thought it best to be nice to the new generations who enter the sport, rather than making them feel like it was going to be hell for them. And I think that spread to Rafa and the other players. Tennis is a hard sport, sure, but ultimately it is a sport; there are many more things in life."

During the "R" years, it wasn't uncommon to see Federer in the players' lounge pushing the baby stroller with his children nor Nadal, a few feet away, drowning his enormous plates of pasta in olive oil. The Spaniard would jump up and down like a kid while commenting on plays during a soccer match on television. He didn't care if he was next to number five, or 250 in the rankings. He treated everyone equally. The ATP circuit at times offered the same sort of environment as a Saturday tennis club. If Federer called Nadal on the phone the day after each victory at a Grand Slam, the Spaniard would do the same for the Swiss. This was the fruit of the seed that was planted by Federer's visit to Nadal in October 2005 in Basel.

Just days after Connors made his caustic observations about the light rivalry, the topic was analyzed by Nadal in the white van that was taking both of us to Manhattan after he had won his first US Open in 2010. It was already dawn, but the Spaniard was very much awake and reacted instantly to the suggestion that the rivalry between him and Federer was too light. "Rivalries aren't light or not light; they're just defined by whether you take them to an unnecessary extreme or not," said the left-handed player who would close out the year as the number one player in the world. "I think that in other eras, maybe rivalries went beyond what was just the game. I think that in this day and age, Federer and I understand clearly that this is a game. And it's normal to appreciate your rival. I have a special appreciation of Federer because I've experienced some very important moments in my career playing against him. I think he feels the same way towards me. Ultimately, you care for your rivals in a special way. I think that Federer, [Novak] Djokovic, Murray, and I all understand that this is a game. We take everything out on the court, but when it's over, it ends there."

The Russian Marat Safin once said that the higher you rise, the lonelier you feel. Nadal, in complete disagreement, answered at once, "I don't feel alone at all. I feel the same as always. There are always going to be volatile people around you, but the most important people who surround me are practically there for life; they're not there because of where I am today."

That gesture that Federer made toward Nadal in Basel was returned in May 2007 in chilly Hamburg. Federer had just beaten Nadal in the final. It was, after five defeats, his first triumph against the Spaniard on a clay court. And then Nadal surprised him with a request that was common in soccer but uncommon in tennis: he wanted Federer's shirt. Federer gave it to him, of course. "It happened to me once before, that a player had come and asked me for my shirt, a Brazilian player did it once. It happens every once in a while in tennis, because so many players are soccer fans and *they* see it happen a lot. Maybe there'll be a change in tennis stadiums soon; we'll start doing everything topless!" he said between laughs. "You never know . . . It was a nice gesture, we know each other well, so of course it's not a problem."

Was it "operation seduction" Nadal had in mind for Federer? Eight months earlier, the Spaniard had seemed frustrated when he talked publicly during an interview in New York about an idea that was swimming in his head. "I would love to play a doubles tournament with him. I'll ask him if we can play together in Madrid."

While Gerard Tsobanian, the executive director of the Madrid Open, was rubbing his hands together, the Nadals realized that maybe they should have brought the topic up with Federer first—and in private. During a press conference at the US Open, Federer confirmed receipt of the proposal. "Yeah, I heard, he sent me a [text message]." Terse, the Swiss star added nothing more. "And so?" was the follow up. "No," Federer said, even more tersely, before realizing that it would be better to explain in a little more detail his rejection of the offer. "I think it's a great idea on Nadal's part, really quite kind of him. It would be a great promotion for both tennis in general and the tournament in particular," he added. "It would be fun, but the thing is that I never play doubles at the end of the season. Plus, if I did, it would be with Yves [Allegro, a doubles player on the Swiss Davis Cup team]."

A Nadal-Federer duo had no precedence in the modern tennis era. While it's true that during the professional era there were duos with such great players as Borg and Rod Laver, Borg and Vilas, or Borg and Connors, there was never a duo comprised of the two highest ranked players in the world. Andre Agassi and Pete Sampras—the great male tennis rivalry before Federer and Nadal's—didn't play together either.

The "alliance" of the top two never became a reality; they were only ever witnessed playing together at informal exhibition matches. They did it on Children's Day at the Australian Open in 2011. Federer and Nadal on the same side of the net, and a picture to remember the occasion, not significant enough to claim a spot in history. Almost six years later, at the beginning of 2012, the Nadals made the same mistake again. Toni Nadal, Rafael's uncle, publicly declared to several media outlets that his nephew was getting ready for an exhibition match in Madrid at the Santiago Bernabéu stadium. It would be a match with a record number of spectators, and the stars would, of course, be Rafael Nadal and Roger Federer. The response was quick, coming from Tony Godsick, Federer's manager: "The idea of participating in this event was presented to Roger, but he turned down the offer."

Godsick added some comments to sweeten the refusal towards Nadal, who wanted to send the funds they raised to his foundation. A few years before, they had played Christmas exhibition matches in Madrid and in Zurich, and everything had worked out perfectly. It was different this time; the Nadals were proposing a game on July 14, in the middle of summer and six days after the Wimbledon final, a tournament that was too important for Federer and after which he always rested. That year of 2012 witnessed his seventh victory over the All England, and he was very far away from the Real Madrid stadium. He needed to be at his best before the 2012 London Olympics, which were planning an unpublished return to the Wimbledon turf less than three weeks after the close of the tournament.

"The event sounds like it will be truly unique, but the date won't work out for Roger, because he won't be competing, and he'll be getting ready for the Olympics, and so he'll be unable to participate," Godsick explained. Nadal received the news in the Dominican Republic. There, lodged in the singer Julio Iglesias's house, he was getting ready to participate in the Indian Wells and Miami Masters 1000. Real Madrid assured that Nadal would play the benefit match with "another first rate tennis player." The goal was to break the spectator record, and the eighty-five-thousand-seat capacity of the Bernabéu would no doubt allow this. The tennis match with the most spectators up until that point had been an exhibition match between Clijsters and the American Serena Williams, with 35,681 spectators. Novak Djokovic offered to come to the rescue, and the exhibition was officially announced. But it never happened.

Nadal was injured during Wimbledon and couldn't compete for seven months. The Bernabéu record would have to wait. Months later, the Serb also took part in the debate about the peace and love environment and did so to retort against Connors. "I completely disagree. I don't think you have to be disrespectful towards your rival to make the competition fiercer on the circuit," he explained while lounging on a brown leather armchair at the Monte Carlo Country Club. "I think that, on the contrary, yes, we're rivals, competitors, and we fight for the greatest sports trophies in the world, but we have to respect one another. You have to have dignity and fair play, because that's the best of what we have in tennis."

The debate kept growing, and the Latvian Ernests Gulbis, a player as great as he was unappreciated, added his own opinion. He's a man with a rich personality who's not afraid to speak up and will not allow the ATP to censor him. "I respect Roger, Rafa, Novak, and Murray," he said. "But, for me, all four of them are boring players. Their interviews are boring." The peace and love years had been unbearable for Gulbis. "It is a joke. It is Federer who started this fashion. He has a superb image of the perfect Swiss gentleman. I repeat, I respect Federer but I don't like it that young players try to imitate him. . . . If I win, the guy on the other side of the net, I have sent him home, that is the reality. I have no interest in appearing nice. On the court, it is a war . . . I would like interviews to be more like in boxing. OK, maybe those guys are not the most brilliant on earth but, when they face each other down at the weigh-in, they bring what the fans want: war, blood, emotion."

Gulbis, it was clear, wasn't interested in being politically correct during that interview with the newspaper, *L'Equipe*. "All that is missing in tennis, where everything is clean and white with polite handshakes and some nice shots, while the people want to see broken rackets and hear outbursts on the court."

During one interview with *GQ* magazine, Murray dropped some hints that were no doubt known to Gulbis but not so much to the general public. If it were up to the Scot, his responses during press conferences would be a lot spicier. That's what you could expect from as big a boxing fan as he is. "I always try to be honest in my answers, but they do tend to be boring so that I don't have to deal with a scandal later. I would say that I'm quite different from what most people believe."

Nadal also got involved in the debate sparked by Gulbis, and he wasn't especially kind. "It's just different values and ways of viewing the world. Maybe he just comes from another culture," he said during an interview with *Marca*. "Everyone is free to think what they want. The sort of attitude that he's promoting in that interview is totally contrary to what should be an example for the youth. Deliberately or not, young people take note of us, and what he said is fundamentally wrong on an educational level."

McEnroe didn't agree with Nadal. During an interview with the *Guardian*, the former number one posed a thought: "I don't know how much the British keep up with Andy Murray nor how much they know about him, but I don't think he's well known in the United States."

Bud Collins, probably the most famous tennis-specialized journalist in the world, was a witness who particularly enjoyed the peace and love years of the world of tennis. Collins, who passed away in March of 2016, was readily identifiable thanks to the unusual pants with outlandish designs and impossible colors that he wore for decades at all the great tennis events throughout the world, but what was important about the American was everything that he saw, everything he knew, and how well he described it. It's no coincidence that he wrote the most complete tennis encyclopedia to date. It was January 2011, the height of the peaceful years, and Collins was fascinated with what he saw. He felt that he was witnessing a special era.

"It's one of the best, without doubt, because between Connors and McEnroe there was hatred, and between Connors and Lendl, lots of hatred. The same thing happened with McEnroe and Lendl. There was no air of friendship, but everyone liked Borg. They behaved with him.

"Borg was discreet and a role model; he was the guy whom everyone admired. When McEnroe played against him, he never threw one of his tantrums. These guys, Federer and Nadal, are different. They are making a great gesture of goodwill that those before didn't. Of course, they're making a lot more money. But there's no envy, and that, to me, is incredible: no envy! They respect each other." Collins sees a precedent to Federer-Nadal: the rivalry between Martina Navrátilová and Chris Evert, the greatest duel that women's tennis has ever had, a story that extended throughout eighty matches. "They were fierce on the court, but they liked each other. They respected each other. I think that word is the key: respect."

With each mention by Collins of the '70s, the image of the players from that era sinks further into the mud. "Connors never respected anyone, and neither did McEnroe. Lendl was a tall and quiet guy, but I don't think he respected his rivals much either. This is a different period, a period of cordiality."

Collins has seen enough tennis that he can carry the comparison several decades beyond the '70s: "Năstase behaved poorly all the time, Laver and [Ken] Rosewall had a good relationship, but neither of them got along with Pancho Gonzales, who was another one who hated his rivals." So he has to go pretty far back: "Fred Perry was really a great guy during the '30s, but a lot of his rivals thought he was a show-off with all the jumping over the net and waving to the stands that he did."

Collins doesn't make any concessions when analyzing the duel between Pete Sampras and Andre Agassi either: "It wasn't like Connors and McEnroe. It was simply cold, distant. They played each other their whole lives, since they were kids. Sampras felt that his game was better, but that people would always find better things to say about Agassi. Sampras didn't like that. And Agassi didn't either."

And though Nadal and Federer might not have liked it, Collins resorts to a pretty unexpected image to describe the relationship between the two during the peaceful years: "When they get together, they're like a pair of enormous panda bears."

CHAPTER 8

Hurricane

SOMETHING WASN'T RIGHT ON THAT night; the streets were empty and the rain had reached biblical levels. Something wasn't right, because water shouldn't be leaking through the roof and especially not into one of the most luxurious suites in one of the most emblematic hotels in New York. Dozy, but vigilant, Adam Helfant called the reception desk in the early morning. "Don't worry," they told him. "It's not dangerous." But the water started to leak in more and more. So much so, that the most powerful name in men's tennis, alarmed, asked for a different room at four in the morning. A couple of hours later, when it was morning and he was eating breakfast, the then-executive director of the ATP was feeling curious about the state of the roof in his original room. "It fell completely in," was the answer from reception.

Three years later, the same situation might have sparked some ironic jokes among journalists, and even in Federer's and Nadal's circles. The two "R"s had felt anything but sympathy for Helfant's predecessor, the South African Etienne de Villiers. But with Helfant it was different. American, and a former executive of Nike, he had been in charge of the circuit during three fairly peaceful years before retiring.

It was Sunday morning on August 28, 2011, when Hurricane Irene struck the northeast coast of the United States. The roof of his suite falling in was just another detail to add to the past fortnight of strange happenings in an unpleasant environment. It had been so tense that such players as Nadal and Andy Roddick had been emboldened with the possibility of a tennis players' strike. Weeks later, Federer would take it upon himself to make that impossible.

Lots of tension. Was it Irene's fault? It had been one of the most worrisomely anticipated hurricanes in history, but by the time it arrived in Manhattan it had been downgraded to the status of tropical storm. Even so, it left at least fifty-five dead in the Caribbean, the United States, and Canada, as well as around $10 billion in damages. Irene was no joke, although there were no victims in Manhattan following a public awareness campaign laden with hysterical edges. Neither the New York City government, in the hands of the independent Mayor Michael Bloomberg, nor the federal, led by Democratic President Barack Obama, wanted to risk repeating George W. Bush's mistake in 2005 of underestimating Hurricane Katrina, which had raked across New Orleans and left 1,836 dead and 135 missing.

But from that Saturday night and into Sunday, Manhattan looked as it never had before: the streets empty, the restaurants closed, the bar windows boarded up. The most crowded and busy asphalt on the planet was as quiet as a graveyard. Only the howl of the wind and the occasional whine of a siren gave proof, every so often, to the fact that there was life out there.

Manhattan had to wait until 6:53 in the morning to confirm that it was safe. Anderson Cooper, a star reporter for CNN Television, aired the question that was running through many people's minds: "I'm really surprised; is this the most we're going to see in terms of rain?" Cooper, at least that once, clung to the facts without embellishment. He had great news. Manhattan wouldn't be flooded, the hurricane winds wouldn't destroy the skyscraper windows. But after days and days of cataclysmic weather warnings, most of his viewers hadn't slept a minute that night; they were expecting more. They expected bad news, very bad. The days of hurricane Irene would be great material for a journalist's doctoral thesis.

Television decided that, at the end of a summer lacking in news, there would be no better way to raise ratings than to present Irene as being the beginning of the end. Judging by what aired on CNN, Fox, CNBC, NY1, and other round-the-clock information outlets, nothing happened in the rest of the world during the weekend of the 27th and 28th, nor even in the rest of the United States; there was only Irene. The forecast catastrophe corresponded perfectly with the concept that the memory of a much more significant event produced, as it would be the tenth anniversary of the September 11 attacks in 2001. Ten years later, the men's US Open final would be played on that emblematic date, although the rains would delay it for a whole day.

Irene ended up hitting the city and state of New York, as well as several other places in the eastern US. Manhattan itself was unharmed, but to the rest of the world Manhattan *is* New York and New York is Manhattan. If someone says that a hurricane is approaching the "Big Apple," the first image that comes to the minds of millions of people is that of a lead-colored funnel bearing down on the Empire State Building. But New York is more than just that one skyscraper and much more than just Manhattan. The state of New York extends for more than fifty thousand square miles and is home to nineteen million inhabitants. The city, with its five boroughs, consists of 300 square miles and eight million inhabitants. And Manhattan, the crown jewel, squeezes a million and a half people into a twenty-three-square-mile area.

None of it mattered; the components of the story were tempting to be able to let it go without exploiting it to the maximum. And although Irene turned out to be kinder than what was anticipated, the weekend before the start of the 2011 US Open was certainly different from any other before it. The tropical humidity, the gray and static-charged sky, and the rain all complicated the activities on the cement courts until, on Saturday just after noon, the players abandoned the installations at Flushing Meadows. The US Open, literally, hung up a "closed" sign. And that's how the best tennis players on the planet spent their weekend: locked up in their hotels.

A hurricane in New York may be unusual, but it's not the first time that the threat came to pass. In 1938, the tournament had ended six days after it was supposed to, and in 1960 hurricane Donna resulted in the Australian Neale Fraser lifting his trophy seven days behind schedule.

The most frequently asked question among the few players, trainers, and family members who spent those hours at Flushing Meadows was this: "What floor are you on?" Some were happy that they weren't too low, because of the fear of flooding—unheard of in the middle of Manhattan—and others, including the Spaniard Feliciano López, on the 42nd floor, were worried about the effects of the winds blowing at more than 100 miles per hour. Such players as López and the Argentinian Juan Mónaco talked satisfyingly about their plays of the day; they had arrived earlier than ever to the club to train during the 8:30 turn in the morning, which no player wants to do. After 11, due to all the rain, it was only possible to practice on the indoor courts, which is what Nadal, David Nalbandian, Andy Murray, Juan Martín del Potro, Maria Sharapova, and Maria Kirilenko did.

The uncertainty was universal, although, certainly, some were more worried than others. "It's scary in a certain way, because we don't know how hard it's going to hit us. And I have a family, and we're in New York, which, you know, isn't a normal city; it's quite a bit larger with all these buildings," Federer said during a press release—many journalists had not been able to land in New York either—before leaving the tournament immediately after to lock himself up in his hotel. "I'm going to follow the news closely, and I'll try to be as safe as I can until we all get over this," added the five-time US Open champion.

What to do when faced with the prospect of spending a weekend locked up in a hotel, in a city with its public transportation shut down, and with closed cinemas, theaters, and restaurants? "Watch some movies," was the solution Nadal offered. "No one knows exactly what's happening. The club closes, everything in Manhattan will be closed," said the Spaniard who would be defending the title on which Irene had decided to play a dirty trick.

That Saturday, August 27 was the chosen day for Nadal and his coauthor, the British journalist John Carlin, to present *Rafa*, the left-handed Spaniard's autobiography. The presentation would be split between a morning press conference with the most important media outlets in the world, and, in the afternoon, a signing session at the local Barnes & Noble on Fifth Avenue. But Irene emptied the press hall, in which the anxiety of many was evident, and caused the event at the giant bookstore to be canceled.

Rafa, the book, would start out on an injured foot. And things would only get worse for the autobiographical work, as it was born alongside one attention-grabbing fact: Nadal, the author, hadn't read his own book, hadn't seen the pages on which his name had been printed as the author in a font twice as large as that of his coauthor's name. One thing is understandable: no one expects Nadal or any other athlete at his level to sit in front of a keyboard to type out his story. No, that's why Carlin was there, an experienced journalist and sharp investigator, author of *Playing the Enemy*—the book about Nelson Mandela that ended up becoming a Hollywood movie under the title *Invictus* and directed by Clint Eastwood. Not having read your own book is one thing, but indicating publicly that you hadn't seen it is another thing entirely.

Taking into account that confession—which, fortunately for him and his management, passed by nearly unnoticed—it was much easier to understand the player's reactions during the eight press conferences he attended during that tournament. "Rafa, in your book . . ." That's how many of the questions that were directed to the Spaniard in Flushing Meadows started. At each press conference, Nadal took questions from one or several of the English-speaking journalists about the book. It made sense, as the book had been published only in English and wouldn't be available in Spanish until the following month. Some of the questions were easy to answer, but others, not so much, especially the ones aimed at the relationship with his uncle, and coach, Toni, a tie which was explained in detail and not without a degree of frankness, in *Rafa*.

As with any book that looks to be a bestseller, *Rafa* forced Rafa to hold a series of publisher-arranged interviews with a selection of media sources. One of these was with Tom Perrotta, a reporter for the *Wall Street Journal*. The interview took place in a car, between commercial appointments, and Perrotta wanted to know, with good reason, why Nadal had been so hard on his uncle in the book. "I'm not a boy anymore," Nadal summed it up. His uncle, he added, couldn't control his life down to the smallest detail anymore. "Before, when he said something, I would follow orders. Now, I can answer back. Sometimes it bothers him, but that's how it goes. At the same time, he has to accept that I'm twenty-five years old, and I have more opinions than I did before."

Those few phrases, full of honesty, were no different than what you would have heard any young twenty-five-year-old say about his father, mother, or, in Nadal's lucky case, an overly present uncle. But, of course, Nadal was not just any twenty-five-year-old young man, and in just a matter of hours, a part of the Spanish sporting world became embroiled in a conversation around one idea: that the end of one of the most productive professional relationships in the whole history of uncles and nephews was coming to an end. And so, the Nadals started seeing on Twitter—the vehicle of communication that was just beginning to impose itself in those days—name after name of new trainers for the player. Toni was soon to be history.

That, at first, disconcerted, and then bothered, both uncle and nephew. Not because Nadal wouldn't have said what he said, not because it's not true that at twenty-five you're different than you were at eighteen. No, what bothered both uncle and nephew was the disturbance that it stirred up, the undesirability of a debate at the start of a US Open at which Nadal was not arriving in his best shape. He had already been mentally tortured in the previous months by Djokovic, who was beating him in final after final during that season. The amazing thing was that the commotion had been started by themselves, through the book first, and then by the interview in the *Wall Street Journal*.

The tennis player said, through Carlin's coauthorship, a lot of things in *Rafa*. But the book does include one absolutely unmistakable error about Nadal, which is that it mentions more than once that Monte Carlo in 2005 was where he had won his very first title. But the fact is that his inaugural title was won during the European summer of 2004 in the Polish city of Sopot. Carlin had probably misunderstood Nadal when he told him that the principality had been the stage of his first Masters Series title. And since Nadal hadn't read his own book, he never had the chance to correct this detail.

The English version was checked over by two people: Carlos Costa, Nadal's agent; and Sebastián, the player's father—Toni's brother. Despite the level of detail with which Nadal, in his book, described how difficult his uncle Toni had been even in his earliest childhood, both the agent as well as the father must have been content with what the writer wrote in the dedication, "A very special thanks to my uncle, trainer, and friend, Toni Nadal." Because that's the truth of it: Rafa is impossible to understand without recognizing Toni's influence on him. And vice versa. It took two Nadals to make one, and there's something there that will never be broken, because their relationship is symbiotic: you can talk to Toni Nadal about one topic and, 164 feet away, two minutes later, hear his nephew make an almost identical observation about the same thing. Which isn't to say that young Nadal wasn't thinking for himself.

"I can say more, and we argue more than we did before, but I still have a great deal of respect for him, that will never change," he said to the *Wall Street Journal* before saying the phrase that would give rise to speculations in Spain. "He has three children, and sometimes he gets tired of traveling all over the world all the time. You never know what could happen in the future."

The future is, in effect, always a mystery. But at the time, at the end of that New York summer in 2011, Nadal honored one of his favorite phrases—"I won't lie to you"—and perhaps leaned a little too far toward excessive sincerity, something which no journalist in his right mind could pass up.

"I didn't read my book," Nadal admitted. "Really, I didn't. I will. I need a lot of focus to be able to read the book in English, and, anyhow, I know my life," he argued. Sure, he did, but Carlin didn't. Not even his agent and father knew all the details. "I'll read it when it comes out in Spanish, very soon. I'll do it because I'm interested in how it works out, right? How it's written, you know?" he continued with complete sincerity. The writer, Carlin, had been a first-rate journalist, but all the anecdotes, the memories, and the experiences were Nadal's, and he was famous for something different, his skills with a racket. The Spaniard had shared the details of his life during long talks with the Brit, Carlin, at Qatar and Australia.

But Nadal is a lucky man. During the same press conference at which he admitted that he hadn't read the autobiography to which he had signed his name and during which he used confusing vocabulary to answer a question about the American Andre Agassi's unconfirmed use of doping, a very strange thing happened that made everyone forget what he had said. On that September 4 2011, the tennis gladiator, the man who had won more than most, the almighty, closed his eyes with an expression of pain, tilted his head back, and started to sink, to slump slowly and inexorably in his chair. "Gentlemen, gentlemen . . ." Rafael Nadal whispered, while a score of journalists had already forgotten that he was analyzing the differences between Gilles Müller and Ivo Karlović's serves. Before their eyes, the second greatest tennis player in the world was falling, and no one knew why.

"I can't keep going," whispered the title defender. "Can you call the physio, please, can you call the physio?" Nadal said with his eyes closed and the pain reflected on his face. Benito Pérez Barbadillo, his press agent and the man closest to him, reacted emotionally and paled. "Your knee," he said. But it wasn't his knee; there was cramping happening simultaneously in his quadriceps and his hamstring. While it was nothing out of the ordinary for tennis players, the spectacle usually takes place in the locker room; it is rare for a player to get twisted up in front of the press.

A couple of minutes later, the room was empty. Pérez Barbadillo was inside with Nadal, and the legendary Manolo Santana, the pioneer of Spanish tennis, went in to see what had happened to the young man who had pushed the boundaries of his successes so much further. Santana left the press conference room promptly after, with Nadal still laying on his back on the rug, boxed in between the wall, a chair, and a desk.

"You're incredible. It's not enough to create a spectacle on the court. You have to do it in a press conference too!" Pérez Barbadillo said before bursting into laughter, along with Rafael Maymó, Nadal's physiotherapist, who had finally arrived after an urgent search.

"Don't laugh, this really hurts!" Nadal complained in an almost childish tone, in pain no doubt, and not very willing to be the butt of any jokes.

María Francisca Perelló was waiting outside. She was Nadal's girl-friend, and most referred to her as "Xisca," while the player called her "Mary." Her gesture of concern turned out to be unnecessary the next day, when Nadal trained as usual dressed in a yellow shirt and red pants, the bull-fighting colors of Spain. It was a subtle sign of strength, a chromatic "I'm at my best," which turned out to be insufficient, as those days in New York ended up reflecting a loss of intensity in the years of domination by the two "R"s.

CHAPTER 9

Madrid

"NADAL DOESN'T KNOW HOW TO play tennis." This phrase, uttered by a Romanian, Ion Tiriac, reflects one of the longest and most personal battles that Rafael Nadal was embroiled in throughout his career. You could say that Nadal won that war, although he lost several battles along the way, and reached the limits of his patience. It wasn't easy for the young man from the small city of Manacor in Mallorca to first understand and then confront the Romanian who was forged as a man, player, trainer, and entrepreneur during the Cold War era. A man who had worked alongside his country's secret service during the years in which the command center of Eastern Europe was in Moscow. A man with a noticeable Argentinian accent known to present his assertions, ideas, and proposals as deeply and accurately as they were sensationalist at times.

Tiriac was one of the biggest tennis personalities of the past four decades. He took up the racket after leaving a career in ice hockey and won Roland Garros in doubles alongside Ilie Năstase, as well as a minor tournament in singles on the circuit. He wasn't a bad player, but his influence and power had always been outside the court rather than on it. His bushy mustache, which was connected to his distinctive sideburns, and his tinted sunglasses, all made him a highly recognizable figure for the public, especially in Argentina, the country that influenced his Spanish during the years he coached and managed Guillermo Vilas.

With a deep knowledge of tennis—he coached Năstase, Vilas, Boris Becker, and Henri Leconte, among others—his tournaments, during his years in Germany and later in Madrid, were always greater than just tennis. Tiriac organized things in a big way, and he did it in part thanks to his great ability to make the host city take many more risks and pay out more than he did. A tournament "made in Tiriac" is always certain to be something different. He himself says, "I have a history. With all due respect and modesty, no one can manage a tournament better than I can."

Tiriac dreams of tennis being more like Formula 1, a select group of players fighting in no more than fifteen or twenty mega encounters each year. The rest of the players, the hypothetical "laborers" ranked lower than number 40 would have to content themselves with playing in a sort of second division. "If it was up to me, I would run tournaments with thirty-two players. Today, what people want is to see the best against the best." He's not the only one who holds this idea, but he is the loudest proponent of it. Speaking clearly is a habit of Tiriac's.

And that's what he did on the night of June 1, 2005, in Paris, which marked the first of his disagreements with Nadal. The air was suffocating on the second floor of the main building of the Auteuil hippodrome, about a mile from Roland Garros. Nadal wasn't yet the winner of the French Open, but he was having a great week; in two days it would be his nineteenth birthday, and five days after that he would conquer his first musketeer trophy. The Spaniard was already "the" player, the man who had just gone through Costa do Sauípe, Acapulco, Monte Carlo, Barcelona, Roma, and who had just begun the conquering of Paris.

Surrounded by Spanish journalists during dinner, Tiriac analyzed the imminent champion. "Nadal's case is interesting because he's a kid who wins matches and doesn't know how to play tennis." It was meant as a compliment, but most of the attendees did not take it as such, and especially not Nadal when the phrase reached him. Tiriac dissected the left-handed player. He was trying to show that considerable future growth was still possible for a tennis player who was already one of the greatest. "His serve isn't correct; he could be serving a lot better," he assured. "He's also not completely developed physically; he could drop a few more pounds, tone himself a bit more," the Romanian added. He recommended that the Spaniard play doubles more often, "Not to volley really, but to learn how to move. "Nadal wins two or three times the points, he could seal the deal sooner," he said.

The analysis was true, and similar to what the American Andre Agassi would say five months later in Shanghai. "Nadal is, without a doubt, a great talent, but he's signing checks that one can only hope his body will be able to pay. He plays hard for each point, and you can only hope he stays healthy, but there is a lot of wear and tear there. A great career depends not only on what he can do, but also on health. You have to stay healthy." Those words of Agassi's were also not pleasing to Nadal, who had to quit that Shanghai Masters due to a foot injury. But Agassi's comment was specific, whereas Tiriac was analyzing all the years of Nadal's evolution as a player. "It's not the power that makes him different; the key is in the acceleration of his racket, which is 10 percent greater than others." The Romanian even threw a compliment directly towards the left-handed Spaniard, although it was too late to win his affection. "Nadal has, above all, dedication more than motivation. Because we all have motivation. I would love to win Wimbledon, but I can't."

Four months after the "doesn't know how to play tennis" comment, Tiriac doubled down. Nadal had just defeated, after four intense hours, the powerful Croatian server, Ivan Ljubičić, 7–6, in the fifth set to win the Madrid Masters Series. It was his first indoor title, a special success in his career because at the time he was still considered basically just a clay court player. And what did Tiriac say during the awards ceremony? "Mister Nadal doesn't know how to play tennis." He explained the statement and added detail to try and explain that he saw in the Spaniard a great champion with much more room to improve, but by then Nadal had already written him off. The young Spaniard took the statement as an affront, regardless of whether or not he understood the depth of what the Romanian was trying to say.

One of the reasons why Nadal and Federer got along so well for so many years is that they share a very basic concept: respect. Respect is almost sacred for the both of them, a detail of some significance in a sport that has included several fairly disrespectful top players. When Nick Kyrgios in 2014 scored a point on the central court at Wimbledon by hitting the shot between his legs, Nadal took note of the Australian's exuberant celebration. He, in the same situation, would have reacted differently. A measured celebration, no smiling, and almost an apology to his adversary for the lucky hit. Exactly the same as Federer would have done, reflecting definitively the etiquette and rules of chivalry of tennis. Nadal understood the technical tennis-related reasoning behind Tiriac's analysis, sure, but he couldn't believe that the Romanian would say it in that way to the entire Spanish press and especially to his own country's audiences in the hour of one of his greatest triumphs. And what was the world of tennis saying during those weeks that Tiriac was claiming Nadal didn't know how play? During those days in 2005 when the Spaniard was dominating on clay and creating impact with his style, with that energy and passion that seemed endless in each match?

- Mariano Puerta, Argentinian and his rival in the Roland Garros final in 2005: "He's a demon! Incredible, incredible! He jumps around the locker room, screaming, 'Let's go, Rafa!' He's destined to make tennis history."
- Agassi, Roland Garros champion six years prior: "Nadal showed that there's a way to play this sport that no one had tried yet."
- José Luis Clerc, Argentinian and former fourth ranked, worldwide: "He's a player to fear. He runs through the locker rooms, jumps up to the rafters! I've never seen anything like it in my life, and I've spent years in locker rooms."
- Pat Cash, Australian, champion of Wimbledon '87: "I lost to him during an exhibition. He was fourteen years old, but I took

heart by thinking that I had lost to a future Roland Garros champion."

- Mark Miles, executive director of the ATP: "I can't remember anything like it in the past twenty years, not since Boris Becker won Wimbledon."
- Mats Wilander, Swedish, former top ranked worldwide, and three times Roland Garros champion: "Nadal isn't afraid of anything or anyone when he plays tennis."
- John McEnroe, American, former top ranked worldwide: "I don't remember anyone as intimidating since Boris Becker in 1985."
- Boris Becker, former top ranked worldwide and three times Wimbledon champion: "Nadal is exactly what this sport needs."
- Roger Federer: "Almost no one plays like he does."

Not one of them had said that Nadal didn't know how to play tennis, although many agreed with the fundamentals of Tiriac's assessment. For that reason, after beating Puerta, during the minutes after his first Roland Garros title, Nadal didn't even look at Tiriac, despite having "invaded" his private box in the Philippe Chatrier stadium to approach and embrace all his family and friends on that dark and cloudy afternoon in Paris.

Tiriac watched him closely from just a few feet away during that instant when Nadal transformed into the Cash who, eighteen years earlier in Wimbledon '87, had amazed everyone in the All England Club when he climbed up into one of the boxes to greet his own. As time went on, that distance of just a few feet would become miles, because Nadal and Tiriac would clash every year. In 2002, the Romanian took the tournament that he was organizing in Stuttgart to Madrid. Things started off poorly because the Czech, Jiří Novák, injured himself in the first final, and Agassi had taken the title without playing.

But Tiriac is tough. Assisted by Manolo Santana, the best Spanish tennis player of all time until the appearance of Nadal, and by Gerard Tsobanian, a French Armenian with an eye for business in tennis, they established throughout the years a series of very high-profile and innovative changes. That was how they decided to celebrate games during evening prime time with models acting as ball girls. A couple of years later, they copied the idea with male models for the WTA (Women's Tennis Association) Masters.

The whole world talked about the tournament in Madrid, which attracted the most famous people in the city every night; many of them knew little about tennis but found themselves captivated by the sophistication and luxury on display before their eyes in the VIP zone, where eating and drinking was an almost paranormal experience, thanks to a catering company that was the same as the one Bernie Ecclestone used for Formula 1.

Then came the construction of The Magic Box, a complex both cold and futuristic on the outskirts of the city so that the tournament could be played in May on a clay court instead of indoors during October. "There is no other venue that can close three fields in five minutes and continue on despite rain," Tiriac proudly declared. He wanted to show that tennis must adapt itself to the needs of television to survive. "You can't just say—he added in his Argentinian accent—'This is London' when it rains, when you have 200 countries watching on television. The sport isn't what it used to be, it's different from twenty years ago."

Tiriac did a bit of everything in Madrid, at times by applying subtle threats. And not-so-subtle ones at other times. His main threat for years was of taking the tournament to Asia if the city wouldn't build him The Magic Box to get out of the Rockodromo, his original headquarters, where he didn't have enough space to unfurl all his ideas.

In the midst of three successive bids to hold the Olympic games—all three failures—Madrid gave Tiriac everything. He was lucky enough to arrive during the years of euphoria and to be done by 2009, when the economic crisis changed Spain. And so Tiriac came to dream of a fifth Grand Slam in Madrid, "What I see for the future, with all due respect to the Grand Slams, is that there should be more room for competition. In prizes, in quality, in infrastructure, in everything." The idea, brought up during an interview with DPA in 2007, was cause for worry in Melbourne, Paris, London, and New York, headquarters of the four greatest tournaments in the world of tennis.

"This is a provocation by Tiriac. The Grand Slams' rights have a basis in the rights of history," Francisco Ricci Bitti, president of the International Tennis Federation (ITF), responded three months later. "Legally, it is possible to make changes, but looking at history, I think it's very improbable," the Italian added. But Tiriac knew very well what he was doing; his idea wasn't baseless lunacy. The ITF Constitution allows the creation of new Grand Slam tournaments or the switching of their base cities. According to article 2.2b, the ITF can "acknowledge other Grand Slams for one or more years, according to the determination of the Board." That is to say, no Grand Slam tournament is assured its home base forever, nor do there necessarily need to be four. There could be more.

Disquieted by the intentions of the powerful Romanian entrepreneur, Tennis Australia, the Australian tennis federation, had undergone some serious self-criticism by December, two months after that interview. "The Australian Open, one of the four Grand Slams, is at a crossroads, and its future position, as well as its existence, is at risk. The demand for tennis tournaments has grown quite dramatically over the last five years, with considerable financial backing in Asia and the Near East."

The Australian Open had been an example of modernity and audacity toward the end of the '80s, when it abandoned the Kooyong Stadium turf and gone, at the time, to Flinders Park. Now it was suffering through a growing crisis. Its installations were no longer the latest technology, and were too small to accommodate the growing number of spectators, which grew from three hundred thirty thousand in 1988 to almost double that number in 2007. Years later, with three roofed stadiums, nearly eight hundred thousand spectators, all kinds of benefits—so basically, much more money for the players—the Australian Open was no longer in danger.

But Tiriac's idea had taken hold. Na Li, from China, said in Melbourne that she would like to see the Australian Grand Slam moved to Shanghai, to which the Australian Cash responded by saying that it would be a shame if "one of the sport's institutions be moved to a country that just started becoming interested in tennis less than a decade ago."

There was more. *"It's said that the Spanish want to buy Australia. Do you think Australia can be a Grand Slam forever?"* they asked Federer before the start of the tournament. "Well, 'forever' . . . I don't know. 'Forever' is a long time, but I don't see a change in the near future," the Swiss responded. The answer wasn't exactly what the Australians wanted to hear. While the Australians were reacting, Tiriac came out to defend himself with a letter in the French *Tennis Magazine*. The publication had been hard on the Romanian's idea. The response was also hard, "Please, stop *demonizing* Madrid and Ion Tiriac."

While Tiriac was defending himself, Tsobanian continued creating motives for nervousness among the four tennis capitals.

"We haven't done any probing into the purchase of the Australian Open, nor do we plan to, but if there were a real opportunity for purchase, we would be willing to sit down and talk. We aspire to have the best tournament in the world, and we believe that this is a worthy aspiration. The creation of a new Grand Slam doesn't depend on Mr. Tiriac, but the question is who has the power to make that decision."

Good question. The answer was complex, because the ITF never wanted to arrive at such a problem in the first place. If the federation that ruled tennis were to someday be controlled by people with ideas similar to Tiriac's, there might be a chance, but the racket sport is very closely tied to its traditions. A new Grand Slam added to the four existing ones would be a true revolution.

Four years later, Tiriac continued with his provocations: "Let the Grand Slams stay; I want the best against the best. I'll be asked to put up the same amount of money that Roland Garros hands out, and that's not a problem. I don't want to make a Grand Slam. I want something better. If I really get crazy, I can make a Superslam." He wouldn't get crazy, nor would he be given the chance. Better, then, to bet on smaller revolutions, to opt for something even more provocative than the beautiful models helping the players. Something like changing the color of the clay that had always been orange, and playing on blue clay.

A decent doubles player, the American Eric Butorac still remembers the day on which Adam Helfant, the then chief of the ATP, proposed Tiriac's idea of playing on a blue court to the Players Council. "He looked at me, I was the first. 'Butorac, what do you think?' And I said yeah, if it was the same clay, and the ball would probably be easier to see on blue, so we should try it."

Helfant then gave Nadal the word. "It's a disaster," the Spaniard said, forcefully. "It's a terrible idea," Djokovic added. "It looks like a circus," Federer concluded. "I wanted to die," Butorac admits today. "I wanted to hide under a table."

Butorac, in 2014, became the president of the ATP Players Council, but at the time he was just another part of the organization over which Federer was president, Nadal was vice president, and Djokovic was a distinguished member. For a player without history or success to be at odds with the three of them was no small thing. Despite how hard the three top tennis players were on the idea, Helfant decided to give Tiriac a chance. And so, at the end of 2011, the players all realized that in May of the upcoming year they would have to play on a surface never before used in the history of tennis: blue clay.

"It's a long story, and I think it's sad that we'll be playing on a surface that a lot of players don't accept," Federer lamented during the London Masters. "But that's how it goes. I don't really know whether to view this as being positive or negative." By that time, Federer and Nadal had open and growing differences of opinion about how tennis should be played, and the Spaniard felt more and more impotent in his attempts to convince his Swiss friend.

During the blue clay affair, however, Federer had been absolutely "Nadal-ish." "I think it's sad that a player like Rafa has had to struggle, in his own country's tournament, against a surface he doesn't want to play on. With regards to this topic, I'm listening to Rafa. And it is sad, really, that we have to play on a surface that not all the players want to play on." Nadal, who is no Tiriac, but also knows how to speak force-fully, was complaining a lot in those days: "I hope I don't have to play on blue grass someday."

Ivan Lendl, the Czech American who dominated tennis for several years in the '80s, commented on the whole business, using that metallic tone of irony that is his trademark: "Let's paint the grass at Wimbledon pink, what do you think?" Neither blue, nor pink. That will never happen at Wimbledon. But just as Lendl had played before on an orange cement court during an exhibition match in Orange County, California—and he still laughs about it—Tiriac and Tsobanian started inviting players in the months leading up to the 2013 tournament to a mountainous region in Catalonia to try the blue clay. A lot of them, especially the women, liked it. The Brit Andy Murray offered the most thoughtful analysis of the innovation among the star players. "It's just a few weeks until the French Open, which is played on orange clay. So it would be better for the players if it took place on orange clay. But I've also noticed that it's sometimes very hard to see the ball in Madrid. I understand the reasons behind this, it makes the tournament somewhat unique and different, and sometimes that's good for the circuit. But the timing is bad for the players. I never played on blue clay, nor do I know what it would be like. It will be a new experience."

Pressured by the public opposition of the greatest player ever to come from Spanish tennis, the Madrid organizers asked that they be given a chance. "We ask for good faith. Let every player who tries the court report truthfully and in good faith just how it feels," Tsobanian demanded. "Do they not go from one color to another during the indoor tournaments? So, where's the problem? We're talking about switching from one color to another just once, not all the time." Tsobanian then ran through a series of arguments in favor of the innovation in Madrid, and reminded that Roland Garros would experiment that year with a pink clay court for promotional purposes. "Is it crushed stone? It is. Is the color different? Yes. Can you see the ball better? Yes. Is it a better experience for everyone ? Yes. So then, what are the arguments against it going to be?"

Nadal held that Madrid is already a complicated tournament due to the fact that it's played 1,800 feet above sea level, which means that it's a contest in which the ball flies fast, which is ideal for offensive tennis and not for men, like him, who stand toward the back to play with top-spin. "I don't support this," Nadal insisted. "You're in the middle of the earth season, and the earth in Europe is orange. You have Madrid and Rome, one right after the other; Madrid is the only tournament at altitude, and now they're changing the clay color. It's a mistake. The players don't benefit at all. Tennis doesn't benefit at all. Only one person benefits, the owner of the tournament. I don't understand how the ATP can accept this."

Tsobanian didn't see anything that backed up the criticism. "Do you know any two tournaments that have the same clay? There are no two tournaments in the world that offer the same sensation when playing. If any player says that, then they're doing so in bad faith." Bad faith from Nadal? Tsobanian hurried to clarify that he absolutely considered the young left-handed player "very well educated." "Rafael has revolutionized tennis, he is a revolutionary, an innovator. His physical play, the rotation of the ball, the sleeveless shirts . . . And our tournament, finally, is the same as he is. We are a young and innovative tournament, he is a young and innovative player. We're identical, Nadal could be our icon."

The idea of turning Nadal into the tournament icon was, because of its impracticality, almost a joke. And Tsobanian knew it. The fact that the competition was sponsored by the insurance company Mutua Madrileña and that Nadal gained millions as the image of Mapfre, another insurance agency, was no small obstacle. But the biggest thing was that the animosity that Nadal felt for Tiriac was still there. He had, since 2009, given him a clay tournament at the height of the dates on which he normally would play the very slow Hamburg, and now, on top of that, he was making him play on blue clay.

"Of course we're not a traditional tournament!" Tsobanian praised himself. "We couldn't be, having only been around for ten years, nor do we want to be. Let us be modern and innovative, revolutionize the sport. Why block us? Ecclestone changes the rules of Formula 1 every week to adapt to what the client wants. This reminds me of the controversy with the models as ball girls eight years ago. Eight years later we're still doing it, because we've done it professionally from the start."

The man who best understood Tiriac smiled widely when he was asked what his dream was for the tournament. "My dream is that on the last day, the winner kneels down on the blue court and kisses it." He dreamed in vain, because everything ended in nightmare.

"This isn't tennis for me. I should either bring some soccer cleats with me or get Chuck Norris to help me learn how I'm supposed to play on this court," Djokovic exclaimed after winning his debut match on the noticeably cobalt blue surface during that unique year of 2012.

The picture was beautiful; the blue gave the tournament an undeniable elegance and distinction, although the players didn't think so, and with good reason: the surface was unplayable. The Argentinian Juan Martín del Potro said he felt like he was performing on Dancing on Ice. Nadal, on the other hand, was not in a joking mood that week, especially not after having fallen in the eighth-finals before his countryman, Fernando Verdasco, a man whom he'd defeated the thirteen times he'd faced him before. Plus, he had lost after being up 5–2 and having the serve in the third set. Furious after the 6–3, 3–6, and 7–5 defeat, Nadal barely waited fifteen minutes before talking to the press, whom he usually makes wait a much longer time. And he immediately fired a shot at the organizers of Madrid going into 2013, "If things don't change, there will be one less tournament on my calendar."

Moments before, Tiriac had witnessed a close-up of Nadal's anger. "Very bad surface, very bad!" Toni Nadal blurted out at him as they passed in the hall. The Romanian kept walking, unperturbed.

Alejandro Ciriza, a journalist from El País, asked Nadal if the fact that the court shortened the distance between the skill levels of the players wasn't positive. "You'll find out," was the brief reply. At the height of his career, Nadal was considered by most anyone knowledgeable of tennis as the best player on clay courts of all time. Before measuring up against Verdasco, he had won 242 out of the 261 matches he played on that surface, and was a six-time Roland Garros champion and an eight-time Monte Carlo champion. But on that very hot spring day in Madrid, everything was very strange. Nadal ended up lost and simmering on the blue rectangle of The Magic Box.

It was a strange afternoon during which a spectator fainted in the intense heat and held up the match for several minutes. During the same afternoon, one of the men in charge of watering the surface tripped and soaked several VIPs in the first rows. In a box, Manolo Santana, the tournament director, watched the match unfold, upset because he knew what was coming.

"This surface destabilizes the game; it's a completely different game, and I won't think of taking risks. I'm leaving with a sore hip from having to adjust my movement all the time," Nadal criticized. "Movement is very important for me, and I couldn't move, I couldn't hit the ball well." "Do you have to count today's loss as a loss on clay?" they asked Nadal. The Spaniard made it very clear: the answer was no. "I count it as a loss, and I'll keep my thoughts to myself. I know I lost to Fernando, something that didn't happen the past thirteen times." Visibly tense, Nadal continued with his criticisms. "You can't support yourself when you serve you fall forward. And now I'm going to Rome with a lack of confidence that I shouldn't have after the work I've been doing. If you put Cincinnati on grass, what'll happen? Are people going to be happy before the US Open? I don't think so. It's a similar situation."

Losing so early in a clay tournament was something that hadn't happened to the Spaniard since he, suffering from blisters, had lost against his countryman, Juan Carlos Ferrero, during the eighth-finals at Rome in 2008. The amount of criticism coming from the players was due to the insecurity that the surface was causing them. Sliding is a common habit when playing on clay, in order to more quickly move and respond to your adversaries' hits. Djokovic is one of the few players capable of sliding on cement, which is complicated and dangerous. But you have to slow down at some point, stop sliding, and that wasn't an easy task at the 2012 Madrid tournament.

"We know there's a problem, sure. The courts are very slippery; there's something not working right," Santana admitted. He had suffered more than most during that tournament. The lights had been on since four in the morning that day at The Magic Box. Andreu Puigserver, the court builder, was looking for a solution, aided by the caretakers of the courts at Roland Garros and Monte Carlo, two of the historic clay court tennis facilities.

They didn't find any, the problem was unsolvable. Very little could be done in the middle of the tournament. And while Santana tried to calm everyone down, Tiriac seemed unaware that this time he wasn't in the position of power to which he was accustomed. He couldn't threaten anyone. On the contrary, he was the one with his back against the wall, and the players were the ones threatening to ignore the tournament next year. "The tournament is on trial for this year? Who says so? The ATP? I don't know anything about that . . ."

Tiriac turned seventy-three years old that day and wasn't taking seriously what everyone else considered to be fact: that next year the clay would go back to orange because the blue experiment had failed. "It looks like the court is too slippery, and that will have to be fixed. But two weeks ago in Monte Carlo, three players broke their feet . . ." the Romanian reminded everyone about the orange court of Monte Carlo. "Today, five days into the tournament, I'm more convinced than ever that the blue clay is a great step forward."

Nobody else thought so, and Tiriac had to explain: "The court is slippery and I apologize for that. We wanted to be sure that no one would get hurt. And as a result, the experts flattened the surface using too much pressure, and when the blue clay was placed on top, it didn't mix with the base of the court. That created slippery playing conditions." The Romanian avoided mentioning something that was leaked by the upper echelons of the contest: In the hours before the competition, the best tournament organizer in history had asked for salt to be thrown on top of the courts. The salt, which in certain circumstances helps compact the clay, was Tiriac's key mistake in Madrid. With all the heat and no humidity, the salt never mixed well with the dust and contributed to the blue courts becoming dangerous, extremely slippery surfaces.

A few feet away from Tiriac, Santana was distressed. "I assume all blame for what happened. I am Manolo Santana, from Spain, for better and for worse. Of course I am disappointed." But Tiriac wasn't, or at least he didn't show that he was. The Romanian acted more like himself than ever during the crisis at his tournament. With the players about to explode, Tiriac gave an interview to the DPA agency and put out another revolutionary idea: in the future, he wanted to play with fluorescent balls. "We'll improve the ball as well. We're thinking of fluorescent green or fluorescent orange, which will catch the light better and will contrast better with the blue clay."

Three decades before, tennis had abandoned the white balls it had used for decades for the intense yellow ones, as they would contrast better with the courts, especially the clay ones, on which the white balls wouldn't last very long before becoming orange. What might have been an interesting proposal in any other context—Tiriac was always thinking about maximizing his sport's appeal for television—sounded to many players like some sort of prank during those turbulent days in Madrid. Not only were they playing on a skating rink, now they were being asked to play some sort of psychedelic tennis.

"If during the coming year they've got the blue clay and fluorescent balls, or whatever, they can have their own tournament, but I won't be there," a very angry Djokovic threatened after also being eliminated early on. During those same few days, one of the Serbian's family members had confessed to one of the members of the organization, "Novak complains a lot, like most kids, but the blue clay thing isn't that bad."

Tiriac could at least count on Serena Williams. "See my socks?" she asked a journalist while lifting up her pant leg. "I love fluorescent colors! I'm excited at the thought of playing with fluorescent balls."

And during those heated chromatic debates, another amazing comment from Tiriac surfaced. "I've never been racist. I have no problem with colors, I've always liked redheads, blondes, brunettes . . ." The joke wasn't exactly taken well in Madrid, but Tiriac, who had flown to Monte Carlo in the middle of the tournament for a dinner with his housemates, was on fire those days. And so he kept opening the old wound of Nadal's defeat, of which he was clearly suspicious. "As a tennis aficionado, I don't understand how you could lose a clay court match with a 5–2 advantage in the third and two breaks. I don't remember anything like that, I've never seen it happen. I don't understand how. He made six out of 34 points. How is that possible?" The Romanian added that he had been talking about his problems with Florentino Pérez, who was the president of Real Madrid and very close to Nadal. "Like Florentino said, soccer players often play in the rain, and they slide a little more, right? And in Formula 1? They risk their lives, right? Motorcycle sports . . ." It was apparent that Tiriac thought the tennis players were overly sensitive young men.

The Romanian assured that he was not bothered by Nadal's and Djokovic's announcement they wouldn't play in the tournament next year and added that he believed in the adage that the best defense is a good offense. "If you make a tournament for just one player, there's something wrong with you. What are we going to do when Nadal and Djokovic go? Are we going to cancel the tournament? Why? This is a question of education for the public and television. When we started, Nadal wasn't here; he grabbed a wild card and lost during the first round."

Despite that his analysis had several valid elements to it, Tiriac couldn't understand that the environment that week was not propitious for challenges, much less for word games. He organized a discussion with Mark Miles, Etienne de Villiers, and Adam Helfant, three ex-chiefs of the ATP, which was directed at that time by Brad Drewett. The three speakers offered him the support that the main players would not. "There is not a more competent and innovative leader in tennis," Miles said. "Show me a single person who's never made a mistake," De Villiers pointed out. "Fluorescent balls? People shouldn't be scared," Helfant offered.

Nadal had already lost, and Tiriac didn't bother to hide how cross he was with the Spaniard. And so he showed Miles, De Villiers, and Helfant the cover of the official tournament journal put out by the local newspaper, *ABC*. The cover was completely dominated by a picture of

Verdasco kissing the blue court after defeating Nadal. "You see this kid? Very different from the other. And he sure did try out the blue clay court at some point in the last few years that it was there for players to practice on." After a while, Nadal uploaded a picture to Facebook of a large fish that he had caught while on a boat. Behind the smiling Spaniard was laid out, in all its immensity, the Mediterranean. Blue, very blue.

A month later, the ATP decided to put an end to the blue clay experiment. "After careful analysis, I've decided that the blue clay will not be used next year," said Brad Drewett, the executive director of the ATP, after a series of meetings that took place during Wimbledon. "We have to be sure that the courts are safe and fair for the players," he added.

It was hard for Tiriac to swallow that reality. For the first time in his life, the players had twisted his arm. He wasn't even comforted by Nadal's praise at the 2013 edition, although Manolo Santana smiled happily when he heard it. "The courts are fantastic, fortunately, and the only thing to be done is to thank the tournament for the investment it has made to make some top-level courts." "I think that we finally have a tournament to enjoy," said a relieved Santana. "We didn't have to talk to the players again to see what had to change; it was very clear."

The tournament had invested upward of a million Euros to change the surface of the three-roofed stadiums and the fourteen exterior courts at the Magic Box complex. The dust, which was orange again, came from a quarry in the River Oise area, north of Paris. "At Wimbledon, we decided to start everything from scratch, the courts from scratch. We hired the experts from Monte Carlo and Roland Garros. It wasn't easy, because due to the dryness and altitude of Madrid the earth doesn't compact as much. We had to dig about three feet below the previous level of the courts, because the moisture was so much lower."

With the players happy and Nadal smiling more than he had in years, the days went by peacefully until someone asked the question, "Where is Ion Tiriac?" The Romanian's quiet absence was palpable. "Let's just enjoy this year in peace," they said in the organization, exhausted by the previous year's crossfire between a good number of the players and, on more than one occasion, the agitating Tiriac, who was a friend of the king of Spain, and, like him, a lover of hunting.

The Romanian magnate was well aware of the jeering he'd received from the public in 2012 and had no desire to be exposed to more. "During the first year, I went out on the court for the final. Last year, I went out on the court with Santana. And who do you think ends up eating shit?" the Romanian exclaimed crudely, weeks afterward at Roland Garros. That's why he had opted not to hand out the trophies in 2013. Everything was left in Santana's hands. "When I played hockey with my club, there were twenty thousand people who wanted to kill me. I understand this public; they pay, they show up, there's no problem," Tiriac assured. "If there was a problem, I didn't go out last year. And last year I let Santana go out first, and I came out thirty seconds later because I didn't want the public hissing at Santana, too."

"Madrid is unique. Look at the weather here in Roland Garros. It's sad that a tournament like this still can't get a roof," the Romanian said slyly, before showing that he was still himself, "I'm 100 percent convinced that the color blue is much better than red. You can see about 30 percent better. It's a shame that the players confused that with the court being too slippery. It's true that it wasn't good. Now they've wasted more than a million and a half Euros in making everything new again. But the future is blue. The track and field and field hockey athletes at the Olympic Games aren't all crazy . . . They play on blue fields."

Tiriac pointed out that Federer, the 2012 champion, hadn't criticized the novelty. "Federer last year didn't bark [sic] much . . . The water exerted too much pressure on the earth, and it was slippery. But you shouldn't get confused; the blue dirt itself isn't slippery. There is no rule in the ATP concerning color, because if there were, you couldn't play on the green courts in the United States." The fluorescent balls would also happen, he added, but the prototypes he'd gotten hadn't convinced him yet.

And then he went back to Nadal, showing that Tiriac would always be Tiriac. "I have an enormous amount of respect for Mr. Nadal. Not just for Nadal the player but for the person as well, but tennis will go on after Nadal and also after Djokovic. Federer is the best of all time, and a great man. You have to respect Nadal because of his strength, for putting out two or three times the effort on the field."

Tiriac was thankful toward the Swiss, who supported him after winning the controversial 2012 tournament. "If I'm skating, so is the next guy, and the next guy. That's what Mr. Federer told me, he is a great man and he won the tournament."

Changing tennis forever would become an obsession for Tiriac. "Tennis is very difficult to change because you have five or six different categories. You've got the ATP; the WTA; the Grand Slams, which are godlike; the International Federation [ITF]; the national federations. How can you go to a table and say, 'Today the tennis ball is 50 percent bigger'? You can't. But the game is impressively fast. Too fast. I would rather see a game between Năstase and Santana. The solution is very simple: a larger ball. Using a larger ball, serves are slower and returns are slower."

Curiously, Nadal would say the same thing as Tiriac a couple of years later. "Players are getting taller, and each new one is serving harder and harder. It's apparent that there needs to be a solution, or soon it will be hard to see the points made," he analyzed during the 2014 Australian Open. "The answer is that the people for whom this sport is their business take the necessary measures to make sure the spectacle is still great for years to come. I don't think it's good, but if that's what the spectator wants, then go ahead . . . If serving to two thousand will make the sport greater, playing quickly and not thinking . . . well, then, that's the path to follow."

Had Nadal and Tiriac ever sat together to talk about tennis?

CHAPTER 10

Manacor

WHAT IS RAFAEL NADAL'S SYMBOL? The horns of a bull. They're on his tennis shoes, on his shirts, on the line of clothing that Nike updates season after season or tournament after tournament. And what did Manacor, Nadal's birth city, do at the end of 2014? They banned bull runs.

Mallorca, like Spain, is a complicated society and sometimes hard for outsiders to understand. The Spanish have discussed for decades if they're Spanish, what it is to be Spanish, and how to behave with those who, even though they are Spanish, don't feel like they are. In that context, the image of the bull is connected in a way that few other things are to a feeling of being Spanish, to Spaniards who have no doubt that they are, although that's just a general statement. Many who feel that they are absolutely Spanish would never go to a running of the bulls. On the other hand, most everyone who rejects being Spanish has a deep-seated allergy to bulls. Barcelona, caught up for years in the debate regarding Catalonian independence, prohibited the running of bulls in 2010. The dream of many in Mallorca is for the same thing to happen, and that, through the passage of time, was becoming more and more likely.

To be Spanish, but not to *feel* Spanish; it happens in Catalonia, in the Basque Country, in Galicia, on the Balearic Islands, in Mallorca, and in other parts of Spain. And in Manacor, of course. The third most important city on the island has forty-three thousand inhabitants, and many of them are much more emotionally attached to anything Catalonian rather than to Castilian Spanish. Their flag is different.

Nadal, whose native tongue is Catalonian—or rather, one of its variants, the subvariant of Mallorcian, which is even harder to understand—is distanced from the argument because he always clearly considered himself Spanish. If there were ever a doubt, you just have to look at the red-and-yellow flag on his tennis shoes, proudly displayed next to the horns of the bull. Nadal's emphatic Spanishness is surprising to many in Manacor, who don't share the same sentiment and who would prefer an idol less attached to that flag, which they would rather see from afar. Of course: there are many others who connect with Nadal precisely because of his sincere Spanishness. Spanish or anti-Spanish, the inhabitants of Manacor naturally get along with Nadal. The tennis player can't live without returning to his city over and over, which wouldn't be as well-known if it weren't for him. The mayor said so himself, "Manacor is eternally grateful to him because his name has given Manacor's life a before and after."

Toni Pastor, who stopped being mayor in 2015, speaks in a dimly lit office, his own, in an unassuming building that houses the city government. The most distinguishing feature is on the facade. "Manacor thanks you," reads the giant sign that covers a good part of the building, with four pictures of Nadal with trophies in Australia, Roland Garros, Wimbledon, and the US Open. How could one not thank him . . . Nadal's career put Manacor's name as well as its people in the media all over the world. The same happened to Mallorca, of course, but the island's need for promotion is infinitely less than his birth city, which has little to offer aside from the traditional pearl trade and the nearby beaches at Porto Cristo.

Manacor, Manacorian. From the United States to China, from Germany to Brazil, through Spain, Australia, and 200 other countries. How can you measure that, how much would such a campaign have cost? Pastor, who was the mayor at the beginning of Nadal's career, shakes his head. "There's no way to know, it's incalculable. And it would have been impossible, even if someone wanted to do it, reaching every corner of the world is only possible thanks to Rafa's name.

"Out of everyone, we have the hardest time valuing and, especially, understanding the great importance that the Nadal phenomenon has for Manacor, because we often don't realize just how important Rafael Nadal is to the rest of the world. I, having had the opportunity to go to some tournaments with him, saw that the name of Manacor is known pretty much the world over thanks to him. Because he isn't just a man who happens to be from here, he is proud to be from here. When he has a moment of respite in his busy professional life, he comes here to enjoy it. For Manacor, this is a unique phenomenon, we're the envy of many cities in the world."

It's very true that the influence of Nadal in Manacor is far greater than what a celebrity of his level would generate in, for example, Barcelona. The modest Mallorcian city never had anything as big as the racket genius. And, as everyone there knows, they'll never have it again. "Manacor is eternally grateful to him; there is a before and after Nadal in the life of the city," Pastor insists.

Nadal is a magnet for those from the south of the island who go searching for beaches in the north and east. There's a sign at the entrance to Manacor that advertises the sale of pears in Spanish . . . and in Russian. Tourists from the former Soviet Union are leaving more and more euros in Mallorca. There isn't much to see in Manacor, a city of small houses, a placid rhythm, and a reserved appearance. The main church, in the center of the city, is one of the must-see attractions, but not only because of the temple. Just about 30 feet away is the Nadals' house, a four-story building in which the tennis player no longer lives, but a good portion of his family does.

"Every day, people stand in the Manacor Tennis Club, or in the Technification Center, looking for a picture of the court where Nadal plays. Many people come to the Office of Tourism Information and ask where Nadal lives, where he trains," Pastor explains. "It's normal to come to Manacor and not see where Nadal trains . . ." the mayor adds.

He had a brief and modest career as a soccer player and happened to meet Miguel Ángel Nadal, Rafael's uncle, in Mallorca.

The Nadals permeated Manacor more than any other family. You had Rafael Nadal Nadal—yes, his two surnames are the same—the grandfather who directed the city's musical bands for forty-one years and whom Pastor defined as "a real character." When asked about the professions he had during his life, Nadal Nadal started listing, "School teacher, court attorney, administrative consultant, and for forty-one years the director of the Manacor Musical Band." Nadal Nadal, born in December 1929, held strong opinions, something which his children and his most famous grandchild inherited. The *Diario de Mallorca* asked him why none of his five children inherited his passion for music. "Marilén had a bit. She went to violin until third year, in the Music and Dance School, but she wasn't up to standards . . ." Retired at sixty-five years of age, Nadal Nadal ponders one idea, "One day I could publish a book about the political mediocrity of this country. I would say a lot of truths."

The *Manacor Comarcal* magazine dedicated a small book to him in 2012 titled, *Teacher Rafael Nadal, living legend with 65 years of musical achievement*. The former choir director saw a different side. "It's not that they dedicated it to me, it's that *Manacor Comarcal* apparently spent four thousand to promote their magazine, not to promote me," he laughed. "In truth, this book doesn't even contain a quarter of what I've achieved on my journey."

Before Rafael Nadal's racket would change the town's life and before globalization would change so many other things in so many places, life in Manacor was pretty clear cut: men were carpenters and women pearl divers. The local economy was based on artisan workshops with two or three people who made custom furniture. One example are the Pareras, Rafael Nadal's maternal family, who descended from the furniture branch. But things started changing in Manacor as well as on the rest of the island, which depended mostly on tourism. "Furniture comes from China now, the pearl business is slowing," explains Ricard, a Manacorian who works in tourism. "During the good times, a married carpenter and pearl diver could live comfortably and save. So much so that many families owned a house in Manacor, another weekend house in the countryside, about four miles from the city, and a third one in Porto Cristo, about seven-and-a-half miles away, the beach home, the summer home."

You can observe some of that when you ask for directions, or some indication of how to get to a determined place in the city. Walking 1,600 feet is, for most of its inhabitants, unthinkable. They would rather use the car, even if they can't find a spot to park it. "A family of four has five cars," Ricard said, talking during the week that *Forbes* magazine published its annual ranking of millionaires. Nadal was listed in 2014 as the wealthiest athlete in Spain and ninth in the world. According to the magazine, a "bible" of great fortunes, the Nadal estate that year hovered somewhere between 150 and 200 million Euros.

The "owner" of Roland Garros likes to become involved in his town. So he donated 150,000 Euros to equip the Manacor Concert Hall. The other half was paid by the local government. "It's a small way to give something back to Manacor," Nadal said during a ceremony in March, 2012. His grandfather was with him and had rejected the proposal that had been heard to name the concert hall after him. "I'm very happy to help, especially during difficult times," the tennis player added, thinking of the current Spanish economic collapse.

Mats Wilander said in 2014 that he sees Nadal and Federer playing "for five or six more years." The Swiss, he predicted, would retire when he was about to turn forty, and Nadal around thirty-three or thirty-four. Whether the Swedish former tennis player is right only time will tell, but there's no doubt that at some point the career of the greatest Spanish athlete of all time will come to an end. "Could you see him as Manacor's mayor?" Pastor smiles and answers without hesitation, "I don't think so . . . I think he's too smart." Nadal doesn't need to be mayor to be the most powerful man in the city. It's already obvious he is. The other thing is that the player isn't the type of person who likes to take advantage of that power.

The city already has a Miguel Ángel Nadal Sports Center in homage to the tennis player's uncle, the former Mallorca, Barcelona, and Spanish selection soccer player. But that installation won't be able to compare to the one that makes the mayor excited: the Rafael Nadal International Tennis Center. "I'm sure that it will be a global benchmark, and there will also be a before and after. That Technification Center, to which I think he'll dedicate a lot of his time, is a very interesting project, with an international school, medical installations, and training tracks. I think Nadal will continue to live in Manacor and dedicate a portion of his time to Manacor. Just having him here is enough to benefit us." Pastor is so excited that he thinks the new center will put Manacor "permanently on the map of top level sports installations worldwide."

Nevertheless, in February, 2008, the mayor saw things quite differently. "We're very worried about the possibility that Rafa might abandon the project," he said in the Manacor Tennis Club, where the player at the time, was launching the Rafael Nadal Foundation. A few feet away, Carlos Costa, Nadal's representative, added to the message, "They're in debt to Rafa Nadal." The story has an inescapable political component. Costa had signed, toward the end of 2004, an agreement with the Balearic government under Jaume Matas, of the conservative People's Party (PP), but the 2007 election put the previous president back in power, Francesc Antich, of the Socialist Party (PSOE). Pastor, the mayor of Manacor since 2003, was given control through the PP. Costa was now convinced that the new government would put an end to the agreement he had signed.

According to the player's consultants, the agreement consisted of three parts: the city of Manacor would provide the lands, the Balearic government would finance the 17 million Euros that it was calculated the project would cost, and Nadal would provide general consulting and decide on the design of the installations. According to Costa, Nadal wouldn't charge anything for his collaboration on the project, but he wanted to be identified with it. During those years, if it rained in Mallorca, Nadal had nowhere to train.

"This all goes back to the end of 2004, after the Seville Davis Cup was won. I spoke with the Balearic government and told them that there were no adequate installations for Nadal, who was on his way to number one, to train in on the islands," Costa remembered. "So they asked me for Nadal's presence at determined events, so they could use him as the symbol of the Balearic Islands. 'You want to use his image?' I asked them. Let's make an exchange then. And so we agreed on the construction of the tennis center." That's what happened: any visitor that came, at the time, to the Balearic islands, even to the small Formentera, would see a life-size image of Nadal welcoming them.

But the socialist interregnum heading the Balearic government stopped the project. "It's been eight months since I asked president Antich for a meeting, but he won't see me, he won't see the mayor of the second city on the island," Pastor complained at the time. "I don't see a lot of interest in the government for Rafa's image. On the other hand, they do care about Paco de Lucía…" he added ironically, speaking about the Andalucian guitarist, well known in the worldwide music scene, who died six years later.

Pastor pressed on: "I have the obligation to think that Rafa's person is far above political matters. But this government is made up of six parties, and each office does what it wants. Now this is in danger, and I think Rafa is surprised, because he gets offers like this, to make huge tennis centers with his name on them, from many other places."

Six years later, the International Tennis Center would still be incomplete, although by the end of 2014 Nadal himself would inaugurate the ground-breaking ceremony. A while before, an embryo of the current project, the Tennis and Paddle Center, had been inaugurated, with Toni Nadal as the athletic adviser, and a close friend of the player's, Tomeu Salvá, another tennis player, in the role of athletic director.

By that time, a few things were different from how they were in 2008. Antich had left the government and Matas was sentenced to prison for one of the multiple corruption cases which were on the front page every day at the island. Pastor, for his part, was no longer in the PP, and promised not to leave politics until succeeding in stopping Matas's successor, José Ramón Bauzá, from being a threat to the Mallorcian language. Too much politics for Manacor, a town just large enough to merit the label of "city."

"Some call it a city, I like to say it's a city because it has forty-three thousand inhabitants and it's the second largest on the island of Mallorca," Pastor explained in 2014. "But it feels like a town; everyone knows each other, which allows Rafael Nadal to live here practically unnoticed, because the people don't bother him, they just think of him as part of the group."

A Manacor VIP doesn't exist, and if it did Nadal wouldn't bother with it. It's not what he likes. When he's in his city, the man who changed an entire era of tennis would rather be with his lifelong friends. One of them is Tomeu Artigues, whom Nadal defeated in final after final in their younger days. "I'm up to my ears in trophies," Artigues said one day in front of the stacks of cups in his room. Did he throw them out? No. He got rid of the most ostentatious stuff and just kept the placards with the writing "second place." Those he framed: the memory remained, but it all took up much less space.

Artigues, Salvá, Nadal, and Joan Suasi, another of Nadal's close friends, are young men with common traditions: beach soccer tournaments, boat trips—a privilege of those who grow up next to the sea—and, at night, two staple locations: Cubic, until three in the morning, and Bauxa, a basement in the center of the city where the nights stretch on until dawn. Every summer, Nadal invited his friends for a few days of vacation. He doesn't like being a star, and with them is when he feels closest to his origins, the "Rafel" of Manacor.

And María Francisca Perelló? Nadal's girlfriend—"Mary"—is the definition of discretion. It's much more common to see her walking the Cholesterol Path in Manacor with her mother than enjoying her boyfriend's fame and money with him in the great cities of the world. The Cholesterol Path is the ironic name that the Manacorians gave the ring that circles the city, a path that María Francisca, wearing a Nike cap to protect her from the sun, traverses regularly with her mother, also named María.

Licensed in administration and business management, Nadal's girlfriend is extremely discreet, to the point that she is perfectly capable of living her life independently of the tennis star when they're both in Manacor. Every once in a while she travels to the tournaments to be with her boyfriend, whom she regularly accompanies to the big finals. There she is seen next to Ana María, her mother-in-law, and María Isabel, her boyfriend's sister. They all follow the Nadal protocol: a row for the men in front and another for the women in the back. If the amounts differ enough to change the rows, Sebastián, the player's father, sits next to his wife. The man-woman split is not exclusive to the Nadals, although they practice it with conviction: in Sa Punta (La Punta), the restaurant that the Nadal family has in Cala Bona, in the Porto Cristo area, the tables are often solely made up of men or women.

Sebastián Nadal, infinitely less extroverted than his brother Toni, is nevertheless the other great key to the family empire. No one could deny his ability to sniff out and manage business long before his son started to rake in the millions. There is a myth in Manacor—which they are proud of, in a certain way—a story that talks about the Nadals' ability to negotiate for millions.

Miguel Ángel Nadal, the soccer player, wasn't satisfied with what José Luis Núñez, the president of the Barcelona team at the time, was offering him to renew his contract in 1997. So his brother made the soccer player's phone ring in the middle of a meeting with Núñez. Who was on the other end? Lorenzo Sanz, Real Madrid's president. Miguel Ángel Nadal greeted him, clearly pronouncing his name, and Núñez understood the message. The renewal, with much higher numbers than previously proposed by the club, was signed days later.

Sebastián Nadal didn't need his son to be a millionaire. He had already been one for a long time thanks to Vidres Mallorca, a windows-building business venture, half of which he shares with his brother Toni. This is part of the reason for something that Toni Nadal always says when the topic is brought up: his nephew doesn't pay him a salary, nor would he want to, because he wouldn't accept him as his boss, which is the reality of the relationship of subordination that trainers have with the tennis players. Toni, of course, didn't work for free. His nephew didn't pay him, the business paid him, a business aided by Miguel Ángel Nadal's success as a soccer player and the resulting economic growth. Another key in strengthening the Nadals' business was their exclusive commercialization of Climalit, a double glazing very much appreciated by the legions of Germans who reside on the island, and which they renamed *Aislaglas*.

Rafael Nadal's father, as a rule, doesn't speak to the press, but in 2006, at the beginning of his son's great adventure, he still did so without the hesitation he developed later. "I'm conscious of what Rafael is, but I don't know if we really know just how large he is. I don't think so. And I don't know if that's good or bad."

While Sebastián talked, his brother Miguel Ángel was telling a fun story about an unexpected encounter he had one night in Barcelona with Manu Carrasco, star of *Operación Triunfo* (known in the English-speaking world as *Star Academy*). It was a conversation among men, with the women at another table. A few feet away, Sebastián was slightly uneasy about the consequences of his son's growing fame, "You have to keep your feet on the ground. If you rise too high, the blows are harder."

Another topic also made Rafael's father unhappy, which was that he couldn't understand the reason behind the constant mention of how educated his son was. "Why does being educated have to be so uncommon? That's what I find strange." To Nadal's father, everything was the same as when the tennis fame had been limited to his brother. "Our family is very well known in Manacor. My own father is a musician, the director of the city's musical band. He directed Alfredo Kraus, something which not many have done. My brothers competed; Toni won at ping-pong, swimming, chess, tennis . . . he would win all four in a week. They would come to the house with his trophies, and we wouldn't even know he had competed! My father wouldn't go watch."

The years went by, and Rafael Nadal stayed as educated as always, a bonus as business seemed to come to the Nadals almost without them having to seek it. Three Mallorcian sisters, Encarna, Lidia, and Isabel Piñero, owners of a group that owns large hotels in Spain and the Caribbean, decided to give the tennis player a house on the edge of the sea in La Romana in the Dominican Republic. The mansion, built specially for Nadal, has an estimated value of $700,000. This was the deal that was being discussed in 2012 in Jimmy'z, one of the busiest nightclubs in Monte Carlo, where a small bottle of beer costs $25. The Piñero sisters were explaining how they had "given" Nadal the house. It wasn't exactly a gift, rather a payment for using his image to promote a complex that was designed to attract more of the rich and famous. At a table covered in glasses of vodka, Red Bull, and blueberry juice sat the creator of a campaign for a brand of rum that Nadal was promoting using a theme that invited everyone to drink responsibly. They were all happy, because Nadal's is one of the best images that can be associated with any product. Even his country's government recognized that when they paid him a fee in the millions in 2015 so that he would be the image for a "Food of Spain" promotion.

Nadal, for his part, was happy, too, because he loved the sea. That's why he invested his own money in a luxurious hotel on the Mexican island of Cozumel and built a huge home at the edge of the Mediterranean in Porto Cristo, the "beach" of Manacor. At his age, it makes sense that he would spend less time in the family home next to the church. The Mallorcians say that when Nadal gets a break from tennis and stays on the island, he can frequently be seen on a back road between Manacor and Porto Cristo at the wheel of a beautiful white Ferrari.

CHAPTER 11

Toni

TONI NADAL HAS MANY THINGS in common with his nephew. One of them is starting phrases with a "no." He wanted to be a tennis player and became a great trainer, but you wouldn't be exaggerating too much if you said that arguing is his favorite sport. And not only his: all the Nadals are overwhelmingly good at debating and arguing, to an extreme. Each might end by giving in to his conversational partner, but the path wouldn't be easy. To win an argument, one must live with Winston Churchill's promise: blood, sweat, and tears. And after every two phrases in a conversation there's that demoralizing "no," which one soon realizes is just a reflex, because the answer often ends up being a "yes," or an "I agree." The conversational partner, finally, breathes in relief.

During a cold November afternoon in Manacor, without missing a detail in following his two sons' soccer training, Toni Nadal explains why he likes debating and arguing so much. "I like to debate because I'm interested in the world. I see discussion as something positive, I think it helps advance society."

"Do you enjoy verbal fencing?"

"No, I enjoy the argument, for you to tell me one thing, which I can refute. I think that things aren't black or white. What I don't understand is people who can't put themselves in another's place. I understand rights and I understand lefts. I might lean more towards one or the other, but that doesn't mean that I'm in the right. The problem is that there's this idea in society that if you're not with me, you're wrong, and you're a bad person besides. And I don't enjoy arguing with a wall, I like to talk."

Jofre Porta, who trained Nadal during the early years, thinks that the Nadals have very well-assigned roles. "The Nadal clan is very neat. Toni shaped Rafa as a tennis player and person, Sebastián takes care of the business, and Miguel Ángel brings the sporting experience." However, when it comes to arguing, things can get out of hand. "In that family, no one turns down an argument, and it can become unpleasant."

Those who have known Toni Nadal for years know of his fierce appetite for debate, for argument. So one time they set a trap for him. First one of them walked up to him singing praise for Carles Puyol, a soccer player for Barcelona, calling him one of the key men for the Spanish selection. "You have no idea what you're saying," they said was Toni Nadal's response. Half an hour later, someone else approached him criticizing Puyol. Toni Nadal, they reported, avidly defended the player. Maybe he still pretends that he was never laid that trap, but during our conversation in Manacor he demonstrates an excellent memory when he recalls an exchange from seven years earlier. "One time, you and I were talking about politics and I was criticizing the left and you told me, damn, but you're on the left. And it's just that I try to be critical of the things I defend. I try to be more critical with what I defend than with what others defend." And just as he is critical even of what he defends, so is he critical of—and hard, very hard—on those he loves.

"Yesterday I was playing tennis with my son, and he said 'I can't get it.' And I told him, 'You can't get it because you're bad.' And it was fine . . ."

"How old is your son?"

"Ten years old."

"And how do he and his other brothers take it?"

"Well, because they're used to it." The toughness he has with his close ones is hereditary. Rafael Nadal Nadal was uncle Toni's father, and the patriarch of the Nadal clan. In an interview with the *Diario de Mallorca* in February of 2014, he showed that he was still, at 85, a Nadal through and through. "What's the Nadals' secret to being good at sports?" the journalist asked him. "I don't know, there are a lot of strange things in life that you don't know the reason for. They have something out of the ordinary. Miguel Ángel sweat through his shirt with Mallorca, I never saw him miss a training once. Sometimes he would ask [Johan] Cruyff, when he was in Barcelona, if he could stay an extra half hour because he trained more than the others. *Rafel*—the grandfather uses the Mallorcian form of Rafael—is an exception to all this. And Miguel Ángel has his boy, also named Miguel Ángel, seventeen years old, who has the same physical build as his father, and could be a top quality player if he did what his father did, but he misses two out of every four trainings, and sometimes he misses all four . . ."

It's possible that the new generation of Nadals don't want to join the Spanish soccer selection or become one of the greatest tennis players of all time. Maybe their cousin, *Rafel*, told them what he told his uncle many years ago: "Toni, I don't know anymore." The phrase, both simple and sincere, passed through the lips of a twelve-year-old Nadal one day when his uncle's criticisms and pressure became too much for him. "It's the most important thing he's ever told me. When I reprimanded him for failing, he told me 'I don't know anymore,'" Toni recalled.

"And did you soften up?"

"Yeah, damn! But, what is sport, competition? Reaching the limit." Since he took control of his tennis and a good part of his personality, Toni Nadal always presented Rafael with problems and obstacles. He wanted him to be ready for any demands, to be the best of the best. When you see Nadal play, when you think of the "impossible" points and matches he's won in his career, it's clear his uncle was triumphant. But, was that amount of toughness really necessary?

"I believe in mental fortitude. When Rafael was little, I understood that it would be tough if Rafael rose to the top. I knew that because of how you count in tennis, the 15, 30, 40, that you need to have a strong mind. I played ping-pong, where all the points are practically worth the same. In tennis, although they might be worth the same, there are points that carry more importance, more tension, such as the 40-all. I knew that he had to be mentally strong, and that's what I tried to get across to my nephew. I come from a generation in which verbal toughness was more accepted. Today it seems like you always have to send positive messages to the world, and it's hard to tell people 'You're not good enough.' I don't think this is good; it leads you to have a false opinion of yourself."

Could a similar amount of toughness be counterproductive? Or not? "No," Toni Nadal says. "I would never be hard on someone whom I didn't respect, whom I didn't appreciate enough. I was tough on some kids who trained with me before Rafael, and it was always because I appreciated them. And I would never be so hard on someone who couldn't take it. I don't say the same things to my son, this one here— he says while pointing towards a boy entering adolescence—that I do to the other one, because I know he can't take hearing certain things. I wouldn't say it ever in my life, I'm not that dumb. Toughness isn't an end, it's a means, with good intentions. What I've always wanted is for everything to be as good as possible for my nephew."

"Did they understand you? Did Rafael's mother understand, does your wife understand?"

"Apparently, I've lowered my level of verbal aggression a lot. My conscience is clean, knowing that I did what I did for his own good. I think they understood. I suppose they can see that I love my nephew."

"And did he understand?"

"Did he understand me? Totally."

You could say that the two Nadals, Toni and Rafael, were lucky to have one another. Toni found a boy who was tremendously educated and, as such, obedient. Rafael found a trainer dedicated 100 percent to him and who turned out to be a sort of second father, considerably more than an uncle. This helps one better understand an image recalled by Ricardo Rivera, a former captain of the Davis Cup Argentinian team, a man fascinated with Nadal—"He's clearly greater than Federer; he did the same, or more, starting out with much less"—but also with the peculiar relationship between uncle and nephew, between the trainer and his player. "It was on a morning before the start of the Australian Open, I see Rafa going to the little window where he can find the balls. He's carrying two water bottles. He was going to train with Mónaco. By themselves. The number one player in the world . . . They started at 11 in the morning and uncle didn't show, and he didn't show. They kept training. Finally, at 11:45, uncle Toni showed up with sunglasses, sandals, and signing autographs. Rafa didn't say anything. Toni said something about hitting his backhand by extending the strike more. Then he added something about how hot it was. At 11:53, eight minutes after showing up, Toni left. Rafa didn't say anything."

That Toni Nadal is frequently late to his appointments is something often repeated by those who deal with him. In addition to that, during the early days of the family glassware business, Sebastián Nadal concluded that his brother was of more use to him training his son full time than by starting debates and games in the factory. All of which contributes to the awareness that Toni Nadal is special, and not always the easiest person to deal with.

He's not just another guy. Most of the international press love him, since he happily talks about whatever you ask him and frequently provides revelations and headlines. Almost everything that the Nadals would like to keep out of the public eye is in danger if it reaches Toni Nadal in the form of a question. He is a free electron, although, in a way, the fact that he may mouth off from time to time may not be as harmful for the Nadals or for Benito Pérez Barbadillo, the player's press agent. Every time Toni talks, he removes some of the huge media pressure from his nephew. By offering up novel opinions to reporters, he draws some of their persistent attention away from the star.

Those headlines that he blurts out spontaneously—or maybe not so accidentally—fly from Toni Nadal's lips in six languages: Spanish and Catalonian, which are his two mother tongues; French; English; and to a lesser extent German and Italian. Kind to the press—except when he's angry about a particular headline, which happens every so often and leads to phone calls and arguments—he is extremely polite to journalists. For its part, the media find him to be a man with time and willingness to talk, smile, and converse about much more than just tennis.

So it's no surprise that Thinking Heads, the business that represents him and has in its address book such names as Lech Wałęsa and Felipe González, promotes him as an "expert in managing adversity, advancement, and values." Toni Nadal studied in Barcelona and lived for a few months in Germany "because of a girlfriend." Within a strongly conservative family, typical of the islands, he was always considered the "red," or the "leftist." Is he really?

"I'm part of the world I live in, and I'm interested in everything that surrounds me," he explains when asked if he really is passionate about politics. "I think that, in theory, it would be much better to live in a more egalitarian society. I don't subscribe to the whole one part or another idea, because I would almost always vote in favor of the people that I think are best at the time. But I do think that society needs to move toward the left, because it needs to move away from inequality. It's not okay for a few of us to be so much better off than the rest of us."

Three and a half years before our conversation, in July of 2011, Toni Nadal held a press conference in a fabulous garden near the All England Club, the home of Wimbledon. It was in the house that the multinational corporation IMG rented. There Toni introduced Banesto, one of the largest Spanish banks, as his personal sponsor, as it had already been his nephew's. Spain was, by then, submerged in a deep economic crisis, which four months later led to an election foreseen in part by the socialist government of José Luis Rodríguez Zapatero, in which Mariano Rajoy's conservative party was victorious. The banks also were the focus of the fury of millions of Spanish citizens, some trapped by mortgages that would often turn into foreclosures after the burst of the "housing bubble." In that context, showing himself as the image of a bank didn't exactly paint Toni Nadal as particularly leftist.

When he's reminded of the topic, he reacts forcefully. To him, one thing had nothing to do with the other.

While his sons were playing soccer and his daughter volleyball, on that cold afternoon in Mallorca in November of 2014, Spain was jumping from one political shock to the next. The latest development in those days—the powerful ascent of Podemos, a new party that galvanized the protests of the "indignant"—threatened to destroy the bipartisanship that had, for the past three decades, defined the political pace of the country. The armies of Pablo Iglesias made the trainer of the best athlete in the country uneasy. "If what they're selling isn't demagogy, I think that's fine, and I think that it's good for people to understand that there are other options in life. The other day I read some of his proposals, some that I think bordered on demagogy. Specifically, I don't think it's totally feasible. If after everything it turns out that it works out, then perfect. Of course, if I'm on the opposition, I can say what I want and everything is fine. An empty gesture is always easy, but later you have to adjust to the reality in which we live, and that's not so easy."

The strongest group among the Podemos voters is the youth, and Toni Nadal saw at the time a contradiction in that. "Yesterday I was in a recycling business in Madrid, and they told me that the people who recycle less are in the eighteen- to twenty-four-year-old range. That's curious. Curious that these people want a better society and won't do something so simple to help make society better. It's curious that these people ask for a better society and then go to a concert and leave the site a mess. It's really easy to ask for a change, but you have to apply that to everyone. I still understand, and unfortunately we see this in the topic of corruption every day; there is a complete duping of the population. And apart from the corruption, which is severe, there's the topic of unemployment, and seeing the social exclusion that many people have makes you feel uninvolved."

When you hear Nadal's uncle talking with such conviction and forcefulness about so many topics, you have to ask: Would you get involved in politics? The answer is astonishing: "I like politics because I'm another citizen, but I think that politics has a problem that has grown a lot lately and may be terminal. The whole world, without exception, speaks only to gain votes and secure their spot in the next election, even while knowing that what they're saying is limited to just demagogy. Am I interested in something like that? No, I'm not interested in having the constant need to trick people."

Pointing out that not all politicians are tricking the public doesn't even give him pause. "Most of them, most of them . . . I guess because we want to be tricked. Most, and I'm not going to give examples, because you have to be careful about what you say. What they're after are popular measures, not measures that are sometimes necessary, but the ones that will be received better by public opinion, even knowing that they aren't right. It's complicated." When Toni Nadal says, "You have to be careful about what you say," he knows what he's talking about. He was still paying the consequences for having mouthed off about Gala León, the first woman in Spanish history to ascend to the post of Davis Cup captain. He questioned her because of her scant knowledge of the male circuit and even questioned her on a radio show, asking if she considered herself better for the post than, say, Juan Carlos Ferrero.

It was harsh, but it was within certain limits. He went much too far, though, when he brought up the "discomfort" generated by having a woman in the male locker room. With the recorder off, the trainer admits that he was wrong to bring that example up because it ruined the rest of his arguments. So much so that during those weeks he was saying over and over again to people, "Me, sexist!?? Let's see what the dictionary says if we look up the word 'sexist.'"

But Toni Nadal likes to argue; he likes to take risks. "It can't be that her only merit is being a woman, because if that were the case there are much more deserving women, such as Arantxa Sánchez Vicario, or Conchita Martínez," he insisted. Despite the explications and arguments he proposed, the damage was done. In the eyes of an important sector of society, it would be hard for him, for years to come, to remove the label of "sexist." Bothered by a descriptor that he didn't believe he deserved, but always with an eye on the soccer field, he analyzed a phrase which he had spoken years before, "A tennis match is a break from everyday life." The statement was not insignificant, nor was the medium in which it was published, a book published in Spanish and titled *Sirve Nadal, responde Sócrates* (*Nadal Serves, and Socrates Returns*). With the prefatory heading, "From the classical philosopher to the elite sportsman," Toni Nadal signed off, along with a friend from Manacor, Pere Mas, on an unusual book that opens with a brief comment from Rafael Nadal, "I don't care if I'm compared to a machine. I know that, more than a tennis player or an athlete, I am a person. When people see us, the first thing they know is this: that we are people above all else."

Mas has a degree in philosophy, but in the brief biography included in the book his life seems to have been much fuller. "He has been a laborer, firefighter, cook, and has worked as a night custodian, hotel director, and farmhand. This is his first book because he believes that love, mythology, Greek philosophy, and sports all help us to be happy."

The Na Camel-la plaza is just a ten-minute walk from the stadium in which the long conversation with Toni Nadal is taking place. The Hípica Cafe, owned by Mas, is in this plaza. And though he isn't there at the time, Mas can be reached by telephone. The book he published in 2008 with his friend, Toni, left him with a bittersweet sensation. "This book, five years ago, would have sold thirty or forty thousand copies," he is convinced, but the economic crisis was responsible for the book selling only about six thousand, a number which is, nevertheless, respectable for the Spanish market. Mas, who started the book as "an amusement," is proud of the work. "I've seen parts of the book plagiarized," he says. "And I don't know if it's because of the book, but ever since it came out there's been a change in radio and television. The word 'heroes' has been used more in connection with mythology since the book appeared. And also [Josep] Guardiola appealed to it with that famous video of Troy that he showed his players."

Although they both signed it, the book was written by Mas. "We had hours of conversation, and I wrote it. Toni read it and suggested changes, and we made changes. He told me at one point that only my name should be on it, but that was unimportant." Six years later, however, one gets the impression that Toni Nadal would suggest a couple more changes in the book. His answers to questions indicate that.

"A tennis match is a break from everyday life? Is that really so?"

"This is a bit of literature. The tennis match, to us, is part of everyday life. It's different when you're young, when you're just starting out. But then tennis becomes your life, and it stops being a break."

"There's another phrase in the book that sparks interest: 'To Federer, tennis is a profession, to Nadal, it is destiny.'"

"This is literature, too; it's expressive. It's too much. To Rafa, sport is what he likes to do, but he has the ability, I think, to do something else if he wanted to. What he apparently likes most in life is sports. He likes soccer more than tennis, but ultimately you do what life allows you to. I'm ecstatic to be in the world of tennis, but if I weren't, then I would do something else, and I'm sure that I would be able to, because there are many things in life. I've never really thought about it because I've been lucky enough to do what I like, especially teaching. Training my nephew is what I enjoy most in life."

Weeks before that conversation with Toni Nadal, the Swede Mats Wilander had immersed himself, during a chat in New York with coffee, in an analysis of the differences between Nadal and Federer. There was a question that he particularly enjoyed: what would they both have been if they hadn't played tennis? "Federer . . . I think he probably would have been a journalist, a reporter. I wouldn't say a writer, a fiction writer. But he's much more interested in tennis than most people realize. He lives to hit the ball, to try out new strikes. If the ball is close to his feet, he passes it in some way or hits it with different spins, and keeps the ball boys busy. He's more interested in the game and in the different aspects of tennis than any other player I've seen. His love of tennis is huge. He's inquisitive enough to be a reporter; he would want to know everything there is about . . . Iraq, or whatever it might be."

And Nadal? "Nadal also loves the game, but with a different culture. It's pretty obvious that he would do something related to sports, he's more physical than Roger, who's graceful. Federer doesn't need to play two hours of sports every day and sweat to feel at ease. Nadal does; he needs that so that he can, ufff, breathe easy."

Toni Nadal smiled at the idea of Federer as a reporter and agreed. And there was no argument with the analysis of what his nephew would be if he hadn't become the king of the racket. "I think so, yes. Nadal is, above all, a competitor. What he likes the most is competition. Maybe once he finishes with tennis he won't play anymore, because what really motivates him is the competition, not the game. We played golf last week, and he got pissed off at me because I'm not competitive. He understands the concept of competition, it's what he wants."

"So you don't see him playing at a mid-level, then. If he can't go toe to toe with the greatest players, then he won't stay in the circuit."

"I've thought that I don't believe he's one of those guys who drag on at that level, because he likes the competition, and if it's not there I think it won't be sufficiently exciting for him. But I don't know, because tennis has been really satisfying for him, and not just because he wins. Ultimately we have to value everything we are doing, but not because of what we are getting out of it. What I mean is that I value being in the London hotel when I'm in front of Big Ben. I value that. I value going to Paris, or here and there. It all counts for something, and life ends up being long . . . If I were here every day [he points at the soccer field], damn . . . And again, tomorrow. So I value what I have."

"Is this the final stretch?"

"I just don't know! I have mixed feelings about that. Years ago, in 2007, 2008, some experts said that Rafael would have a short career, and when you would ask me I would always say the same thing. I hope they're wrong. So I just don't know. I don't know if it's the final stretch. That there's less time left . . . sure! You don't need to be smart to know that. The truth is that Rafael has been in the circuit for twelve years, ten years in the top three, ten years of winning at least one Grand Slam. It's not easy. The truth is that we've had problems, but we'll see. I don't know if we're in the final stretch or in the midst of the journey. We'll see," Toni Nadal said in November 2014. Next year, the streak he was talking about was cut short. His nephew ended up fifth in the ranking, and, for the first time since 2004, he didn't win a single Grand Slam.

"What's left of that Toni who wanted to be a tennis player?"

"I started playing tennis late, at fourteen years of age; but I won't lie to myself, I wasn't good enough. At best, I would have started at fourteen and been good at twenty-two or twenty-three. But I try not to trick myself, I don't think that's something smart people do. I wanted to be a tennis player, but when I saw that I couldn't . . . I wasn't bad, I was in the second category, nationwide. I had a pretty good backhand."

"You hear about a certain 'genius' of Toni Nadal. There are some mythical resonances around the decision that your nephew, despite being right-handed, should play with his left."

"That's not true. Rafael played everything with both hands. Rafael is left-footed, he played soccer with his left, and when he wanted to hit hard, he hit harder with his left. So I thought he should play with his left. Nowadays he only uses his left to play tennis, everything else he does with his right. It was never an intentional decision of mine to make him play with his left. He played with both hands, did everything with both, and I've always been motivated by logic. He was very good; at eight years old he was the champion of the Balearic under-twelve, and when he was ten years old I made him play with one hand. He wasn't sure, so I told him, 'Hey, how many do you know in the top ten who play on either side, with both hands?' 'None,' he told me. 'Well, you won't be the first.'"

"So it's just by chance, then? A stroke of luck?"

"Well, I don't know if it's a stroke of luck, because maybe if he had played with his right, he would have played better, I don't know."

"If there's something that Federer has always regretted, it's that Nadal is left-handed."

"Okay, but tennis isn't just about Federer. He had to beat a lot more people if he wanted to win. One of his biggest problems with serving is due to his playing with his left. He has to coordinate his serves a lot more, and that's what is hardest for him."

Toni Nadal's mention of his difficulties serving—which characterized his nephew's career—brings up the memory of a conversation at the beginning of the year with the Australian Ken Rosewall, one of the greatest tennis players in history. Rosewall believes that the explanation behind his weak serve is that as a child he was forced to play with his right, despite having been born left-handed. This time, Toni once again doesn't argue the point. He responds by making the motions of serving with his arms. "It could be, it could be . . . If you ask Rafael to make this motion with his right arm now, he does it well, and with the left... Sometimes when he would try, he would tell me 'You see? I do it naturally like this. And like *this* it isn't natural.'"

"The rules allow for serving with one hand and playing with the other."

"Yes, it's possible, but by now it's a little late, it isn't the right time. Years ago, I remember that Carlos Moyá wanted to make changes to his backhand, and I remember I told him that at twenty-eight years of age I wouldn't make a change. 'I think you're wrong, you're number five or seven in the world at hitting a drive, what are you going to change now? If you did this at eighteen years old, it's feasible and positive. What are we going to change now?' I apply that to myself now as well."

"Nevertheless, during the 2010 US Open, Nadal served very well. It was key for him winning the tournament."

"There's a simple reason for that. Just like a blind man hears better, when I arrived at that US Open, Rafael was playing pretty poorly, and we couldn't do anything right in training. He had to serve better, because if not nothing would go well. I think it forced him to make a decision in his mind. He held the racket like in Wimbledon. And it's not that Rafael has always served poorly, it's that he has no continuity, he oscillates too much. At one point, he might serve more or less well, and then, suddenly, he starts serving poorly, because he lacks that natural coordination of movement."

"Moyá and Porta say that if he served better he would play worse."

"It's possible, it's possible. The truth is that in the US Open he played really well, and he served well."

"*Sure, but that was a tournament; the appraisal refers to his play in general.*"

"Yeah, I understand. Federer, when he plays well, also plays better towards the back, because it becomes easier for him to hit from there. His play style would definitely be different, it's true, but I don't know if he'd play better or worse."

"*Are players obstinate? Federer took a long time to change his racket. And when he did, it was a success.*"

"Change happens once you understand that change is necessary. If you're not sure, it's harder to make the change, it won't work. It works when you're convinced that it's necessary. When Rafael ended 2011 having lost six times to Djokovic, when the season was over we talked about it. I told him, 'Man, there are some things you need to improve. You have to jump when you hit the winner, you have to do this and we'll train for it.' He knew what he had to do, and that's why it worked well. Federer, on the other hand . . . The racket makes it easier, but it's also his mind that tells him that he has to do it. He knows it's the right call, but additionally he makes two tactical changes; he's more aggressive and gets closer to the net. That's what makes him play better."

"*In that book you signed off on with your friend Pere Mas, you say that Federer doesn't have the ability to feel 'true' suffering.*"

"I think that was something he wrote. I can be pretty vehement when I talk, but I don't say things like that. Federer has less of an ability to suffer than Rafael, that's true, and less than Djokovic, but he wouldn't have won as much if he was incapable of suffering. Not so much physical suffering, but the capacity for mental suffering is necessary, because you can't win otherwise.

CHAPTER 12

Basel

LIKE SO MANY SEVENTEEN-YEAR-OLD ADOLESCENTS, Roger Federer and his good friend Marco Chiudinelli would get terribly bored on their nighttime weekend outings in the oftentimes overly peaceful Basel. The trip to McDonald's was mandatory, as was the trip through the game room. They almost always rode into the city on their bikes. And they almost never went with girls. "I was one of those guys at the party who hid in the corner, crippled by shyness," Federer admits when he talks about it. "I started to gain confidence once I started winning at tennis."

Roger and Marco were joined at the hip. The two young men loved tennis, soccer, and Chiudinelli especially also loved music. Both their lives consisted of daily practice and tournaments on the weekends, a schedule that inevitably made night life rare. Drinking? No sign of that. Roger and Marco didn't touch alcohol. They were such avid friends and athletes that there wasn't room for anything else in their minds.

It's not hard to realize that Federer fits in with Basel; they're made for each other: a calm, cosmopolitan city with a diversity in language and ethnicity. Federer answers questions in English, German, and French in press conference rooms all over the world, something for which he was, in a sort of way, destined. René Stauffer talks about this in *Quest for Perfection*, a well-documented and complete biography of Federer. When the future tennis player was born in the Cantón Hospital in August, 1981, Robert and Lynette had already decided that their baby would be named Roger, because "at some point it would be good for him to have a name that could be pronounced in English."

The fact that Federer's parents had more than the usual portion of foresight is something that becomes undeniable once you arrive at one of the key stages of the Swiss man's career: the tennis club where he started playing. Only the chirping of the birds breaks the silence and adds a bit of vibration to the fresh, end of October air that is saturated with the odor of dead leaves and ocher covering everything. On the neighboring street, St. Galler-Ring, bikes go by every so often, as well as cars that seem to be equipped with silencers. Before arriving at Old Boys, you see a club with several soccer fields, a sporting installation deserted at this time. The houses and departments of the area have at most three or four plants. The calmness is very Swiss, but there's a decidedly German ambience. Is Basel a more German city than it is Swiss? Isn't Federer, or couldn't he have been, almost German? The Basilea-Mulhouse-Freiburg airport actually has Customs offices for three countries: Switzerland, France, and Germany. It's no wonder, then, that Federer is so international, that his parents gave him a name that would sound good in English, and that the player himself would enjoy his mastery of a language that wasn't his native one.

There are nine courts that make up Old Boys, and only the two covered ones are having any action that day, while the club coffee shop is half empty and lethargic. The two covered courts are the Roger Federer Center Court and the Marco Chiudinelli. Even the boards give the sense of being extremely Swiss: rectangular, small, white with black lettering, unpretentious.

Federer is now very far removed from daily life in the peaceful tennis club, but history still resonates there. So says Franz Camenzind, more than eighty years old and the oldest partner at the club. "I've been a partner at this club since 1945, one of the six hundred honorary members that there are in total. I'm the oldest partner in the club, the number one," he says with poorly hidden pride. When Federer was born, Camenzind had already been playing in the Old Boys club for thirty-six years.

And he was still there in 2012, when he was remembering a bygone era of tennis, much different from today. "I still play tennis every weekend; I play doubles. I started here in 1940 as a ball boy. Until 1950, 1955, there were ball boys for every match, and then only for the championships, and then they were gone altogether."

Camenzind was a witness of Federer's tough days, when he drove his parents and his first trainers crazy. "I've known Federer and Chiudinelli since they were small. I've seen how Federer's racket would occasionally fly from one court to the next." That racket-throwing and racket-breaking Federer was always contrasted against the obedient Nadal, who had the idea drummed into him that breaking a racket was a lack of respect towards the other children.

Camenzind, who had been playing tennis at Old Boys for sixty years by 2005 when Nadal and Gaudio faced off, doubts that the Spaniard was always so impeccable. "Who knows? Truthfully, we don't know what Nadal did when he was young." What the number one partner at Old Boys does know is that Federer surprised him. "I never would have thought that Federer could be number one. Now we have two hundred boys in youth practice. Who knows, maybe another good player will pop up."

Federer and Chiudinelli, when they were teenagers, were so sporty and "proper" that they had a hard time fitting into the curious environment of Zum Wurzengraber, an impossible locale in the heart of Kleinbasel, the most alternative, or less perfect, area of the city. The Zum Wurzengraber was, until 2012, an unavoidable stop for those who wanted to see the real Kleinbasel night life. Upon entering, a visitor would get the feeling that he was somewhere that the Spanish film director Pedro Almodóvar would have gone if he had filmed in Switzerland. Full of outlandish decorations and barely acceptable food, the Zum Wurzengraber filled up on weekends and was the type of place that only the average person would visit, not stars. Although if you looked closely, Fränzi, the owner, could be considered a star. She had overly large hoop earrings, huge, '60s-style glasses, short and well-tailored dresses with colorful designs, lots of makeup, short hair with thin bangs tinted bright red, and an indeterminate age: Late sixties? Less? More?

Fränzi worked in the kitchen, the bar, and at the register, without pause. Years before, she had collected a legion of fans in Barcelona, where she was considered one of the best waitresses in the city. She wasn't far from Almodóvar there. Many clients from that time still remember her, and help her in different ways to the point that the locale, which closed the doors of its building in 2012, was assured a new location thanks to the support that Fränzi received from some of those same clients. In that new locale you would find Siwi, Fränzi's daughter, who was a true "heretic" in Basel.

"I hate Roger Federer. I hate him." Siwi is a simple girl, not brilliant perhaps, but she stands by her thesis with sympathy, decisiveness, and conviction. "I hate him. He has so much money. He could hand it out," Fränzi's daughter says again. She is a tireless waitress, and much less eccentric in her style of dress than her mother. They both, however, share a squat physique and a long face that leads into a diminutive torso, the waist and chest almost hard to separate. They are quite recognizable; there's no denying that they're mother and daughter. Siwi's gaze lights up again. "What sort of pride could the son of someone who just hits balls with a little racket have?" she asks, while jokingly and mechanically imitating the motions of a serve with her wrist.

Fränzi and Siwi, despite the significance they have for the "Basel underground," are still just anecdotal, because Federer is admired and loved in their country to a degree that perhaps no athlete has ever before achieved. That doesn't mean that there are no criticisms, which started to grow during the recent years of Federer's career. Criticisms which, as often happens, are directly linked to his success, or lack thereof, at sports. So the negative comments that started appearing in 2013, Federer's lowest year since his ascent to the top, became less frequent during the months following his comeback. His successes helped, his hand-over-hand fight for the top position in the world, and above all, his conquest of the Davis Cup in France in November of 2014. "The newer generations are big Nadal fans," one spectator explained on a gray Autumn afternoon at the tournament in Basel, where Federer had first evolved from a ball boy to a several-time champion. And it's the truth. Toni Nadal, in fact, had once gotten tickets for a Swiss group who was desperate to see his nephew play at Roland Garros.

Supporting the "outsider" to the detriment of one's "own" is not new; it happened towards the end of the '80s, when the German *Tennis Magazine* regularly received letters from Germans who criticized Steffi Graf, the number one player in the world. Her game, they said, couldn't compare to "the plasticity and beauty" of the Argentinian Gabriela Sabatini's game. *Smash*, the main Swiss tennis magazine, also, on occasion, received letters criticizing Federer. They called him a "sore loser," "arrogant," and until the success of 2014, could not find sense in his erratic conduct in chasing the Davis Cup.

As it happened, Federer's aura, in October of 2012, was showing some small cracks that weren't there before. That October, as in every year, Rotschi went home to play in front of his audience. This time, there had been anger against him ever since the tournament, and a lack of understanding on the part of his Davis Cup teammates. In 2012, the agreement that Federer had previously signed with the organization in Basel would expire: half a million dollars to play each iteration of the tournament, plus the VAT, plus the official prizes. Again the number one player in the world and the Wimbledon champion a couple of months prior, Federer was in a good position to renegotiate the agreement. What Tony Godsick, his agent, asked from the tournament set the normally serene Swiss men's hair on end. The number was never made public, although several local journalists have said that is was closer to $2 million each time he played the tournament, rather than the million that is usually agreed upon for arrangements of a similar magnitude. Whatever the number, the reaction of the tournament showed that it was certainly high, more appropriate for what Federer or Nadal would charge from tournaments with a bigger pull and more economic power than the one in Basel. "We're not Qatar," was the ironic comment of René Stammbach, president of the Swiss Tennis Federation.

And while the discussions continued and veteran members of the tournament organization accused Godsick of an excessive ambition and desire for money after having left IMG, the talent management company, a couple of questions were circulating around in St. Jakobshalle: Does Federer care about the Davis Cup or not? Does he really want to win, or does he just pretend to be nice when he mentions it time and time again as a goal?

Swiss Tennis had gotten excited at the prospect of an idea that was proposed for February of 2013: playing the first round of the Davis Cup in Basel, against the Czech Republic. There, on Federer's territory, in a stadium of nine thousand spectators, the pressure on Tomáš Berdych and his team would be guaranteed, and the home field advantage would be significant. But Federer wasn't convinced by the deal. He felt that by using Basel as the locale he was basically being ambushed, being forced to play. He made this known to the federation, which changed the location to Geneva and a stadium of five thousand seats, half an hour from Lausana, the land of Stanislas Wawrinka, the number two Swiss player. A very strong player from deep in the court, and owner of a huge backhand, Wawrinka's tennis career was inevitably overshadowed by the real-life legend that is Federer. He would later take a turn for the better, but up to that point, in October 2012, he had played Federer thirteen times and had lost twelve. It would still be a few months before his impacting title in the 2014 Australian Open, a year which changed his life. Four years younger than the seven-time Wimbledon champion, Wawrinka was the undeniable victim of a complex when the net was between them.

But during those days in Basel, when he was eliminated in the first round of the tournament, Wawrinka spoke clearly off the court: his ties to the Davis Cup were absolute. "You don't need to keep asking me, I will always play in the Davis Cup," Wawrinka had said in 2011 to Stammbach. And when, a year later, he was asked about Federer's doubts, his words left no room for doubting. "No, I don't understand Roger, I don't know why he won't be at Geneva in February against the Czechs." "Disappointed?" they asked him. "I'm used to it," he answered quickly, shrugging his shoulders.

The thousandth "no" from Federer to the Davis arrived exactly twenty years after the greatest Swiss achievement in the tournament, the 1992 final against the United States. That time, two men, Marc Rosset and Jakob Hlasek, had climbed their way to the decisive encounter and had put the United States' back to the wall. No small feat, because the North Americans were playing with Pete Sampras, Andre Agassi, Jim Courier, and the legendary John McEnroe in doubles. That final in Texas ended with the home team winning, 3–1, although not without a fight, because Switzerland wasn't far from winning the doubles point after Rosset's successful strike against Courier, at the time the number two player in the world.

It took Switzerland twenty-two years to play in the Davis final again, a paradox when you realize that for more than a decade they had the man whom many people consider to be the best tennis player of all time.

CHAPTER 13

Mirka

"Crybaby!"The hurtful insult cut through the air at the O2 Arena, a dream stadium in which to watch indoor tennis. There may be no video that shows the word coming from the lips of Mirka Vavrinec on that Saturday in November of 2014, but there are several photos in which Stanislas Wawrinka is looking directly at Roger Federer's wife. His look hovers between angry and tired, clearly overcome by the situation. The number two Swiss player is prepared to receive Federer's serve, at an advantage of 4–6, 7–5, 5–4, and 40–40 in the London Masters semifinals. Five days after that match, both players would fulfill the Swiss dream of finally winning the Davis Cup.

Wawrinka is a sensitive player, and he frequently becomes embroiled in long discussions with the chair umpires, which he usually ends up losing. He appears not to be able to stand for injustices, and his explosions are a bit agonizing, with an air of surprised complaint, as if he were incapable of understanding how a decision could be made that would harm him. He has "thin skin," it's relatively easy to make him lose control, and his rivals know this. But he is also deep and intelligent. In January of 2014, he caused a sensation in the Australian Open when the cameras focused on the words he has tattooed on his left arm: "Ever tried. Ever failed. No matter. Try again. Fail again. Fail better."

The quote, from Irish writer Samuel Beckett, isn't meaningless. "It's how I see life and, especially, tennis."

But on that London night, Wawrinka wasn't thinking about Beckett. He had more urgent things on his mind. Just moments before the cry of "Crybaby," Wawrinka had complained about the yelling by Mirka, who was sitting in a box at the edge of the court. "She did it in Wimbledon," he lamented. Sarcastic and subtle, or more likely cruel, Federer's woman summed up the whole situation in one word: crybaby.

That night ended with Wawrinka defeated despite having four match points and with a strong argument between himself and Federer in the stadium's gym. John McEnroe said he had witnessed the tension between the two players, and, if there was anything that they absolutely mustn't do at that point in the season, it was fighting. He meant in theory, of course, because the sport can often be surprising when human conflicts are solved in strange ways. When an exhausted and sad Wawrinka stepped into the press conference room, it was already morning on Sunday, but none of the journalists knew what McEnroe would say hours later on Twitter. They only knew about the protests of the second best Swiss player during the match, which anyone there could see, although they still weren't totally sure of what had happened.

Wawrinka didn't help to clarify things much. When he was asked what happened during those moments, his answer was as slippery as an eel, impossible to grasp. "Nothing special. A tense match. It's never easy." Federer didn't clear anything up either. "I clearly had good luck tonight," the Swiss said after a win that would end up being a Pyrrhic victory, since the next day he would withdraw from playing in the final against Novak Djokovic, alleging back problems. It was the third time in his very extensive career that Federer would quit a match.

The O2 Arena is a special place. Watching tennis there is a pleasure, but it's not really a tennis stadium. Rather, it's a multipurpose stage used often for music. Indeed, before entering the complex where the stadium is, a visitor can take a quick trip through the history of rock. Once you leave the subway station, North Greenwich, a succession of photos to the left of the path that goes to the stadium captures decades of music industry highlights:

1951: Frank Sinatra plays the Desert Inn

1954: Elvis Presley, *That's Alright Mama*

1954: Muddy Waters, *Hoochie Coochie Man*

1963: Beatlemania

1964: Rolling Stones, *Satisfaction*

1969: Woodstock

1971: Marvin Gaye, *What's Going On*

1972: David Bowie, *Ziggy Stardust*

1974: Kraftwerk, *Autobahn*

They're all names of musical influence throughout more than sixty years. The milestones, whether they consist of names like Bowie or in "states of being" like Beatlemania, are all small legends superimposed on large photos that show the evolution, not just of music, but of society as well. Looking at them, activating something in your memory, remembering the first time you heard each one. It makes you want to stay there all afternoon.

1974: Bob Marley & The Wailers, *No Woman, No Cry*

1975: Led Zeppelin, *Physical Graffiti*

1976: Sex Pistols, *Anarchy in the UK*

The photo, in sepia tones, shows the faces of the young men of the Sex Pistols in the '70s. It's a concert, one of them yells at the camera, showing his teeth. Others of the same age surround him; they're at most eighteen. On the night that the "anarchic" Federer faced Wawrinka, maybe one of them was in the stadium. They would be at least fifty-five years old now.

1979: The Specials relaunch ska in Great Britain

1979: Sugar Hill records hip hop for the first time

1981: Duran Duran, *Planet Earth*

1982: Michael Jackson, *Thriller*

The photos are more colorful and less sepia, the clothes and haircuts are '80s style, and the austere, tough leather jackets of the '70s disappear.

1983: Metallica invents speed metal

1984: Prince, *Purple Rain*

1985: Live Aid

1985: Madonna, *Material Girl*

1986: Bon Jovi, *Livin' on a Prayer*

1988: Madchester, the second summer of love

1991: REM, *Losing my Religion*

1991: Nirvana, *Smells Like Teen Spirit*

1995: Blur versus Oasis

1996: Spice Girls, *Wannabe*

1997: Robin Williams, *Angels*

1997: Puff Daddy, *No Way Out*

2000: NSYNC, *No Strings Attached*

2000: Eminem, *The Marshall Mathers*

During those years between Robin Williams, Puff Daddy, NSYNC, and Eminem, Federer's name had started to be heard in the tennis world. To hear Wawrinka's, you would still have to wait.

2003: Beyoncé Knowles and the triumph of R&B

The same year of Federer's great triumph, also in London, the beginning of the long series of titles at Wimbledon.

2005: Live 8

2006: Take That plays again

2007: The O2 opens

The tennis players miss that photographic musical journey because they enter the O2 through the back door, having traveled on a boat from their hotel at the edge of the Thames, the quickest way to get to the other side, that of the renovated London East End. For the spectators, on the other hand, seeing these photos again and remembering those bands was a bit of a consolation after a final that wasn't. Still, they got to see some tennis.

Andy Murray was playing Mario Kart, a popular Nintendo video game, when he got the call: they didn't need him. The Brit was in London, officially on vacation after being steamrolled in his last match of the year, 6–0 and 6–1, by Federer in fifty-five minutes. Murray played an exhibition match with Djokovic on that strange Sunday, and uttered the phrase of the night, "I have to apologize because, clearly, I asked too much of Roger on Thursday."

Not always understood by his compatriots and occasionally drained by the pressures of a sport that he doesn't always enjoy, Murray possesses something that distinguishes any true Brit: a command of irony. That quality is quite infrequent in tennis, a huge business in which what you say, what you don't say, and how you say it, somehow always translates to money. Every player's image is cared for, under total control, well managed, and most of the time having journalists nearby is a problem for that carefully constructed profile.

So, on that unusual Sunday afternoon in which the Masters—a tournament played since 1970—was without a final match for the first time in history due to Federer's back injury, the ATP communications department opted for keeping Federer away from the media. By that time, thanks especially to the work of British journalist Simon Briggs of the *Daily Telegraph*, the whole world was up to date on that outburst of "crybaby" that Wawrinka received. The logical thing was to ask Federer what had happened, but that wasn't possible. The governing body of men's tennis hid the player, and offered the media an ATP "interview." The so-called "interview" consisted of six questions, but none of them even came close to the incident that had taken place Saturday night.

The injured Federer was, without a doubt, disappointed by not being able to fight for his seventh Masters title, but for a man of his capacity and self-control in front of the media, answering a simple question about what had happened on Saturday wouldn't have been a problem. The ATP saw it differently, and the media would have to wait until Tuesday, in the French city of Lille, to hear Federer.

The questions at press conferences are studied in minute detail. The players take close note of who is asking, what they're asking, and how they are asking it. The ATP communications department does the same thing, as well as the players' agents, their press agents . . . and the journalists themselves, as they make use of transcription services during the biggest competitions to record every question and every answer. And so, after weighing the situation a bit, one journalist attacked the topic, the outburst of "crybaby" that intrigued the sporting world, with an elegance of clarity. *"As you know, it's not just your back that has generated a lot of interest in the past couple of days. Could you tell us a bit more about what was the cause of the anger between you and Stan on Saturday night?"*

Federer's answer floated like one of those slow backhands with slice that he executes so perfectly. "Well, I was actually on the other side of the court, I was pretty far away. We had a conversation after the match; everything is very relaxed with regards to the situation. We're old enough, we have Severin [Lüthi] as a trainer, and the captain of the Davis Cup, our friend, who was also there. I just wanted to know if there was any rancor, because it was one of the noisiest moments during the whole match, clearly lots of noise. Like I said . . . There aren't any resentments or anything of the sort. We're having a good time here. We're friends, not enemies. But it was obviously one of those moments, one of those heat of the moment things. I don't think there's much else to say about at this point." It was pretty clear. Federer didn't need any communications department to protect him; he is more than capable of handling these situations himself.

After facing a Teflon-covered Federer, the press turned to Wawrinka. *"Stan, the chair umpire from Sunday night, Cedric Mourier, gave an interview today in which he says that you told him that Roger's wife was the one talking to you during the match, and he saw that you were clearly irritated by the situation. Is that so?"* Wawrinka, who owns an even better backhand than Federer, opted to answer with a deep top-spin. "First of all, I'm not sure that he's allowed to talk about that. And, yes, it's like Roger said. First of all, we don't have a problem. We talked about it after the match. Not just about that, but about a lot of things. We know how to handle small things like this when they arise. As far as the match, it wasn't the first issue that happened over the course of the game. I don't think the chair umpire did a great job, exactly. As you saw at the beginning of the third set with the overrule and everything, there were already some problems. But again, I don't have much to say on my part, because the issue is just being blown out of proportion by the press, by all of you. But for us, there isn't really anything. It took us five minutes to talk about it and then to move on and think about our next big shared objective: the Davis Cup this weekend."

"One more question. Now that Cedric said what he said and mentioned your wife by name, do you have any comments to add to what Stan said?"

Federer responded using the same cold ferocity with which he deals with his opponents on the field. "In the first place, the chair umpire doesn't have permission to give interviews. Whether or not my wife is mentioned by name is not important, it really isn't. I think everything has been said, the situation is totally relaxed, I don't know what the big deal is."

"Did you feel obligated to have a conversation with your family about how they react on the field? I know that in the heat of the battle, tensions run high."

"You said before that it was your last question. Now you keep going," Federer answered, smiling. And then the moderator from the International Tennis Federation (ITF) decided to intervene. "Can we please move on to another topic? Another question in English?" With Swiss elegance and precision, the scandal was defused. The blame lay with the chair umpire for not controlling the situation, and with the media for insisting on inquiring about what happened.

"What does Mirka mean to you?" The question is posed to Roger Federer while he is on a layover. He is surrounded by desert, a vast extension of sand that ends in a soupy ocean, but for the moment he is in a different setting: The air conditioning lets him ignore the strong heat of Dubai, and a television spotlight brightens the dimly-lit corners of the small television studio in which the interview is taking place. It's February of 2007, and he is starting his fourth consecutive season as the top player in the world. Federer is at the peak of his career; he's unstoppable, a winning machine who plays well. "She's just a colleague," he responds in German, joking. But then he gets serious, because Miroslava Vavrinec deserves that. "Naturally, she's the most important person in my life, along with my parents. And I'm very happy for all that she does

for me. She will always be my wife, or my girlfriend. Everything she does, she does because she enjoys helping me. If she stopped enjoying it, she would have to stop doing it."

In 2007, Roger and Mirka were a young couple in their twenties, Myla Rose and Charlene Riva hadn't been born yet, and especially not Leo and Lenny. They had an alliance sealed in fire since a nineteen-year-old Roger, on the first of October in 2000, had kissed Mirka for the first time. It was during the closing ceremony of the 2000 Sydney Olympics, and Mirka was surprised: "I didn't know that Roger was so much fun."

Fun or not, they soon became a couple, and then partners. Vavrinec, born in Slovakia, moved to Switzerland when she was two, and rose to number 76 in tennis worldwide, but rarely occupied much space in the Swiss press for her athletic achievements, which are summed up in forty matches won out of ninety-nine played, and no finals during her four-year career. A foot injury caused her retirement from tennis and opened the way for her to become, according to the Swiss newspaper *Blick*, "one of the most sought people in the world of tennis business."

That lasted for a while. Mirka, three years older than Federer, whom she married in 2009, took care of managing the top player's relationship with his sponsors and with the press. She was especially in charge of saying "no," and the word left her lips frequently. Federer felt a bit guilty then, that she was always "the bad guy." Finally, he freed her from that responsibility; he thought it unfair. "Mirka watches my back, she takes care of everything," Federer recognized more than once. "When Roger wins, it's like I'm winning, too," Mirka points out.

Absolute symbiosis, total agreement. "Mirka is everything: girl-friend, organizer, stylist," the Swiss magazine *Schweizer Illustrierte* once wrote. And Mirka didn't deny it. "Yes . . . my hand is there," she would say when asked about Federer's "style." At the beginning of the relation-ship she nearly had to drag her boyfriend to the hairdresser, to control his preference for letting his hair grow and tying it up with a not-so-glamorous rubber band. The succession of photos of his celebrations with the Wimbledon trophy held above his head enable one to see Federer's aesthetic changes.

During those first years, the Federer clan rented a house just a few steps from the All England Club, and Mirka would put together a stellar meal every night using the sixty pounds of food she brought from Switzerland. She liked to cook. "We love Swiss food so much! It's a relief to eat at home after having to eat every night at restaurants or in the hotel," she recalls. Through the years, both of their lives became more complicated and sophisticated at the same time, although the future Mrs. Federer knew from the start that she would not lead a normal life. "Sometimes I realize that I don't have any time for me. I don't do sports, and I'm carrying a few extra pounds, I know that." Mirka, who said during the interview with *Schweizer Illustrierte* that she was "technically better" since she has been playing with Federer, believes that the fact that she played tennis was essential. "I think that's why we understand each other perfectly. No other woman could put up with so much tennis! Tennis is everything in our lives. Every day, every minute. If he wants to sleep late, I don't bother him when I get up early to go jogging. And if one night he wants to watch a soccer match with his friends, I leave him alone."

Mirka wasn't bothered by traveling in Federer's wake and thus making her own desire for professional growth secondary. "Roger shows me his love every day. He tells me 'thank you' every day, very sweetly. He takes care of me, he spoils me." Mirka, to be sure, believes absolutely in the pact she sealed with Federer: "He's the greatest in the world, that's a unique thing in life. My time will come after the tennis. That's what we both agreed on." Federer agreed when that phrase was mentioned during the interview in Dubai. "Exactly. For example, if we're on vacation I do everything she wants to do. If she wants to go shopping for ten hours, I go with her because she has to wait for me for ten hours at every tournament. I don't have a problem with that."

It's evident how proud Mirka is of her husband. During the first years of his success she made an understandable comparison, although in a sporting context it's curious. "Apart from Kournikova, there are few that can claim that luxury," she said, commenting on Federer's five appearances throughout a single year in *Vogue* magazine. The Russian Anna Kournikova, one of the great beauties in the history of tennis, and owner of an interesting play style aside from an excess of double fouls, would close her career without ever winning a tournament.

During those years, Federer started to become interested in dressing well, and to that end he counted on the advice of Trudi Götz, the "czarina" of fashion in Switzerland. "Roger grew up," Götz, who knew Federer in 2002, remarked. "He has a look suitable for James Bond. And Mirka looks like a diva. I love them both." So much love came with its perks: Roger and Mirka were Götz's guests every year at the Prada showroom in Milan, where they could at their convenience try on clothes that wouldn't appear in shop windows in Zurich for another six months.

Götz is a public figure in Switzerland, were she is respected for her years of work and the luster that her shop, Trois Pommes, adds to the already elegant Bahnhofstrasse, Zurich's main artery. But every celebrity has bad moments. One of them happened after a visit from Oprah Winfrey. "This happened to me very recently in Zurich," the famous television presenter said during an interview with Larry King in 2013. "I walked into a name brand store and said I wanted to see a bag. 'No,' the clerk told me. 'That's too expensive for you. It was designed for Jennifer Aniston, etcetera, etcetera.' I wanted to do like in *Pretty Woman*, come back the next day, buy everything and tell them they'd made a big mistake. But I didn't, that girl probably worked on commission."

The crocodile-skin bag cost 35,000 Swiss francs and was from the renowned Tom Ford collection. Götz later explained that there were no racist intentions on her clerk's behalf, but Winfrey already has had too much experience with those affairs: As she also related to Larry King, towards the end of the '90s a store on Madison Avenue in New York closed its doors in her face. They later explained that they had recently been robbed by "two black people," and they were scared.

Mirka soon started to enjoy that life of luxury, which included visits to exclusive hotels like the Burj Al Arab in Dubai, a seven-star hotel that seems out of this world. Or to the Arts hotel in Barcelona, the Huvafen Fushi on the Maldives, or Le Touessrok, the best hotel on the Mauricio islands, located on its own island with a coral reef included.

Years later, in 2012, Federer bought a sixty-two thousand-square-foot plot of land on the slope of a mountain with an unbeatable view of the area known as the "gold coast" of the Zurich Lake, according to the newspaper *Blick*. And next year there were photos of the eighty-six thousand square feet that Federer owns in the mountainous area of Valbella, in the Graubünden canton, where he built two complexes: Bellavista A for himself and his family and Bellavista B for his parents. If they get tired of winter, they can always take a five-hour flight to the two-thousand-square-foot flat in the heat of Dubai.

Such real-estate assets were possibly in their future, but not yet a goal, during the years that Götz opened the doors of glamour and a different image to Roger and Mirka. The leap to a higher level of fashion for the Federers was left to another woman, a Brit who had settled in New York, Anna Wintour. The daughter of Charles Wintour, who was the editor of a British press institution, the *Evening Standard*, Wintour has since 1988 directed *Vogue* magazine, a must-read reference for fashion and trends. Known for being difficult—some would even say arrogant—her attitude gave Wintour some benefits. There was a time when the business paid for her to take trips on a Concorde airplane between New York and London, together with her husband, who is South African, as is Lynette, Federer's mother. A pageboy bob haircut and extra-large glasses are Wintour's trademark. She is as respected as she is feared because of her influence in the fashion industry.

"Roger was a provincial Swiss, and Mirka wasn't sophisticated either," remembers someone who asked to remain off the record, a man who has been in the tennis circuit for twenty years and knows them both very well. "Anna Wintour changed them."

There was little left of the provincial Federer on the night of August 23, 2012. Fifteen days before, he had turned thirty-one years old, but the celebration has been delayed until just days before the start of the US Open. He had just won Wimbledon the month before, his tenth Grand Slam title, and Wintour was of the opinion that the celebration should be big. And "big" means inviting Nicole Kidman, Bradley Cooper, Keith Urban, Óscar de la Renta, or Diane von Fürstenberg. They came to the Beatrice Inn, an exclusive hotel in the West Village. It hadn't been opened yet, but very few things are closed to Wintour in New York when she wants them. And what she wants can sometimes be absolutely bold. It was her idea to reach a new world record, which was the 832 pages that made up the September 2004 edition of *Vogue*. And it was her idea to show on her debut cover in November 1988 a nineteen-year-old Israeli model wearing a pair of 50 dollar jeans, and a T-shirt that was worth ten thousand dollars because of the diamonds with which it had been encrusted.

That she can be frightening was proved both to Winfrey—her again—and Hillary Clinton. To the first she said that she had to lose twenty-two pounds before appearing on the magazine cover, making her a definitive victim of the famous 118-pound limit. If you were over that weight, appearing on the cover of the magazine was overwhelmingly difficult. The problem with the potential candidate for the presidency at the time was of greater significance and, in a certain way—because of the editor's reaction—an inconsistency based on the reasons why she vetoed the television star.

Bill Clinton's wife was initiating her own fight for the Democratic primaries against Barack Obama and was wary of seeming "too feminine" if she landed in the pages of *Vogue*. Over the course of more than two hundred years as an independent nation, only men had been in command in the White House. A woman who appeared in *Vogue* might not be trustworthy enough to carry the nuclear briefcase, as measured by some adviser whose job it was to predict how potential voters would react. The 1998 cover of Hillary, photographed by Annie Leibovitz, was a long time ago. At the time, she was the First Lady, not a candidate for the top governing post in the country. But Wintour thought otherwise, and she made it known in an open letter to Hillary

Clinton in the February 2008 edition, "Imagine my amazement, then, when I learned that Hillary Clinton, our only female president hopeful, had decided to steer clear of our pages at this point in her campaign for fear of looking too feminine. The notion that a contemporary woman must look mannish in order to be taken seriously as a seeker of power is frankly dismaying. How could our country come to this? This is America, not Saudi Arabia."

Since almost nothing is forever, Wintour not only organized fund-raising dinners for Obama, but in 2013, with Hillary considering a new presidential attempt, she shared an event with her at Little Rock, the capital of Arkansas, the Clintons' "hometown." Peace had been made, and Hillary added her name to the list of Wintour's friends, which ranges from Cate Blanchett to Calvin Klein, and includes Mario Testino, Justin Timberlake, LeBron James, Miuccia Prada, and Pharrell Williams. And Roger and Mirka, of course. Right at the top.

Federer is very clear about the fact that he owes a lot to Wintour, because it's thanks to her that he developed a sense of fashion. "All this started with a celebration that I had to go to after getting a title. I didn't know what to wear," Federer recalled in 2014. The celebration was a dinner that Wintour organized in his honor. "I learned that a dark suit is better at night. I always remember that tip." Far removed now from that provincial man some saw in his beginnings on the circuit, Federer going into his thirties had become familiar with life in the Hamptons, the exclusive ocean-side area just an hour from New York. And he liked it. "You hear all those things about the Hamptons, but then you go and you find that it's between a relaxing bay and the sea and that it can be really peaceful, except on the summer weekends. Then it can be pretty hard, very similar to a Swiss skiing season."

You can't say that Wintour "hung on" to Federer's success. Her aim wasn't to make friends with the champion. The editor was fifty-two years old when, in August of 2002, she greeted Federer at the US Open. "I didn't really know who she was," Federer admitted years later. He was barely twenty-one at the time of that encounter; he still had that pony tail and long hair, and was still just a very promising player, but not yet the best.

Joshua Levine, a reporter for the *Wall Street Journal*, interviewed Wintour in 2011 in her office in *Vogue*'s editorial department, which he describes as "artistic and tidy." She had been awake since five in the morning. She normally did this to play tennis at six, but during that January she was up in dimly-lit hours before dawn to glue herself to the television so that she could follow her friend in the Australian Open. On that day, Federer struggled to defeat France's Gilles Simon in five sets. "'At least he's still in the race,' she said after the match, visibly relieved," observed the journalist, who had earlier obtained a brief remark from Federer about his relationship with Wintour. "I get all kinds of ideas from her, what to wear in and out of the court, photograph sessions, sponsors, everything." Federer emphasizes that Wintour never asked him for anything in return. "But that day will come, and when it does, I'll be very happy to work with her."

CHAPTER 14

Lille

THE HOT AIR HIT ROGER Federer's face, and, ignoring his fame and determined to be a part of the crowd, he stuck his head out of the taxi window to shout out his joy to the Manhattan streets. He was young, he was in the center of the world, and was bent on enjoying a night in the Big Apple. In the seat next to him, the Austrian Stefan Koubek was shouting, too, just as happy and with his head also out the window.

As time went on, Federer would stop being so spontaneous. On one hand, because you don't do the same things when you're thirty that you do when you're twenty, and on the other because fame started to set him limits. More importantly, when you're married and a father your time and priorities shift. Also—he says this himself—because Mirka is central to his life: she organizes it, just like his mother did when he was young, and Federer feels comfortable with this arrangement.

"Her support is tremendous; without her I couldn't do what I'm doing. If she came to me one day and said, 'You will retire tomorrow,' things would potentially be quite different," Federer told the *Age*, an Australian newspaper, in 2013. "Then I would have to talk to her about it, but she believes that I can still achieve a lot of things, and she supports me a lot. She loves, like I do, life on the circuit. She thinks that it's fantastic that the kids are around me and in the tennis world. We think that's a great education for them."

Two years later, Myla Rose and Charlene Riva's education was a topic of growing importance, because they would soon have to enter elementary school. How would he solve the issue? This is what Federer was asked in Australia in 2015. "I don't much like talking about these things in public, because everything has to be analyzed. The idea is to have them in the circuit while I'm playing, and we'll eventually arrange private classes. Probably. We'll see." His extreme discretion when it comes to talking about personal topics is well known, although the question required Federer to admit that reality was winning out over his dreams. "I never thought this would happen. I never thought I'd still be playing, but I'm happy with how I play and the little ones love it."

Within Swiss tennis there was a widespread belief that floated around for a good part of Federer's career: his repeated absences from the Davis Cup were due to Mirka's lack of a desire to let him be "loose" for a week in the team environment. That can't be proved, although the Federer who shouted on the streets of Manhattan was the same guy who, when speaking French, frequently used a slight cuss word, *connerie*, and was the same Federer who, after a 2004 Davis Cup series, celebrated hard in D!Club, a nightclub in Lausanne. Mirka, still young and perhaps understandably insecure about the relationship, didn't like to see her boyfriend so out of control and so interested in the festive night life with his friends.

During those years, Federer began a strong friendship with Gavin Rossdale, who would become the front man for the rock band Bush and who was married at the time to the singer Gwen Stefani. British, born in London, Rossdale has Scottish roots and is a tennis fan. A talented player and a common presence at the famous tournaments, he every once in a while tries out his two-handed backhand with Federer. "Have you ever been close to beating him?" *Details* magazine asked Rossdale in 2010. It was the typical sort of question that tried to find something out through provocation, but Rossdale wouldn't be manipulated. "No, the truth is, that's not really what it's about. My fun with Roger is limited to just hitting the ball around enough for him to get some exercise.

That's my Wimbledon, hitting the ball around with Roger without him wasting his time. Of course I've gotten a few points, sure. If you get in a good serve, you can score a point on anyone in the world, but could you do it for five sets? Probably not."

If with Myla Rose, Charlene Riva, Leo, and Lenny, the Federers seem to have shown a good imagination for their children's names, the Rossdale-Stefani couple would bring their friends fully back to reality; they're just two boring conservatives. With names like Kingston James McGregor, Zuma Nesta Rock, and Apollo Bowie Flynn, the Rossdale-Stefanis showed that you can always go further.

Rossdale, who in later years followed Federer to several of the world's main tennis stages, is the Swiss player's friend, yes, but his passion for tennis is genuine. He's not just an obsessive fan, he's interested in much more than just what his friend does. "I like to see players who have class. Roger, of course, but almost all the players in the top one hundred are very good. There aren't any with defects. The athletic level of the greatest is phenomenal, they give the impression that they would be good at any sport. There is an intense level of art in tennis, a lot of passion, and compromise. I enjoy and value the game for what it is."

One of Rossdale's favorite players is Latvian Ernests Gulbis, the same man who once defined Federer, Nadal, Djokovic, and Murray as "boring." Gulbis believes, as do many other participants and observers of the circuit, that Federer is too "Swiss," a concept that views order, predictability, and a certain lack of passion as bordering on boredom. A similar idea was expressed by the Argentinian writer Ernesto Sabato in his chapter, "Report on the Blind," from *On Heroes and Tombs*: "The first time I traveled through that country, I had the feeling that it was swept every morning by the house maids (and throwing the dirt away, of course, in Italy). And so powerful was the impression that I reconsidered the national mythology.

"The anecdotes are essentially true because they're made up, because they're made up piece by piece, and adjusted precisely for an individual. Something similar happens with national myths, which are made for the purpose of describing a country's soul, and so it occurred to me at the time that the legend of Guillermo Tell (in English, William Tell) faithfully describes the Swiss soul: When the archer hit the apple with the arrow, right in the exact center of the apple, they lost their only historical chance at a great national tragedy. What more could you expect from such a country? A race of watch-makers, in the best of cases."

Two Swiss tourists, years ago, were interviewed by an Argentinian reporter in Marruecos, a restaurant in the middle of nowhere, halfway between Zagora and Ouarzazate. The Argentinian wanted to know if they concurred with Sabato's analysis. The two agreed and listened to the idea with interest, asked more about Sabato, then admitted that the tie between mythology and the supposed Swiss perfection and precision is very accurate. "The only thing I don't agree with," said one, a student of economy and an ultrapolyglot, "is in the Guillermo Tell thing. Our national hero is Roger Federer."

It is in the interest of every national tennis hero to win the Davis Cup, but Federer had a historically distant and complicated relationship with his competition. With good reason, perhaps, because the players agree that a series in the Davis drains them physically and emotionally for nearly three weeks: the week before the clash, the week of play, and the one after. Even if you win, even more than the boost it provides in confidence that is always useful in the sport, the Davis exhausts you. Not to mention what it's like if you lose!

And so, Federer always had to be begged, preferring to watch the Davis from a distance. But he would appear, surely, to save his country in September, when participation in the worldwide group ends if you lose in the first round, which happened to Switzerland frequently. It's been a long time since 1998 when Federer traveled to Spain as the fifth player on a Swiss team led by Marc Rosset, who had been one of the members of the finalist team in 1992. "He seemed shy at first, but was the complete opposite later," Rosset recalls. "I came back from practice once, and he was playing PlayStation in my room. I walked in and he didn't move; he stayed focused. 'Excuse me, can I use my room?' I asked him. Then he understood. He was really confident; he wasn't at all afraid to go in my room and use it, even if I wasn't there. But I liked the kid."

Sixteen years later, Federer had very different things on his mind than PlayStation. It was 2014, and he had a unique opportunity: the field was favorable, and Stanislas Wawrinka had gone up a category after winning the Australian Open. It was, clearly, now or never. So he arrived at the finals against France in Lille, the second chance in history for Switzerland to win the Davis and the first for Federer and Wawrinka. There was fear in Switzerland after the unexpected tension between its two ace players, but the sport brings with it surprises. Sometimes, everything can be forgotten after a good drink.

"Roger, I still love you." Unmistakably drunk, hair a mess and his eyes showing signs of agitation, Wawrinka demonstrated one of the possible solutions to confronting a team crisis in sports: arguing hard first, and drinking, perhaps even harder, later. Wawrinka's declaration of love for Federer was the culmination of 185 frenetic hours for the Swiss team at the Davis Cup, between the nearly three-hour battle in the semifinals at the London Masters, and when the trophy was raised high eight days later at Lille.

During that time, all kinds of things happened. Federer won a two-hour-and-forty-eight-minute Masters semifinal after scoring four match points on Wawrinka. Mirka, according to a general consensus among the English media, yelled "crybaby" at her husband's rival in the last stretch of the match. The two players, John McEnroe pointed out, got into a shouting match in the tournament's gym, and then Federer injured his back and refused to play the Masters final against Novak Djokovic.

On Sunday morning, when Federer tried to leave his bed after the court battle with Wawrinka, he found that he could barely move. "I practically couldn't get out of bed," the Swiss star recalled two months later in Australia. Lille, the location of the Davis final, is connected to London by a direct train that crosses under the English Channel. That same Saturday night, Federer called the Swiss team's doctor, who was already in France, for him to come see him in London. "He was there when I woke up. He examined me and said 'You can't run, so you can't play.' 'Are you sure?' I asked him. What he did was let the area heal on its own, except for some minor treatment to help it relax. It took me two-and-a-half days, or three, before I could run again. And I took medication, strong medication. On Wednesday night, when I played a bit in Lille, I felt for the first time like I could run again. And I told myself, if you can run, you can play."

While Federer was getting his back looked at in London, Wawrinka had entered the tunnel below the channel and emerged in France to get ready for the final. Many thought that the Swiss team would split apart, because there had already been tension from prior years between Federer and Wawrinka, due to the latter's anger at the former's refusal to be what some perceived to be a "loyal" member of the team. The concerns were high in Lille: Would they be able to adapt to the clay after weeks on fast courts? Would they repair their bonds? Would Mirka sit in the stands and encourage Wawrinka? And, most importantly: Could Federer play, or would captain Severin Lüthi have to bet on Marco Chiudinelli, number 212 in the world ranking?

Federer didn't train on Monday or Tuesday, worried about his back. He hit the ball around lightly for twenty minutes on Wednesday with his close friend Chiudinelli, another thirty on Thursday, and, clearly still limited in his movement, was steamrolled in Friday's debut by Gaël Monfils. At the time, however, the environment in Switzerland was increasingly positive. Wawrinka, during a great exhibition match at the start, had dominated the top French player, Jo-Wilfried Tsonga, and Federer—having been given some "more information" about the state of his back—seemed to be exuding confidence. On the opposing side, an old injury bothering Tsonga left him out of the doubles on Saturday in which Richard Gasquet and Julien Benneteau were vaporized by Wawrinka and Federer. Switzerland was stroking the cup with the apparent attitude of a team that expected to be keeping it.

Mirka, mother of four young children, didn't show up at Pierre-Mauroy Stadium during the entire weekend, which left Federer in an unusual situation, but one which he always enjoyed: spending a week with friends and teammates, fighting together toward an objective. And, if everything went well, celebrating afterwards.

A man of talent, Federer is also a man with luck, because the stars aligned, and he was able to seal the deal, 3–1, with a luxurious backhand drop that left Richard Gasquet powerless. But in the photos of the win in the final match, Wawrinka was always at the center of the team, next to the trophy.

"Roger, how unlikely did this victory seem exactly a week ago, when you had to stop playing? How much team work was necessary to make this victory possible?" was the first question at the press conference after the incredible victory.

Federer: "Good question."

Wawrinka: "Good question. It was for you, so you have to answer [laughter]."

Federer: "I know. [laughter] Good question. Clearly, we are very, very happy. We've had a great time since the match point."

Wawrinka: "Yes, exactly."

Federer: "Stan is the one who put us in such a great position for Sunday."

Wawrinka looked at Federer with wide eyes and a half smile while saying "No, no," to which the seventeen-time Grand Slam champion answered with his own smile and a "Yes, you did it."

With Lüthi between them, Wawrinka threw out that "Roger, I still love you" that encapsulated the captain's job. Severin is Federer's trainer, but he was able to join the two teammates and avoid the disintegration, or self-destruction, that the Davis Cup teams sometimes inflict on themselves—for example, as had happened to Argentina in the 2008 final that they lost against Spain.

"Today we saw how quickly things can change," Wawrinka pointed out during a brief lapse of sobriety. "At the start of the week, there were a lot of things written about Roger and myself, about Roger's back . . . What ended up happening was the complete opposite, and we can be proud of that." So proud, that the immediate expectations were very clear, "The likelihood that we will be drinking alcohol tonight is very high."

A Davis champion fourteen years before Federer, the Spaniard Alex Corretja, thinks that the title was key for the Swiss. "Federer could be pointed at in his country and told that he wasn't dedicated to the Davis. That's why it was so important for him." Winning a Grand Slam is the pinnacle of tennis, but conquering the Davis is also huge. And, in a certain sense, superior. "When he goes to a restaurant in Switzerland, the expressions of gratitude coming from everyone will be much greater than after his seventh Wimbledon title. People identify a lot with the Davis Cup."

"This weekend was an extra test of his genius." Mats Wilander, a Swede, former number one worldwide, and three-time Davis champion, wrote this in a "Federer ecstasy" column for the sports newspaper *L'Equipe*. One of the greatest in the history of tennis, Wilander enjoys being a witness to the great moments of the sport, when he can, and during that weekend in the north of France he sat next to the reporters on the steps so he wouldn't miss a thing. The Swede always has an attractive vision of tennis, a unique and candid point of view. Sometimes he guesses correctly in his analyses, and at other times he is quite wrong. The best example would be his prediction in January 2013, days before Nadal would return to the circuit after a seven-month absence due to an injury. "Even though his name is Rafa Nadal, this year he is an outsider in Paris," Wilander said in Australia. "It is the year for Andy or for Novak to win Roland Garros, and for Federer as well, obviously, although he already won it."

Wilander was convinced that Nadal would pay the price for his prolonged absence. "I think it will probably take time for him to be himself again, and especially for the rest of the players to think of him as the old Nadal." The other players "lose a lot of respect for the ability" of a tennis player after such a prolonged pause, the Swede insisted. He would later lament those comments, as the Spaniard closed 2013 with ten titles, among them Roland Garros and the US Open, and solidly installed himself again as the number one player in the world. It's clear that you can't be right every time.

Wilander did, however, hit the target when he dissected Federer, the Davis champion. The Swede, who at the end of 2014 could predict the Swiss star playing "for four or five more years," confessed himself surprised by the capacity for improvement shown by a player who had already won everything that tennis has to offer, except for an Olympic gold medal in singles, and who is, on top of all that, a father of four. "I can clearly see Stefan Edberg's influence in his net play," the Swede pointed out. The right side volley much more solid, and the decision not to play out long points and to resolve them up front, are other contributions by the part-time trainer whom Federer hired at the end of 2013.

But beyond Edberg, and beyond his great talent, mobility, and a physique perfect for playing tennis, Federer had another undeniable ally in 2014: his new racket. Miguel Seabra is a Portuguese journalist specializing in tennis, who had claimed for years that Federer should change his racket. The Swiss played during his youth era and his first years as a professional with a Wilson Pro Staff, 85 inches, the same racket as Pete Sampras. Then he moved on to 90, but he soon saw himself at a disadvantage against his rivals, who all had wider hoops—between 98 and 100 inches—technologically more modern racket contours, and novel adjustments to their grips. Federer delayed for a significant amount of time in facing that reality. At times, it's hard for the greats to admit that there are some aspects in which they're just the same as everyone else, that the model of the racket influences their game a great deal.

After falling in the second round of the 2013 Wimbledon, a tournament which he had won a year before, Federer surprised everyone; he registered at the last moment for Hamburg and Gstaad, and went to both appointments on clay, which he normally didn't play anymore in those days. He wanted to try his new racket, with a larger hoop. The experiment ended poorly, because he lost to the Argentinian Federico Delbonis in the Hamburg semifinals and against the German Daniel

Brands in his debut at Gstaad. Federer seemed desperate. His strikes, uncontrolled, seemed almost rude. It was as if he were no longer the master of his game.

But the experiment, in the long run, was a success. Federer confirmed that the racket he had gotten from Wilson wasn't adaptable to what he needed, and he went back to what he had always used, a more than twenty-year-old antique, but with some changes. The 2014 season saw him reappear with his new racket. The change, combined with Edberg as a brilliant addition to his team, was a success: Federer ended the year as the second best player in the world and fighting until the very last week for the first spot. Nine months earlier, in March, the world ranking had placed him, incredibly, in eighth position, a spot he hadn't occupied since October of 2002.

The new racket is, in theory, a 97 hoop model, although that information should be taken with a grain of salt. Many of the great tennis players use prototypes, rackets made "to measure." Federer's, according to people who are close to him, might have a couple of inches more or less than the official model. It's a unique racket, which exists only for him. It's not sold in any stores. Whatever the design, it was the racket he needed. Ever since he started playing with it, Federer noticeably improved the power and effectiveness of his serve, as well as his backhand, which is much more solid and with more top spin when he needs it. He misses less often with his right, although he might take more risks than he did before with that strike. The racket lets him play "easier," with more power, effect, and security. During that year in 2014, he was getting more unusual hits, hits at key points, which aided in his comeback. And if you add to this the fact that Edberg helped him get his game in order and added a new facet to his net play, you'll understand how Federer became successful again after a depressing 2013 in which he won only one tournament.

There's no magic in that racket; in fact, it's just the opposite. What it did, in truth, was to allow Federer to appreciate a technological leap which his peers on the circuit had embraced years ago. Among them Nadal, whose Babolat racket allows him to achieve hits that would be very difficult with the rigid Wilson. During 2014, Federer won seventy-two matches, more than any other player, and played in more finals than any of his rivals: eleven. On the same day that Nadal opened an academy with his name on it in Mallorca, Federer was enjoying, in his own country, a series of celebrations for the first Swiss title in the history of the Davis Cup. More than ten thousand people greeted the team in Lausana, Wawrinka's native city, where the Helvetians gathered at the special request of Federer. "Our cup! Our heroes!" is how the newspaper *Blick* summed up the feelings of the small nation.

There was no evidence that the Spaniard—four-time Davis champion—had congratulated the Swiss, but there's no doubt that during the agonizing weeks of 2014 the two players were eyeing each other, very attentive to what the other was doing. The ambition was the same as always, defeating the other in the race to be the greatest in history. Without the Davis, or the Olympic gold in singles, Federer was at a disadvantage against Nadal. Now he had the Davis, and in Río 2016, his last chance.

CHAPTER 15

Shadows

Does Roger Federer have a dark side? Not exactly, but there are some things that the Swiss player regrets today.

Irascible, disrespectful, conceited, unprofessional: Federer was all these things in his early years as a professional, during which he remembers himself as "savage." "I didn't know how to handle things," the Swiss star admitted in *Years of Glory (Die Jubeljahre)*, a book written by journalists Marco Keller and Simon Graf, which compiles the great successes of Swiss tennis in the past couple of decades.

"I still feel like I did when I was fifteen," Federer remarks during an interview for the book, published in 2013, in which he confesses that he was embarrassed by how badly he had behaved on a tennis court. "It was in Rome, in 2001. I was playing with Marat Safin; each of us was behaving worse than the other. After the second set, they showed [on the stadium's giant screen] how furious he was, and then how furious I was. He and I, he and I, he and I . . . As I watched it, I felt profoundly ashamed. And I told myself, 'This really can't go on like this.'" It did go on, however, days later in Hamburg. The Argentinian Franco Squillari defeated him, 6–3 and 6–4, in the first round, and Federer himself remembers the encounter as being scandalous. "I was one match point down, I played a good point, and went up to the net and he, who's left-handed, hit me a crossed backhand.

I missed the ball; in fact, it ended up between the racket and the ground. I looked at the ball and thought, 'What am I doing?' And I smashed the racket. Later I reconsidered. 'Starting now, I won't say another word again, ever.'"

Federer had a long history of poor behavior with his racket in hand. And during the interview with *Die Jubeljahre*, he doesn't hesitate to admit that in 2000 in Barcelona he was disrespectful towards the Spaniard Sergi Bruguera, a two-time Roland Garros champion. "I lost 6–1 and 6–1. He, a week earlier, had lost 6–0 and 6–0 to Sébastien Grosjean in Casablanca. I walked onto the court without even a trace of respect for him. I didn't respect Bruguera. I thought I would easily defeat him 6–1 and 6–1. But this was a Roland Garros champion. I underestimated him, I panicked, and then I didn't know what to do. Everything was being broadcast live on Eurosport . . ."

To think that Federer would be content after not giving it his all during a tennis match sounds like science fiction today, but that's exactly what happened in 1998. "I went from playing in front of ten thousand spectators in Basel to playing in front of empty stands," in satellite tournaments. It was the same year in which he scared himself after feeling satisfied with a loss in the final of the juvenile US Open against the Argentinian David Nalbandian, one of his nemeses in the beginning of his career. He felt that he'd played a good tournament. Until he stopped to reconsider. "How could you be happy with a loss?" Federer says he asked himself soon after the match in New York. "Come on, get to work!"

Those were the years in which Nalbandian confidently summed up his strategy for defeating Federer: "I throw him several high backhanded shots, switch to the right, make him run, and done." Things changed over time, and Nalbandian retired without achieving any of his three wishes: winning the Davis Cup, a Grand Slam tournament, and an Olympic medal. Federer analyzed the player from Argentina in 2007 during an interview with DPA. He was fully aware of the incredible defeat that Nalbandian had suffered against the Cypriot Marcos Baghdatis in the 2006 Australian semifinal, "The truth is he lost a lot of matches that he should have won. I think he missed the opportunity to score on the top player in Australia last year. He could have left the court as the winner of that final, who knows . . . And maybe that's why he wasted some of his opportunities and then spiraled downwards after. It seems like it's hard for him to keep his skill up for the whole season. Despite that, I think that he's a super player, one of the best to hit the ball in the entire circuit. Simply put, he plays very nicely."

Federer, during his first years on the circuit, also hit the ball nicely. He was a conformist, heir to the adolescent who, in the Swiss federation's school in Ecublens, would cause such a fuss during practice that the trainer would kick him out. In that, he couldn't be more different from Nadal, who would follow even the most unusual instructions from his uncle Toni, and was incapable of throwing a racket. "It's not that I specifically tried," recalls Federer, "but when it happened I was happy. I would ask, 'Am I out?' And the trainer would say, 'I don't want to see you again.' And I would think, 'Perfect!' I would go to the showers and get on the bus home."

A part of the old Federer was still there the first few times he crossed Àlex Corretja on the circuit. "I remember him with that famous pony tail, with a really good right, using Sampras's Wilson. A really good slice backhand, really good serve, and . . . very unorganized, very unfocused, playful, and very adolescent. He joked a lot in the players' lounge and laughed really loudly . . . He was a little juvenile. He was always on the Internet watching the 'head to head' matchups and yelling loudly about who was overtaking who!"

In that aspect, the Swiss was similar to Nadal, although the Spaniard absorbed the statistics without yelling. "You would watch Federer train and think to yourself, this kid is really talented, he plays so easily. I remember one anecdote. I beat him at Roland Garros in 2000, and at the end of the match my father says, 'This kid plays really poorly, he misses a lot.' And I told him that he's really good, that he'll be the top player in the world."

Two or three years after that match at Roland Garros, Corretja had a feeling. "I noticed that he was changing; there was someone who

Even as a child, Rafael Nadal knew what it took to win trophies. (*Diario de Mallorca*)

The author interviews Nadal in 2011 in London. (*Benito Pérez Barbadillo*)

The author interviews Roger Federer in 2010 in Lisbon. (*Torneo de Estorial*)

Roger Federer and Andre Agassi in 2005 in Dubai. (*Dubai Duty Free Shop*)

Nadal knows soccer: it was 2008 and he preferred Messi over Robinho, and he bet on José Mourinho as manager. (*Sebastián Fest*)

Nadal displays his prowess during a soccer game as a tribute to his uncle Miguel Ángel. (*Diario de Mallorca*)

Federer and Nadal pose at Roland Garros in 2005. (*AP Photo/Christophe Ena*)

Federer and Nadal after Nadal's 2008 Wimbledon victory. (*AP Photo/Anja Niedringhaus*)

With a 2009 win at Roland Garros, Federer tied Pete Sampras with fourteen Grand Slams. (*AP Photo/Bernat Armangue*)

Federer's wife Mirka and twin daughters watch an exhibition match at Melbourne Park in 2013. (*AP Photo/Aaron Favila, File*)

Nadal with Guillermo Vilas in 2006 after Nadal broke Vilas's record of fifty-three consecutive victories on clay. (*AP Photo/David Vincent*)

Nadal practicing before the 2015 Australian Open championship as his uncle and coach Toni Nadal looks on. (*AP Photo/Mark Baker*)

Federer reacts after defeating Nadal in the 2007 finals at Wimbledon. (*AP Photo/Alastair Grant, file*)

Nadal celebrates after the 2014 Australian Open semifinal, in which he defeated Federer in straight sets. (*AP Photo/Eugene Hoshiko*)

Federer and Nadal greet each other in India in 2015. (*AP Photo/Tsering Topgyal*)

(*AP Photo/Tsering Topgyal*)

made him click, that someone who you always need and who makes you see how good you can be." Little by little, Federer changed, and one key factor in that was Mirka. "Our relationship quickly became something serious. Thanks to her, I grew up faster. She's older than I am, and women mature faster than we do anyway."

He pegs the other key factor to January 2004, when he won the Australian Open and became the top player in the world. A year before, he had lifted the first of his seven Wimbledon trophies. "I got home, and I asked myself, 'Now what?' I'd accomplished everything I ever dreamed of as a kid. I was happy, but I thought, 'It would be good if you were capable of repeating these achievements, of feeling these sensations again.' I always knew I had talent, but I had no idea that I could achieve all this." By controlling his demons, Federer became what Philippe Bouin, for years the greatest tennis writer at *L'Equipe*, described in a few words, "McEnroe's hand, Lendl's thirst for victory."

Federer sometimes has strange responses. After winning the title at the 2014 Davis Cup, the international media wanted to know if he would play the first round in Belgium in 2015. "I'll probably decide that once the Australian Open is done. I've been talking about it . . . It's clearly very hard to leave your seat after having won the Davis Cup; that was always an objective of mine, of the Swiss federation, of the guys on my team, and for myself, after playing for fifteen years. Yes, I'll talk with the captain, see what his plans are for himself, for me, for everyone. After that, I'll need some more time. I'll probably decide after the Australian Open."

Federer would end up *not* playing the series in Belgium, nor would Wawrinka, and Switzerland would lose. Many would have liked to hear that conversation between the player and the captain, Severin Lüthi, who has a steady job during the year: training Federer. Dubai was the stage that Federer chose to officially declare his withdrawal from the Davis. The explanation he gave bothered many who were involved with Swiss tennis, as well as the International Tennis Federation (ITF). "It wasn't a difficult decision. I played for so long that, after winning it, I think I can finally do what I want, to be quite honest."

Federer speaks nearly perfect English, but his choice of words sometimes play against him and gives him an air of arrogance that concerns him less in other situations. "It was a huge load for me during my career and one of the things that caused the most difficulty in life, I have to say. I've always felt that there's too much blame shifted on you on behalf of the federation and the ITF, more than any other. So I'm happy that I finally faced the situation." And then the Swiss star added a comment which he had already made in Lille but which few people took seriously at the time: the title in 2014 was more for his teammates than for him, "I did it entirely for the guys, more than for myself. To be honest. I really wanted Michael [Lammer], and Marco [Chiudinelli], and Stan to win, because they deserved it. That's why it was really clear to me that I wouldn't play this year."

During September 2011, an organization known as Reputation Institute became known to tennis fans after it placed Roger Federer as the public personality with the best reputation in the world, surpassed only by the former president of South Africa, Nelson Mandela. As the son of a South African, it was a complete honor for Federer to be in this position, one more aspect to add to his image as a "special" athlete. Things were different for Nadal. The leader of the fight against apartheid caused some problems for the Spaniard who, while on a trip to Disneyland Paris after winning his eighth Roland Garros in 2013, expressed on Twitter his sorrow for the death of the South African. Mandela died six months after the tweet, and although it wasn't Nadal, but his social media team who sent the message after receiving erroneous information from the Disneyland Paris authorities, the screw-up was obvious.

Life doesn't always smile on the Federer clan. In 2005, *Blick*, the most read newspaper in Switzerland, revealed a strange situation that involved Miroslav Vavrinec, Mirka's father. Some investors who controlled a "sex yacht" that was working at full speed off the coasts of Monte Carlo during the Formula 1 Grand Prix, had managed to trick Vavrinec and placed him as the president of an enterprise linked to the business. Upset at the headlines chosen by the newspaper—"sex scandal" next to a picture of the player and his girlfriend—Federer took to the phone and called the owner of the powerful editorial group Ringier, which publishes *Blick*. The situation dissolved quickly.

Marco Chiudinelli is a good player. He rose to number 52 in the world ranking and, when he came to the end of his career, had accumulated about $2 million in prizes for his success in singles and doubles. Two million, minus the many expenses of course, but Chiudinelli has managed to live off tennis, which is something not many can say. Blond, tall, and with the appearance of a model, he is, nevertheless, no Roger Federer with a racket, although he is one of his best friends.

"I never even dreamed I would be a tennis player. At sixteen, they called me out of the blue to be a part of the Swiss juvenile team. I wanted to be a business administrator, so I hadn't set myself any goals or dreams," he explained in 2012 during a talk in a players' lounge in Basel, which was about five degrees too hot. "It was hard for me to adapt. I played until I was twenty-two, but I didn't sleep much, I didn't have a very professional life. Until I said to myself, 'Alright, if you're going to do this, try to do it right.'"

At the time of that interview, Federer was still the president of the Players' Council, and Chiudinelli did not have his friend's capacity for multitasking. "Roger is very balanced, with his feet on the ground. That's why I'm not surprised he can look out for everyone's interests, those of the players who aren't stars and the doubles players."

There is something, however, that Chiudinelli denies emphatically: the "cliché" of Federer as being serious and formal, and Nadal as being fresh and spontaneous. He says it's just that, a prejudice, at least as far as his friend is concerned. "It's true that the Swiss—because of how our country works and how we are—tend to think things through twice and to not react on our first impulse. But it's a cliché to think that Nadal is spontaneous and passionate, and Roger is just serious and formal. Roger can also be passionate outside the court; he also does his things and has his moments. What happens is that we don't tell those things to the reporters."

CHAPTER 16

Doping

"*RAFA, WHY DON'T YOU DOPE?*" The month of December in 2006 was slipping away. Nadal was twenty years old; he had finished another season to remember, with a second Roland Garros title and the Wimbledon final as new milestones. The second best player in the world clearly understood the question. It was asked in "Argentinian," with an accent on the last vowel, in an empty room in Sa Punta, the family restaurant in Porto Cristo, one of the many magical spots on the island of Mallorca. He wasn't being propositioned with a transgression; he was being asked for the opposite reason, a more profound one: his philosophy with respect to doping.

"*Why don't you dope?*"

"Because I don't see sport in that light," he answered with absolute conviction. "Sport is competition, giving the best of what you have, not what you don't have." The reasoning, impeccable, would leave Nadal's lips a countless number of times throughout a career in which there was always a number of fans and reporters who were suspicious of his physical exuberance. Suspicions are free, but the concrete truth is that few tennis players were ever submitted to more antidoping drug tests than Nadal. And no positive result ever came up.

That's one thing Nadal and Federer have in common; they never tested positive. In every other way, they're different. While there's no memory of a journalistic article with even the slightest suggestion that Federer might pursue forbidden assistance, the Spaniard read and heard his name associated dozens of times with more or less clear insinuations. Never with any foundation nor with any proof. It was already so in 2006. During that frank conversation in Porto Cristo, Nadal made it clear that he had had enough of the insinuations surrounding Operación Puerto. Behind that curious name was a police operation that revealed an extensive doping operation in Spain.

Operación Puerto started out promising a lot but ended by delivering much less, with cycling complaining that it was the only sport with penalized athletes. Eufemiano Fuentes, a doctor on the Canary Islands who was doping athletes, had hinted during private conversations that there were also soccer and tennis players involved and even said as much during an interview with the French newspaper *Le Monde*. Just bringing it up made Nadal uncomfortable. Very uncomfortable. When faced with the question about Fuentes and *Le Monde*, the Spaniard reacted as he usually does when he would rather not talk about something: he denied knowing anything. "No, I didn't hear anything about it, didn't hear anything."

"Nothing?"

"No."

"Nothing?"

"No."

And then he let loose. "The truth is that these kinds of things don't worry me too much, and it's already been proved that the things in that newspaper aren't very credible." With "that newspaper," Nadal was referring to what had been published by *Le Journal du Dimanche* in May of 2006. The French newspaper connected the Spaniard to the doping scandal without providing more than anonymous comments from other players. That was something that convinced the Nadals they weren't loved much in France. "It's all the same. When things like this come up without proof, it's always something stupid. It's better not to get involved; ignoring it is the best you can do. You have to be conscious of the fact that if one of these writers, who are so smart and know everything . . . if they were on the circuit and knew how things worked, they would know they can't write that. On Saturday, at nine in the morning, they came looking for me at my home for a doping control test. Here, in my home. Nine in the morning."

What Nadal was describing as almost breaking and entering, or as something very nearly inconceivable, is in reality part of what is required of any elite athlete: there are tests, everyone is required to submit to them, and the control staff can appear unannounced. That's how it is, no shortcuts. But in his youthful twenties, Nadal saw things in a different light: How dare they come to his family home in Manacor on a Saturday morning? "My mother called me and said, 'The doping people are down here.' 'Alright, send them up,' I said. It was easy, because I had just gotten up, and when you get up in the morning, it's much easier to go to the bathroom . . ." he remembered easily. It was the sixteenth control he'd had to submit to in that season. A third of them were also blood tests.

Syringes, Nadal admits, aren't exactly something he enjoys. "I'm getting used to it now," he says, laughing, "because I've been tested several times. But I would get dizzy before. I fainted once, because I don't like blood at all." The later years forced him to get used to syringes, and other perhaps even more difficult procedures. But at the time, only the punctures bothered him.

Nevertheless, what bothered him the most and still does is being watched and followed step by step when he's given a doping test, although in time he would learn that it's a fundamental necessity for the seriousness and validity of every control and was even beneficial for him. "When you've signed the paper, they follow you to the bathroom, and they watch. You go shower, and you have to shower with the curtains opened. Incredible, it's criminal. [It happens] in the circuit, but in my home, too. Once you sign you're under control, in case you would switch, or something . . ."

Having started, Nadal made a comment that those close to him would regret being made public. "And the thing is . . . they treat us like delinquents, and it's one thing to keep in mind, because I don't see any of the politicians going through doping control tests or anything. And so why should athletes?"

Politicians submitting to doping tests is one of the typical ideas that gets thrown out during a heated debate between friends or at the family dinner table, but no one expects it to come from the lips of one of the most famous athletes in the world. After all, he and his family were used to dealing with politicians in Spain and at an even higher level.

But the comment was timely. On one hand, millions of Spaniards would support it without a shadow of a doubt. On the other, during that December in 2006, there was a story circulating of a satirical Italian show, *Le Iene (The Hyenas)*, that had performed involuntary doping tests on about fifty members of parliament. During several of them they found evidence of consumption of cannabis and even cocaine. Nadal's eyes widened in surprise when he heard about the Italian experience. He felt, perhaps, redeemed. "Well, maybe there should be more of that. Because it's not okay for us to be treated like criminals; I don't think it's right. I don't know how we, the athletes, have allowed it." It would be good to "do something," he added. "I'm willing, because of everything they make us go through. Because they treat us like criminals, I think it's pathetic that [the Argentinian Guillermo] Cañas went to the US Open [in 2005] and they wouldn't let him in. Why? Because he's killed someone, he's raped someone? Maybe he just took an aspirin he didn't know he couldn't take. And, then, what's this?"

As time went on, Nadal's public declarations insisting on his annoyance with the doping control system became habitual. The business would almost form part of his claims in the years during which he was part of the ATP Players' Council. He was predictably unsuccessful. After declaring his indignation against "the politicians," Nadal took a couple of steps back, "It's all the same to me, I'm just another player. I accept the doping controls, but they seem exaggerated." His intention, he said, was just to make clear what "wasn't right." "Two years ago, I had just lost a five set match in Australia against [Lleyton] Hewitt, a match in which I had a lot of options to win. And in the hallway, as soon as I walked out the door, they handed me the paper to sign for the control. And I didn't sign, I didn't sign! They follow you every-where. I think you have to be a little smart, use your head, wait ten minutes before coming out of the locker room, and calm down a bit."

Calming down when talking is key for any public personality, and with time Nadal would learn that you can't state your opinions about a topic as delicate as doping without being careful and precise. What you talk about in an intimate family environment can't be transferred to the public sphere without filtering.

Which meant, of course, that the topic should be left off the agenda. Obsessed with the topic, Nadal's family started to video record the con-trollers to document how they disrupted their home. Every once in a while, players, trainers, and close acquaintances would see the vid-eos that the indignant Nadals showed on their laptop at tournaments around the world.

Months after that interview in Manacor, a photograph made an impact on fans, rivals, and journalists. It was January 2008, and an image of Nadal during one of his trainings before the Australian Open was circulating around the world. If the Incredible Hulk played tennis, anyone would have said at the time that he had been reincarnated in the Spaniard. The only thing missing was the green skin. Obviously, photos only capture an instant, not the absolute truth, but that image certainly shook a lot of people and scared the Nadal clan. Those bound-less muscles, that huge dorsal, and that fierce look on a stony face just instants before hitting a backhand were certain to cause excitement in the minds of those who were always insisting that the Spaniard's phy-sique wasn't normal and that he must be getting external help.

Paul Crock, an Australian, is a photographer for the French agency Agence France-Presse (AFP), and was the author of that impacting image. He remembers the moment well. "It was one of those really hot days they have at the Australian Open, and Rafa was on one of the back courts training without a shirt on. I took that picture and others, and that was that." Crock has been photographing tennis players in Australia for a decade, which allowed him to follow Nadal's evolution. "He was a big guy at the time, now he's thinner." The "angle of the photo had a great influence" on the result, the photographer admits. "This is simply and plainly what we do; we take pictures of the training sessions. That was an open session, but there weren't many people."

Time went on, and photos like that one became no longer possible because Nadal's physique changed. The body of an athlete isn't the same when he is approaching thirty as when he is twenty, although the player would deny year after year that he had lost weight, or that his musculature had decreased. He also self-imposed a measure as simple as it was practical: no more training in public without a shirt.

The Nadals' complaint about the antidoping control system continued until 2009, when a figure of decisive influence in tennis sent them some advice through a mutual friend. "Tell Rafa to calm down and to talk less about the whereabouts rule," was the message. The "whereabouts rule," as it is known in English, forces the sports player to communicate a fixed time and place in which he can be found every day if there is a need to be submitted to a control. As athletes tend to train starting at nine or ten in the morning, they often sign off saying that they can be found in their homes between seven and eight in the morning. When the control comes, many of them complain about having to give urine or blood samples so early at their homes. "Tell Rafa to calm down, because doping is a very sensitive subject. Look at what Federer did; he came to me two years ago and said he had a problem. They rang his doorbell for the control at six in the morning. I talked to the Swiss antidoping agency and everything was resolved." The fact that the higher-up would emphasize Federer's intelligence didn't imply that he was unaware of Nadal's. "Nadal is a very good guy, very educated and intelligent, but he's too surrounded. When there's so much money at play, a lot of people show up. And the Spanish are unorganized."

There is a former tennis player who doesn't exactly engender sympathy among his colleagues, Christophe Rochus. At the end of 2010, the Belgian talked openly about doping in an interview with the newspaper *La Dernière Heure*. He said he was "fed up" with the "hypocrisy" in tennis, and stated that he wouldn't be upset if doping was legalized within his sport. "There is a lot of cheating, but the thing is that no one likes to talk about it," he claimed. "I would like to end that simulation; the hypocrisy is exasperating."

Rochus, now retired, rose to number 38 in the world ranking in 2006. He never won a title, but he played two finals, measured up against Nadal twice, and lost. The first time, in Australia in 2009, he lost to Nadal 6–0, 6–2, and 6–2. The second time, three months later in Barcelona, it was 6–2 and 6–0 for the Spaniard. It's clear that Nadal doesn't bring up pleasant memories for Rochus, who, every time he decides to speak to the press in his country, throws a layer of suspicion on the entirety of tennis. "I've seen things, like anyone," he told *La Dernière Heure*, without adding any details. "To me it's inconceivable to play for five hours in the sun and come back the next day like a bunny," he added. "I remember a match with one player, whose name I won't mention. I won the first set easily, he went to the changing room and returned completely different. He got a 5–3 advantage in the second set, and when I tied for five . . . his nose started to bleed. I told myself that was all very strange."

Two years later, Rochus came back to that topic in an interview with another newspaper in his country, *La Libre Belgique*. Those days, Rochus was talking about the confession by the cyclist, Lance Armstrong, of doping. "Is doping a reality in tennis?" the reporter asked him. "Of course it's a reality," Rochus responded, convincingly. "The sport has become more and more physical, so there is, inevitably, more temptation to consume performance-enhancing substances. And now, with the Armstrong thing, we have to admit that the fact that someone has never come back positive doesn't mean that that person hasn't doped. If you can use good doctors to do personal controls, you can consume undetectable substances. So, in my opinion, the antidoping controls are useless and don't really prove anything. As far as Nadal, rumors are just rumors, but everyone is asking the same question: how can you be so strong in Roland Garros and a month later, not in, apparently, any condition to play. That's why it's so suspicious, even if we don't have any proof. Maybe he really is injured."

The reporter picked up the gauntlet and pushed the idea further. "You have to admit that all those pauses of Nadal and others are really intriguing . . . " And Rochus charged on enthusiastically, "That's the idea! To keep it from being obvious! Everyone tries to obscure it. The less you lie, the less explanations you give, the better. Let's take Robin Söderling. He won Bastad in 2011, and since then has not returned to play tennis. Apparently, he's really sick [with mononucleosis], when I know that he was unbeatable back then. We can't deny how hard that is to hear. He was at the peak of his career, and the next day it is said that he can't play tennis . . . I really believe that's incredible."

Rochus's words reached Nadal's ears soon after, and in an interview with the Spanish newspaper *Marca*, Nadal listened to the next question: *"Have you had the chance to cross paths with Christophe Rochus since he insinuated that your long break, as well as Robin Söderling's, could be a possible consequence of doping?"* Nadal, habitually careful when it came to speaking about the subject, dropped a bomb, "I haven't crossed paths with him, and if I did, I would say a single word to him. I don't feel offended. It's easy, when you're sitting at home, to say things to try and be the center of attention when you're not anymore. He was in the limelight when he played tennis, not a lot; he wasn't that good, but if he wants to be in the limelight for saying stupid things, let him say what he wants. I don't feel offended by someone like Rochus, even if he says stupidities."

Nadal likes to argue, and if he can do it to defend a friend, even better. He has a fierce sense of loyalty, and the Spaniard doesn't pull punches when it comes to defending something or someone he believes in. So, when the Frenchman Richard Gasquet tested positive for cocaine in 2009, Nadal became the public defender for the player whom he had bested the thirteen times he had played him between 2004 and 2014. It was Nadal who first brought up the theory of the kiss that Gasquet had given a girl at a nightclub in Miami. The girl, popularized as "Pamela," had consumed cocaine, alleged the defense for the French player, who would ultimately come out of the case nearly intact.

Despite not shifting a fraction of an inch in his opinions about the procedures for doping controls, Nadal changed his habits about the way he made public comments. He was more mature and had the experience of having dealt with the subject for years. The Spaniard understood that he would have to ease up on repeatedly complaining about the controls. Spanish society and media had heavily moderated the public's tendency toward feeling like a victim of some "international conspiracy" (generally on behalf of the French, British, or Americans) any time one of their own athletes came back positive. Apart from that, Nadal was already a star who excelled at the sport, and hearing him say week after week that the antidoping system was unfair and inadequate didn't exactly help his image. And a good image, as everyone knows, is the foundation for better contracts and more money.

Nadal's protests transformed into an entirely new proposal: full transparency and disclosure of information. "From my point of view, the controls should be made public. People on the street don't know all the controls that we pass or don't, so I don't see any reason not to make each control that's done public." The statement was given in February 2013 at Viña del Mar, the Chilean tournament that saw Nadal's return to tennis after seven months' absence due to a double knee injury.

Nadal, who can be as persistent when trying to bring up a new topic as he is on the tennis court, insisted on speaking about it days later in San Pablo. "It's necessary to divulge when, and how many, controls happen. I'm here to take as many tests as they want, and when they want. If I have to do one every week, I'll do it no problem." A doping control every week and in the public eye; it wasn't the same Nadal as six years previous. The idea did make sense, because it's extremely difficult to know how many controls each tennis player takes throughout a year.

The controls can come through one of three routes: the Tennis Anti-Doping Program (TADP), the National Anti-Doping Agencies, and the World Anti-Doping Agency (WADA). There is nowhere online where you can easily find how many controls have been administered among all three possibilities. The information is scattered; it is revealed belatedly and in an incomplete and not very clear manner.

Nadal's proposal on his South American tour reached Roger Federer's ears days later as he was playing the tournament in Dubai. "Sure, it's an idea. I'm in favor of transparency and aggressive controlling, I always have been," the Swiss player said. "It's important for us to be sure that the integrity of the game is maintained where it needs to be. The tours, the players, we all have agreed on the attempt. I think that there's a great urgency for us to be sure that our sport stays as clean as is possible. It's very important."

Although Nadal was happy, that same week in Acapulco, to hear that Federer agreed with him—"I'm happy that we're on the same page here, it's important"—the phrases that the Swiss player used didn't imply a true agreement. While the Spaniard proposed instantly communicating who was being controlled, the Swiss resorted to using the usual terminologies when speaking about the tricky subject of doping: "transparency," "integrity," "clean sport." They seemed to agree, but Federer and Nadal were talking about very different things. Nadal never explained how the public controls would be put into practice. Behind his proposal was his desire for everyone to know that he is one of the most controlled players, something which also applies to Novak Djokovic. And, in the process, that it also be clear that other players are controlled less.

A top ten player submits, on average, to ten controls every year. If players like Nadal accumulated, season after season, sixteen or seventeen tests, it meant that there were other men among the top ten who were controlled maybe five or six times: a third of what the Spaniard did. The complicated doping control system in tennis includes a set group of players to be controlled. That set group is made up of the top fifty in the worldwide ranking and the ten best doubles pairs. Of course, other players outside the elite are controlled, but if you have success, testing is unavoidable.

Those responsible for the TADP didn't think that Nadal's proposal to make all controls public seemed very reasonable, "Our philosophy is that we don't want to give too many details to the players who will be controlled, so the system isn't easier to trick." The Italian Francesco Ricci Bitti, president of the International Tennis Federation (ITF) and a man of influence in the WADA, reacted with a touch of irony, perhaps surprised by the proposal of a player who, for years, had dedicated himself to criticizing the system. "It's good to see that top players like Rafael are so open to talking about this topic, but there's a limit. We can't divulge everything; if we did, we wouldn't have surprise controls. We have limits, as set by confidentiality." A veteran leader, Ricci Bitti receives criticism with a specific philosophy. According to him, there is no way for everyone to be in agreement when it comes to the matter of doping control." The topic of doping is a lose-lose situation. If there are many positives, it's bad. If there aren't, it's also bad."

At the time, the Nadals were somewhat sensitive to the subject of doping because, ever since he returned to the circuit after seven months absence between 2012 and 2013, the Spaniard had been subjected to a great number of controls. "There are players who are controlled much more than others, who get pointed at more. If someone returns to play, they get controlled more. I haven't been informed, but it would have to be so in [Rafael] Nadal's case; he would be tested six, seven times because he is returning to play," Ricci Bitti explained. Nadal's family remarked sarcastically that the top leader in tennis was so poorly informed that it was he, himself, who had asked them if he had been controlled and how many times. "In tennis, the top forty male and female players are analyzed the most. When someone falls outside the top fifty, it's less likely for them to be analyzed," Ricci Bitti continued, while providing examples using first and last names: "Serena Williams was outside the top fifty for a time."

Days before, the Serbian Novak Djokovic, the top tennis player worldwide, had stated that he hadn't been subjected to a blood test "in the last six or seven months." Ricci Bitti, who argued for years with the ATP, WTA, and Grand Slams about how the costs of the antidoping system would be allocated—an incredibly modest $2.5 million—didn't put much stock in what the Serb has said, "The Djokovic thing has more to do with the control plan, which is something that changes day to day." A man of very ample experience in the Olympic world, the Italian resists defraying the entire bill for the controls, and he does so with a logical argument. "Antidoping costs a lot of money, and what you invest in doping you take away from development."

The main function of the ITF is to develop and expand tennis throughout the world, but the amount of $2.5 million destined for the doping control system, in a sport that moves billions a year, speaks clearly to just how relative is the commitment of the governing bodies. If Ricci Bitti adds that "only five or six countries do it well" as far National Anti-Doping Agencies are concerned, the picture becomes clear. Or, perhaps more likely, dark.

Dark and thorny. The tennis world didn't always behave as it should have. When Andre Agassi admitted in *Open*, his autobiography, to having consumed methamphetamine crystals in 1997, many widened their eyes in astonishment. But when they read that the ATP pardoned the American, despite his having come back positive, those same eyes popped straight out of their heads. Agassi recalled in *Open* the moment when an ATP doctor called him in a melancholy tone.

"I thought he was going to tell me I was about to die." Something like that, because the doctor had called to tell him he had come back positive for "crystal." "My name, my career, everything was on the line now. Everything I had achieved, everything I had worked for, could turn to nothing in no time. Days later, I sat down to write a letter to the ATP, full of lies and with a few truths."

Agassi contended that he had consumed the substance without realizing it when he drank from a friend's glass. It wasn't much different from the argument that the Argentinian Mariano Puerta gave after testing positive in the 2005 Roland Garros against Nadal. Agassi continued playing without issue and revived his career with a title from the 1999 Roland Garros. For Puerta, who was a repeat offender and whose explanations were implausible, it was the end of his life in sports. Fertile ground for those lovers of conspiracy theories and for those who believe that the "first world" players can't be touched, that those who pay the price are always the weaker ones. "Punishing him would have been a huge embarrassment and a serious strike against the integrity of the sport. It is, anyway," Stephen Bierley wrote in 1999 in *The Guardian*. "Many could opt for understanding it, given the circumstances of his life at the time. For others . . . it diminishes the credibility of tennis and its governing entities, especially of the ATP." In those days, the ATP was directed by the American Adam Helfant. In an interview, the DPA news agency asked him if he expected new developments in the "Agassi case." "No, I don't think so," Helfant said. "It happened a long time ago, he made some remarks in his book. We investigated and found that the case was handled [in the ATP] appropriately. We didn't see anything we could do, given that it happened so long ago. And the decision was made independently of the ATP."

Mats Wilander has his own opinion of that decision. The Swede was one of the greatest tennis players in the past few decades, but tennis had no mercy when, after he came back from retirement to play doubles alongside the Czech Karel Nováček, the former top player in the world tested positive for cocaine in 1995. A man whose career extends much farther than tennis: a commentator for Eurosport and *L'Equipe*, head of an original project known as Wilander on Wheels (WOW), the Swede spoke without keeping anything back. And from a conversation with him that took place in January 2013, in Australia, just days after the memorable interview of Lance Armstrong by Oprah Winfrey, the context is almost perfect. Few characters are more different from one another than the manipulative former cyclist and the politically incorrect former tennis player.

"It's like tennis just rediscovered the topic of doping this week, even though it's always been there. Isn't that a bit hypocritical?"

"I think that doping is talked about in every sport and all over the world, not just in tennis. Obviously, during these two weeks, it is "the" topic, but with all the controls that are done, I don't think that doping can hurt tennis. I imagine that the governing bodies of tennis would allow someone who came back positive to keep playing. Yeah, there were cases in the past. Players were caught who had involuntarily doped, players were caught who had consumed recreational drugs, and there will be others, I suppose, who won't. I think that's society, society isn't clean. I don't think you'll ever find an aspect of life, of work, of corporations, of government, or any place in the world that's clean. That's the main thing."

"When you see tennis matches, do you believe what you see? Is it real?"

"I believe it, I believe it. I could easily play four matches of five sets in eight days, and play five hours every day. No problem. But today, they're much faster, they train much better. And look at what they eat, at what they drink, they're recovery drinks. Look at the supplements and the vitamins they take. Look at the rackets, although the rackets don't necessarily help the physique. Simply put, they train much better, they're great athletes. The tennis players are, nowadays, some of the best athletes in the world."

"The debate surrounding doping is strange at times. For example, you are on the historical list of doping in tennis. Do you think you should be on that list?"

"It's just that I don't think that is doping."

"That was exactly my question. You didn't dope to play tennis and raise your level of performance."

"But it was illegal."

"Yes, it is. Does a positive for cocaine help the fight against doping?"

"I don't think so. What I think is that the reason why the recreational drugs are included in the controls is in case the person who gives a positive has a problem. And the reason why we try to detect steroids and all those things is because they damage your health. And because it's cheating. That's the big difference."

"But then seeing your name on a list of tennis players that doped isn't exactly correct."

"It doesn't matter. If you come back positive, you're on the list. True or false, I don't think it matters. That's just life."

Wilander was surprised to hear about the "biological passport," a system that, through the constant control of determined parameters over a period of time of a year or more, can establish, even without a positive, if an athlete is punishable for doping. The Swede didn't know the system, which tennis would just start using during that year, but was already a habit in cycling. Nadal didn't know about it either, during that interview in June 2013, which was more than just surprising. *"Do you know what the biological passport consists of?"* Joan Solsona, a Spanish reporter, asked him. "Not really, to tell the truth," was Nadal's remarkable response, after which he added a bit of a confusing explanation. "It's that tennis is pretty much separate from doping and the problems that other sports have. There are very few positive cases. And it isn't because we're not being controlled. We pass the same controls as everyone, or more. I don't think that doping in tennis makes much sense. It makes sense in sports that depend exclusively on tolerating more, or putting up with more. There are more aspects to tennis, technical as well as mental. I don't know what the biological passport is, but anything that makes the sport cleaner, I support." That Nadal didn't know what the biological passport was, a topic already discussed at length in the sporting world at the time, didn't stop him from insisting on his proposal at the time, "We come back to the same thing. You wouldn't be asking me these questions if the controls were public. That's the path to follow for the whole world to know who passes and who doesn't."

The concept behind the very publicized idea of a "biological passport" is a regular tracking, over a prolonged period of time, of values in the blood and urine of an athlete. If those values show suspicious or impossible fluctuations, the heads of the antidoping system have a valuable weapon to close the fence around an athlete. So valuable, that they can suspend the athlete even if they have never given a positive result on a control.

The conversation with Wilander continued until the Swede was won over by a certain skepticism. "There is, obviously, a financial component in all this. Can you control everyone? Clearly. Is it worth it? Quite probably. But I think the problem in sports, not just in tennis, is that they don't necessarily do everything to make sure they're clean, because you don't want to invest billions of dollars. We trust that tennis is clean, but we can't be 100 percent sure." That analysis was more common to Wilander, who was so often fond of doubting and making everything relative.

The Swede attentively listened to a theory: many people would rather dope and live a life at the extreme, even if they would die at forty or fifty, rather than to live to ninety or one hundred after a "boring" or "normal" life. That could be said in the '80s and '90s, according to the results of a survey that laid out the "Goldman dilemma." Would you take a drug that would guarantee you an Olympic gold, however, you would also die five years later? In those years, 52 percent of those surveyed responded in the affirmative to the question, which was originally proposed by Bob Goldman, an American researcher. The study, based on the questions asked of 212 elite athletes in the United States, was repeated every two years, and the results varied very little until 2014, when the *British Journal of Sports Medicine* found that only 1 percent responded affirmatively. Had the athletes finally wised up? Experts looked at the results with skepticism, especially considering the context of a society in which the pressure is on being superhuman and on the consumption of all kinds of substances in order to relieve the demands of everyday life.

Wilander also sees it like this. "The world is full of junkies. Some are addicted to adrenaline, others to endorphins, others to drugs, others to alcohol, others to speed. Some are addicted to the game. That's how it is; it's full of addicts, of junkies looking for a high. There isn't a single tennis player who isn't looking for that feeling, that high. That's something that I can guarantee 100 percent. And that high doesn't come from drugs, it comes from the adrenaline, from the endorphins, from happiness. Everyone, quite probably 90 percent of the population, is addicted to something in life. To anything. Sometimes it's legal, other times illegal. Highs and lows, that's what life is about."

CHAPTER 17

Laboratory

TENNIS IS OFTEN PERCEIVED POORLY. It is viewed suspiciously, and it's not illogical to do so when you see two men furiously hitting a ball and running for five hours in 95-degree heat in the middle of the day in the Australian summer, or in hot and humid Miami. They do it one day, then play again one or two days later. Sometimes it's even another four-hour match. This happens over and over during the course of an entire season. It doesn't seem human.

But Agassi thinks yes, it's possible. "When I played, I did so with a certain sense of urgency, with the attitude of a sprinter in a marathon. I knew I had more or less four hours before I started to decline physically," he explained in January of 2013 in the midst of the charged atmosphere following Armstrong's confession.

"I see them play now and they're more calculating, they play slower, so six hours now isn't the same as six hours when I played. Plus, they're in much better physical shape; they seem to have a much stronger lower body than mine, probably not the same if we're talking about upper body. My game didn't consist so much of using my legs; rather it was about moving the ball to all sectors of the field. So, yeah, I think it's possible. I think they're conscious, from a very young age, of the importance of being prepared."

Whether or not you agree with Agassi's analysis, it's worth it to take a look at one fact: the numbers in 2012 show that, out of all the controls done in tennis, about 29 percent were blood tests, a number which increases to 38 percent in cycling, and 50 percent in track and field. The blood tests, it is common knowledge, go much further than urine tests and can detect a much wider range of substances over a longer period of time. To catch someone who is doping with a growth hormone, you need blood tests, which are also necessary for the biological passport. Erythropoietin (EPO), on the other hand, is detectable through urine as well as blood. What does EPO do? More oxygen to the blood and, as such, more physical depth and resistance. So, EPO helps increase the performance, and thus the ability to win and to charge more to athletes, cyclists, tennis players . . . and soccer players.

What did soccer do in 2012? Ninety-nine percent urine analyses and 1 percent blood analyses. Roger Federer, who, aside from being a great tennis player is also a sharp politician, knows all these numbers, and surely knows not to take Joseph Blatter seriously when he says, "There is no indication of doping" in soccer. Certainly not in soccer, the most popular and competitive sport on the planet, the glass ceiling everyone wants to reach, the ticket to money and fame if things go well. That's why the Swiss tennis star reacted without hiding his annoyance to an unexpected show of demagogy from Djokovic, which would have been bad enough on its own but came out worse coming from Federer, the second greatest in the world.

One night in November 2013, Djokovic took advantage of the dozens of reporters from all corners of the globe to attack the antidoping system during a press conference at the London Masters. In the cold hallways of the O2 Arena and in the exclusive corners for VIP guests, the topic of discussion had a first and last name: Viktor Troicki. The Serb had avoided a doping control in April of that year in Monte Carlo. He asked the doctor in charge of the control if he could do it the next day, alleging that he didn't feel well. Despite the fact that the doctor authorized it, Troicki was responsible for knowing that postponing a control is not possible, for which reason he received an eighteen-month suspension, later reduced to twelve by the Court of Arbitration for Sport (CAS).

While Nadal stuck to his new style—"it's a complicated situation for everyone, I believe in Viktor, but someone has to make the decisions"—Djokovic decided to set the press conference hall on fire. "This proves again that the system set in place by the World Anti-Doping Agency (WADA) doesn't work," the legendary Serbian read his notes from a piece of paper. "I don't trust them anymore, I don't trust in what is happening," he added. He was walking on the tightrope of irresponsibility.

Postponing a doping test for a day is an unheard of situation in the hyperprofessional world of the sport. There are methods to erase, in fewer than twenty-four hours, the traces of the consumption of certain substances. No serious control system, then, could allow for picking testing days and times "à la carte." Djokovic knows this.

Federer didn't let the Serbian's comment go without comment, and a day later he exerted all his weight as the president of the Players' Council. "When you get called to do a control, you have to do it. It doesn't matter how bad you're feeling, I'm afraid. A next-day control is not a control anymore, from my point of view, because who knows what happened that night. . . . I trust the system, for the most part, because I think they are very professional," he added just in case someone hadn't understood.

The ITF, the WADA, and even the ATP were furious with Djokovic, who, because he had come to his friend's defense, didn't hesitate to attack the entire tennis control structure. But the Serb was lucky because Federer, in his enthusiasm for the subject, let slip a phrase that irritated the ITF and swept attention away from what Djokovic had said, "I feel like they're not testing us enough. They didn't give me controls in Basel, or Paris either. Here, they did one after the first match." "I simply think that they should be doing more controls. I know that the budget can be small at times, and all those things. . . . I just feel like they used to give me more controls, I think they did twenty-five tests in 2003, 2004. It's clearly gone down since then." He also added, "Last year, when I won in three tournaments in a row in Dubai, Rotterdam, and Indian Wells, they didn't control me in any of the tournaments. That's not good enough for me."

The ITF hurried to correct the Swiss. "Statistics don't support the suggestion that there are less controls than before. Roger Federer was controlled, on average, eight times a year between 2004 and 2006, eleven times a year between 2007 and 2009, and nine between 2010 and 2012. What we don't know is the amount of tests done by the national agencies, and it's possible that those controls have been more frequent in the past." The man behind the ITF's statement, the key figure in the tennis antidoping system, a man whose name is known by few, not to mention his face, and with whom almost no one talks, is Stuart Miller, the master of the laboratory secrets (*interview conducted in January 2014*).

"Doctor Miller, I know for a fact that you like tennis, that you go to matches."

"I'm paid to work for tennis, so of course I have to watch them."

"Are there situations where you're watching a match and say to yourself, 'That can't be, we have to give that player a test?'"

"It could happen, yes. To be honest, things like that are very rare. There have been situations in which something happened that led us to administer specific tests to a player with very little forewarning, yes . . . But, as a rule of thumb, watching a match on television doesn't make you say, 'We have to test this person immediately.' You need to remember that we're based in the United Kingdom. If something happens in Australia, you're probably sleeping, so we can't react instantly."

"When you watch tennis matches, do you notice any changes in the landscape that might have been influenced by the growth hormone (HGH)?"

"The thing is, it doesn't work like that . . . That's a perception, and perceptions are never simple, you can't base a doping case on perceptions, you need concrete proof. What you can do is use perceptions as a step in the path that leads you, along with other information, to detect the consumption of a substance. For example, if you see a player running twice as fast as another, then you might have the impression that something is going on and then do something based on that."

"Is HGH a new danger in the doping world of tennis? How do you confront it?"

"I don't know when it became a danger, but what we do know is that it can potentially be used in tennis to enhance performance. The problem with HGH is that the window of opportunity to detect it is very brief, that time between when the substance enters the organism and the moment when it's not detectable any more. Originally, we only had twenty-four hours, now we have a week."

"I don't ever remember a positive for HGH in tennis."

"There never was, and that can be a result of the control program being relatively new. The substance is hard to detect, but the fact that we haven't found it doesn't mean we should stop looking."

"And genetic doping? Is there really a danger of someone trying to alter the genetic composition of athletes to make them stronger, faster, and more competitive?"

"Looking toward the future, it's something which some people might be tempted to use. It's already forbidden, detecting it is a challenge, but there are tools like the biological passport, the great advantage of which is that you don't have to detect the substances themselves, just their effects."

"But the biological passport can't detect gene doping, am I correct?"

"No, the passport cannot detect gene doping. I'm not an expert on gene doping, which is still very new; there is a lot to learn about how it works, how it changes the body, and how to detect that. It's a long journey."

"That means that, for the time being, the sport isn't ready to detect gene doping."

"The sport is working very hard on gene doping, but I think it's correct to say that time is still needed to develop and test methods that will get us there. Let's admit, there's a lot of room for improvement in other areas, such as autogenous blood doping, which is probably another big challenge. It's easy to detect that. I've injected myself with someone else's blood in order to improve my athletic condition and performance, but it's much harder to prove that I've extracted my own blood, and transferred it back into my body with reinforced red blood cells. We also have to control that, so there's a lot more to do."

"*But the biological passport would work for that.*"

"For blood transfusions? Yes, you can do that with biological passports because you'll see the effects on the red blood cells. There are other ways, too. If you keep blood in plastic bags, a part of that plastic will pass into the blood, these are the so-called plasticizers. Although it wasn't part of the case, there were detectable plastics in the case of [the Spanish cyclist] Alberto Contador, which suggested that the blood had been stored in plastic bags."

"*There haven't been any positives in tennis, so far, for that type of doping, right?*"

"No, and we analyze samples of blood transfusions. The biological passport will let us detect cases of blood doping as well, but there haven't been any so far."

"*The biological passport will start to be implemented in September 2015 with about 150 players; is that correct?*"

"That was our initial group. We'll start with the best players, but there will be more in time. We need between three and five samples to start to generate the passport."

"*Another of your responsibilities is coordinating with the national anti-doping agencies. I would imagine some agencies are very good, others not so much, and some practically nonexistent. Which countries work really well as far as their agencies, and which ones don't?*"

"We have a good relationship with a lot of agencies, and there are many good agencies, although I don't have experience with all of them. The largest, like the ones in the United Kingdom, the AFLD in France, the USADA in the United States, the ASADA in Australia . . . There are many good ones. Norway, for example, has an excellent ant-doping agency. They are all very professional, they all work under the WADA's code. Some are larger than others, others have more resources than some, but that doesn't mean the smaller ones are less competent."

"*How is it working with a national antidoping agency of a country that has the top, second, or third to the top player in the world? Is the work more intense in those cases or does nothing change? Spain, Serbia, Switzerland . . . Is there more contact and joint work with those countries due to the fact that they have great players?"*

"Not necessarily. As you can imagine, those countries are interested in their players forming part of our group of controlled tennis players. We talk a lot with those agencies, we know they're active, even though they don't necessarily have to call us, because the national agencies only need to talk to us when they want to do controls in a competition at an event that is under our jurisdiction. In any other situation, they can do controls without asking us for permission. What we do want is to coordinate our efforts, so if they're thinking of doing a control, they can look first to see if we're going to do one. That's the benefit of having a centralized database in the WADA, because all of our planning is stored there. The people who have access to that database can see if there are controls planned, and they can also call us and ask us. What we don't want is to waste resources by having two organizations show up at the same time to control the same player."

"How does a player find out that they came back positive on a control?"

"They receive an email and a letter in the mail at the address they registered in their file."

"Which organizations control a tennis player?"

"There are three possibilities: the Tennis Anti-Doping Program, the national agency belonging to the country they're playing in, and the WADA."

"It's complicated to have a global statistic that reflects all the controls a player is submitted to . . ."

"The WADA publishes reports that contain, save in a few exceptions, all the controls done by all the agencies to all the players. And they are publicly accessible. It's the best place to get centralized information."

"You would have read that Nadal is demanding that the controls be made public. What do you think about that? What does public mean to you, what would change?"

"Our policy is to follow the WADA's code with regard to what is made public. We publish a report at the end of every year, we say how many tests were done, we mention every player subjected to a control, and we say how many they did. I think that the people who are asking for the details of specific tests to be made public will have benefit in the short term. If they were controlled many times during a short period of time, it would become clear that they were the object of a rigorous program. But there could be other situations and other players or other sports in which less controls are done, and that could lead to certain speculation about how many opportunities they have to dope, and it would be completely unfounded. Our responsibility is to look out for the sport's best interest, so we only report once a year."

"Do you have personal contact with the players?"

"Yes, we have contact with players."

"And when they ask for public controls . . . what do you understand by that? What are they referring to, exactly, keeping in mind that up to a certain point, the controls are public?"

"I never talked to anyone about the subject. I heard the same suggestions that the controls be public. We're in contact with a lot of players, but I have to say we don't have many asking us that."

"At first glance, it seems simpler and cheaper to send people to any European country to control players than to do it in, say, a country like Argentina; is that so?"

"We work with a business that does the controls and counts on a network of local staff. Very seldom do we have to send people on long-distance flights in order to collect samples, very seldom."

"You're referring to IDTM, the Swedish enterprise, right?"

"Yes, IDTM, International Doping Tests and Management. They work for many international antidoping organizations and federations, they have a network of people who do controls all over the world. The benefit we get from that is that the tests are consistent, their people all have the same training and follow the same procedures in Doha, in Wimbledon, or in Rome. That's one of the other benefits."

Miller is a scientist and an expert, but first and foremost, he is a Brit. He talks in a quiet, at times monotone, voice, always tries to be proper, and apparently nothing agitates him. A great expert in biomechanics, his responsibilities in the ITF also include studying and approving anything related to technical equipment, especially the balls and the rackets. You get the impression that Miller speaks very little with the players and also that the players are mostly uninterested in talking to him. A dialogue between the deaf is seldom good, but that distance could prove to be positive in a certain light: he is able to preserve the independence of the organism that has, like it or not, the power in its hands to ruin a player's career. The ITF took complete charge of the doping controls in 2006, when the WTA accepted transfer of those prerogatives and joined the ATP. During that year, three cases of doping were announced: one during the qualifying rounds of the Australian Open, another during the Challenger tournament, and a third during a wheelchair competition. It is very apparent that the controls happen in tennis, as apparent as the fact that the sport, for better or for worse, never had a Ben Johnson, or a Marion Jones. The most similar cases were Agassi's nonofficial doping and Maria Sharapova's suspension in 2016.

CHAPTER 18

Plasma

"Do I HAVE TO GET stuck more times? Then put me to sleep." All champions have their limits, even Rafael Nadal. The first time he arrived at building number 10 on Beato Tomás de Zumárraga street, the left-handed player didn't know what he would find. He did know, in fact, why he had gone to Vitoria, the small and tidy capital of the Spanish Basque Country, where eating is regarded as an art form. Nadal wanted someone to get rid of the knee pains that had been tormenting him for so long. He wanted to play without suffering again, and he had been told that Mikel Sánchez was the doctor who could perform that miracle.

Sánchez, a smiling and persuasive doctor somewhere between his fifties and sixties, had the solution: regenerative surgery, enriched plasma. And he also had a syringe that promised to hurt a lot. The doctor recalls, "The first time I gave him an injection, he told me: 'Do I have to get stuck more times? Then put me to sleep.'"

Sánchez can clearly remember that first encounter with Nadal, the man who made his novel treatment famous. It's simple in theory: blood is extracted; it is put in a centrifuge for eight minutes, the red and white blood cells are removed, and you are left with a dense liquid, rich in platelets: enriched plasma. Enriched plasma, growth factors, stem cells . . .

names that are almost unsettling. What is that about stem cells? "Tissues are made of cells and a matrix. All tissues wear down and regenerate for maintenance, but they don't always wear and regenerate at the same rate," Sánchez explains. "When there's more wearing than regeneration, there is a degeneration of the tissue. What regenerative medicine tries to do is to recover that balance. When a tendon is broken, you seek to cure the tendon so that it is in as much the same shape is it was before the injury as possible."

Sánchez enthusiastically explains. He knows the topic isn't simple and that it often generates unfounded feelings of suspicion. So he refers to the animal kingdom as an indication that he didn't make it up himself. "This is something God invented, or nature, or whoever, during the evolution of the species. A lion, a dinosaur, they heal, or healed, the same way we do. What we've done is to observe what nature does. What we know is that all tissues work through cells creating matrices or cells. You stimulate them into making more or less, to specify when and how. Those stimuli are provided by proteins that we have in the platelets in our blood, in the plasma, and what we do is stimulate a lot of cells into working all at the same time. That's how we achieve faster and better quality healing."

Doctor Sánchez pauses to allow so much information to be digested. "Those proteins are called growth factors, and that's why it's called plasma, rich in growth factors. The plasma is blood that we've removed the red and white blood cells from, and to which we've added platelets. It's plasma enriched with platelets containing growth factors." Confident that he is being understood, Sánchez details the next step: centrifuging the blood. "It's very fast, it centrifuges for eight minutes. If we do it too quickly, the platelets can break. If we do it too slowly, the balance is broken. This plasma, once it's ready, is injected into the site where we want something to heal. How the plasma is prepared is important, and also how it's injected, where, how much, in which sites . . ."

It's common knowledge that the natural intestines used on a tennis racket come from cow stomachs. You need two-and-a-half cows to create a standard grip. So tennis owes a great deal to this peaceful herbivore. Additionally, the sport is in debt to the sheep. That one is harder to imagine. But it is so: Sánchez and his colleagues inject blue-colored plasma into sheep to see how, and in what quantities, it is distributed throughout the organism. "It's a good-sized animal, with enough blood, and relatively cheap."

Lions, dinosaurs, sheep . . . Sánchez clearly knows what his favorite examples are, and he also knows that a light touch of humor is necessary to help in assimilating so much scientific information. "It's not common to see a lame lion or to comment, 'Look at how bad that wild pig's osteoarthritis is on the hill there.' It's not common because they're always doing exercise, and have healthier cartilage than we do. Cartilage injuries are mostly a human pathology. We have become sedentary animals. I have Chondromalacia patellae. Every year, before the skiing season, I jab myself."

For Nadal, finding a treatment that would allow him to recover what he'd lost was like being born again. With time, the stem cell treatment was being used on other parts of his body. First, in December 2013, in Doha, he celebrated not having knee pain in his "everyday life" for the first time in years. Then, twelve months later, compressed into the back seat of an Opel Corsa driven by Benito Pérez Barbadillo through the intricate roads near Manacor, Nadal was telling the Spanish journalist, Ignacio Naya, why they had made "two holes" in his back, just like he had explained two days before to another Spaniard, Javier Martínez, in an interview in *El Mundo*. "They take the plasma from your own blood, centrifuge it, and are left with the growth factors that they inject into you to regenerate," he explained to Martínez in London during a pause at a poker game, a new interest of Nadal's which was somewhere between a passion and business.

If the injections into the knee tendons were painful, the back treatment sounded nothing short of terrifying. "The methodologies between different treatments aren't very different, I don't think, it's just that this is a little more aggressive because they have to make a couple of holes in your lower back to extract the stem cells from the iliac crest. Afterwards, they have to cultivate and reproduce to try and make the regeneration of the tissues faster."

The combination of holes in the back and stem cells extracted from the iliac crest was a bit much for a weak stomach, but Nadal had no recourse but to explain everything in detail. To the displeasure of the rest of the clan, his uncle Toni had revealed the back treatment during an interview with the DPA, thereby destroying the plan to keep it a secret behind the appendix operation which the player had undergone at the time. Naya, who is now a chief of Sports in that German agency, managed to find a way to elegantly ask Nadal, three weeks later, about the business that sounded excessive to the layman, although it was perfectly reasonable to an expert. *"According to you, the stem cell treatment requires making holes in the iliac crest. Are you pushing your body too hard, or is it not as aggressive as it sounds?"* Nadal responded without hesitating:

"I would never do anything that would put my future health at risk just to prolong my career in sports. My personal life and happiness extend much further than my tennis career. That's what comes first. Beyond that, I'm not doing anything that hasn't been suggested by doctors. I have a group of highly professional doctors who try to help me keep my body as healthy as possible, even if incidents like what happened this year happen."

The tennis player had his responses memorized, because the holes in his back had associated his name once again with the cursed word "doping." After Toni Nadal's revelation, the sports newspaper *As* had published a flashy article in which the headline stated that the treatment the player was undergoing was considered doping in Italy. That statement, inaccurate, bothered Nadal in ways you couldn't imagine. Days after the article in *As* had been published, the player took advantage of a question from Juan José Mateo from *El País* to get a small bit of revenge. *"After the treatment was made public, we've seen headlines stating that it's forbidden in other countries,"* the reporter asked. Nadal answered with cold fury, "Incompetence makes it possible to disseminate erroneous information. How is it doping? First of all, you would need to know what the technique is. Second, if there was even the slightest risk that it was doping, why would I dope? My way of viewing the sport, without a doubt, and it pains me to even have to say it, is that I would hang my racket up, as high as I could, so I could never get it back down, before I would cheat and throw away everything I've done all these years. Everyone has a limit. Bodies have a limit. You can't trick yourself, or trick others. That's what doping is—tricking the whole world—and the first in line to be tricked is yourself. And on top of that, you're risking your health."

In order to write and talk about the matter, he had to do his research, and lots of it, because he was treading on dangerous ground. A little earlier, the treatment that would change Nadal's life and career was considered doping by the highest authority on the subject: WADA. Sánchez, himself, explained it honestly, "When you say you're treating an athlete with something that comes from blood and is called growth factors, it sounds huge. It sounds too much like growth hormone." The name wasn't the only aspect that attracted WADA's attention; the organization based in Montreal had also become interested in the results, which were both good and fast.

Sanchez continued, "The antidoping agency said, 'Let's go see what this is.' And for a time it was doping, it was on the list of forbidden practices, and you had to ask permission before doing it, which didn't make sense. If I have a muscle injury and I have to ask for permission from an anti-doping agency, which would take ten or eleven days to answer, then I'm not interested in doing it. There was a convention in Lausana in 2012 with experts from all over the world, and they concluded that there was no basis for considering it doping."

Which wasn't to say that any form of reinjecting blood with a syringe was fair game. "The reinfusion of blood with a high concentration of red blood cells to increase oxygenation, and consequently performance, is one thing: it's doping. But here we throw out the red blood cells, we get rid of them. We're left with a bit of plasma, a third or just over half of a cubic inch, with platelets. That's not doping, it's just the opposite."

And so, without the label of doping, Nadal's main problem was putting up with the pain of the treatment. Couldn't you resort to using less painful needles on Nadal and all the others who were submitting their joints to multiple injections to regenerate them? Sánchez smiled, shaking his head. "The problem isn't the needle, but rather the volume of liquid that you have to insert into one spot. The injection is just an instant and done; the problem is what's going in, between five and ten milliliters of liquid. It's painful in the tendon because it expands very little, it's not very elastic. In the muscle, on the other hand, the pain is very little because it's more elastic, you can fit more. The tendon is collagen, very dense."

Nadal's problem was in the tendons, meaning that the pain was unbearable. That's why the player opted for being put completely to sleep each time the dense liquid was injected into the tendons in his knee. Sánchez added, "You can't fit much into a tendon, and you have to press a liquid in there. We can't use a local anesthetic, which generates a completely opposite effect at the cellular level. So what we do is use a general anesthetic, sedation, but then you have to go to the operating room with anesthetics, which is a little more complicated. That's how it was finally done to Nadal, because it had to be done several times."

The sacrifice was worth it. Sánchez was perhaps saving the career of the biggest sports player in the history of Spain. "Nadal doesn't like it at all when we talk about his injuries. It's kind of like talking about a racing motorcycle breaking down," the doctor said. He might not like it, sure, but talking about Nadal without mentioning his injuries would be talking about an incomplete Nadal. He is both: his successes and his injuries, some injuries which greatly increase the merit of his career, a career in which he suffered important injuries every year, some of them very serious.

The degeneration of his knees certainly was. Nadal wears a size 8 shoe, and his feet are unusually small for his height and weight.

"He's like an elite soccer player; he has small feet like the Brazilian player, Sócrates," points out Jofre Porta, who trained Nadal when he was a child and then a teenager. "That's why Nadal's weak physical link is in his knees. At six feet tall, a tennis player usually weighs 172 to 174 pounds. Rafa, at 185, is pulling about nine extra pounds. And that hurts him." So much so that the wear on Nadal's knees became irreversible. His body was, and is, wasting more tissue than it is capable of regenerating. If he kept up that pace without finding a solution to his problem, his career would end up in the history books at an age similar to Björn Borg, twenty-six years old.

The first time they stepped into Sánchez's office, the Nadals came up with a theory: everything originated from the player's problems when stepping, which in 2006 led to the fabrication of a pair of special insoles in order to change his step and avoid the excess of stress on the tendons. "He had a degenerative tendinopathy," Sánchez explains. "The Nadals' theory makes sense, but I didn't know him before so I can't confirm that it was the cause. When a tendon is put under too much stress, more is wasted than what is generated. It's very difficult to prove, but it's a possible hypothesis." Sánchez once made a comment to the newspaper *Marca*, that the first time he examined Nadal's knees, he couldn't believe he was playing tennis under those conditions. "His ability to play through pain, to suffer and still win, is enormous."

And Sánchez's ability to change many people's lives also seems amazing at that time, from the king of Spain to Nadal, and including the cyclist Joseba Beloki and the soccer players Xavi and Carles Puyol. The Portuguese Cristiano Ronaldo was also anxious to visit Vitoria. "A lot of foolish things get written, of course. Take Beloki's case, for example. Nadal's problem is one of overuse; he wastes more of his tendon than he can generate, due to his style of playing, to how violent his play is. Beloki's problem was different, he fell, destroyed his elbow and hip, and was able to get back on his bike in six weeks. With Beloki, we gained more than a month and a half on the time that we had predicted. They wrote us from the University of Nantes to ask us how we managed it."

You can tell that Sánchez is passionate about what he does, but he also demonstrates an important degree of confidence and audacity. A few feet from his office, he has a device that seems like science-fiction: a 3D printer that makes naturally-sized bones. "We see patients suffering from the effects of other injuries. What we do is to scan and print their knee in 3D using a synthetic material, so we can rehearse the surgery before operating on the patient. If we don't like the result, we print again and change our technique so we're completely prepared when we go into the operating room." If a machine that prints life-size bones is impressive, the future that Sánchez envisions is twice as impacting. "In the future we'll be printing medicine to order, and living tissue. Now we all take the same stuff, even though we're different. There will be a machine that can create an individualized pill and tissue from cells. The future is unforeseen." The doctor offers to show the machine and explains how they fixed a knee that wasn't exactly in good shape. "We had to insert half the tibia from a cadaver into that knee. We'll be able to fabricate the structure of an individual's bone, using a printer that will contain cultivated cells so we have a unique matrix and cells. That will be the future. And the biggest challenge yet is the cartilage. A hip or knee prosthesis, which is something that presently gets results that are quite effective, is ultimately a failure of regenerative medicine, because you're substituting a part of the organism with something made of metal and plastic. The challenge is in getting a tissue to truly regenerate."

Sánchez was already a recognized professional before Nadal consulted him, but the boost that the tennis player gave his image was enormous. "There are always trends, and people think that if this doctor fixed this famous person, then he must be good," Sánchez admits.

For over a decade, when he was at the top, Nadal had to figure out how to train and play through the pain. Perhaps one of the peaks of his suffering came during the eighth-finals match at the 2011 Wimbledon against the Argentinian Juan Martín del Potro. The Spaniard was shrieking battle cries from the middle of the court because of the unusual pain in his heel. His father later admitted that he had never seen him in so much pain.

But Nadal was also yelling out of anger towards the Argentinian, whom he said complained that Nadal had been given preferential treatment because of his pain in the middle of the match, although Del Potro swears that it was exactly the opposite: he insisted that he had asked the chair umpire to give his rival all the time he needed.

Nadal did not believe, nor did he accept, that excuse, and he didn't hesitate to retrace his steps back to the press conference room after he had already left, to stand firmly in the entrance and glare at the journalist who had said that Del Potro denied his accusations. "None of that. I know what I saw and heard," he said with his features tense, and not at all attempting to hide the fury he felt, despite having won the encounter. It's not surprising, says a man who knows Del Potro more than most. "Juan and Rafa are friends for the photo shoot, but they would claw each other's eyes out if they could."

That drama on the British turf served to demonstrate, indirectly, the incredible ramifications of having "Nadal's business." Everything he touches—and everything that touches him—can turn into gold. Having successfully attended Nadal, the appropriately named "Hope" clinic, the clinic at which Sánchez works, finds that its phones explode with new calls.

The Nadals, who are not in the habit of giving away business, kept the name of the clinic where the left-handed player had been attending a complete secret after that tense match with Del Potro. The idea was to avoid, at any cost, that the London clinic and the doctor in question receive any benefit from the good publicity that always comes from attending a sports superstar. Not only that; for several hours, Nadal's presence in the Wimbledon quarter finals was not at all guaranteed. The announcement that he would, indeed, play his match against the American Mardy Fish wasn't made through any statement or press conference. No, it was done through Facebook. Dozens of thousands of clicks, traffic to the player's page, and more and better business for the player's enterprise.

That Sánchez's treatment helped Nadal is something that seems difficult to refute, although the doctor himself talks about the weight that the "placebo effect" carries with athletes. But the "placebo effect" is one thing, saying that the treatment had no real effect despite the clear ramifications is something else. The Spanish Carlos Arribas, a writer for *El País* and one of the journalists who best understands and explains the topic of doping, wrote toward the end of 2014 an article in which he played down Sánchez's treatment. "Recently read in a tweet from Karim Khan, editor of the scientific journal, *British Journal of Sports Medicine:*

Player: Will stem cells cure my back pain?

Doctor (lie): Yes.

Doctor (truth): No idea, but it's very unlikely. Would you like to be a guinea pig?"

The beginning of the article was devastating, and Arribas added that Nadal would find it difficult to see the humor in the dialogue made up by the British specialist. "But the efficiency and the safety of the treatment give birth to controversy in the scientific world and among traumatologists ever since its use struck a chord with the media after, according to the *New York Times*, it saved Bartolo Colón's, the Yankees pitcher, shoulder and elbow and relaunched his career in May, 2011."

Sánchez's method, which according to the doctor himself is practiced in fifty other centers in the world, although a scientific journal elevates that number to seven hundred, is also seen negatively by some of his Spanish colleagues. Traumatologists from prestigious specialized clinics in Madrid charge, while always asking for anonymity, that the method is mostly effective at gathering money.

In his article, Arribas quoted experts who were both in favor of and against the treatment. "'My personal experience and that of the people I know who use those techniques is very good,' says Luis González Lago, a Spanish traumatologist who works for Baniyas, a soccer team from Abu Dhabi. González Lago, who used to play handball in the Atlético de Madrid, is a great supporter of regenerative medicine."

Juan Manuel Alonso, a member of the medical committee of the International Association of Athletics Federations (IAAF), does not agree, wrote *El País*, "Obviously, I cannot be in favor of stem cell treatments because it is still an experimental therapy, and it is done without any scientific data that shows its benefits and risks over a long period of time, which are unknown. I don't consider it as something serious." Alonso is a colleague of Karim Khan's in the sports medicine center Aspetar, in Doha. "If athletes want to be guinea pigs, go ahead, but they need to know: a doubtful outcome and unknown risks in exchange for a great deal of money, about 7,000 Euros per injection."

Alonso added that the owners of the clinics that offer the treatment use the apparent miracles that they achieve to cure the impossible injuries of famous athletes as advertisement. "It has given birth to an industry that is very criticized by the scientific community but takes advantage of the news that is spread about success with celebrities," read *Nature* magazine, speaking of the effects of the operation in the Dominican Republic.

Arribas's article was surely read by the Nadals, but it would be difficult to convince the player that Sánchez's treatment is much more expensive than effective. The Roland Garros megachampion didn't just experience how the injections made his knees feel better: while the needles were injecting the enriched plasma into a sedated Nadal's joints, the tennis player was overcoming an almost built-in disadvantage he had against Roger Federer. "Federer hasn't had injuries from excessive exertions, and he's been playing tennis for years," Sánchez remarked. The extra pounds that Porta had mentioned that Nadal was carrying play a part also. "Of course, but those are hard to lose because they're not from fat. But it's a factor. There are a lot of factors. Nadal has fantastic physical qualities, better than average; he's good in every aspect. If he had a bad physique, he never would have gotten so big, but the fact is that if you have worn a down tendon that is still degenerating, and you keep doing what you're doing, you'll have to keep getting injections."

Federer again: "His style of play and his physique give him a good balance." That the doctor who gave Nadal's knees their life back would compare him unfavorably to Federer was a bit note-worthy. "Don't tell poor Nadal that," the reporter joked. And then, Sánchez adds surprisingly, "No, he was the one who said that about Federer. The little I know about tennis is what they taught me."

CHAPTER 19

Body

"I'm sorry, I don't have my identification again . . ."

"Please, Rafa, you can go in."

Rafael Nadal had just lost a Grand Slam tournament with a degree of severity quite unusual for him, and an hour after the defeat against the Czech Tomáš Berdych he moves around the hallways adjacent to the players' changing room at the Australian Open. It's January 2015, and you could say that 99 percent of the world's population knows who Rafael Nadal is. Obviously, this would include the guard at the back entrance to the locker room, on top of which he had seen him enter and exit a dozen times those days. It also helps that Nadal is in Australia, a country in which, when faced with something out of the ordinary, a smile is always the answer.

It's not like that at every Grand Slam, although the basic rule is the same in all of them: even the best-known players in history must have their identification hanging from their necks in order to access the different areas of the tournament. This includes the changing room, an area that the players feel, with good reason, they practically own. Other players of his caliber would not even bother to apologize to the door attendant for not having their identification; they would just walk in. But Nadal, in that regard, is different from most.

The ID card of the nine-time Roland Garros champion is in the hands of his uncle Toni on that 27th of January 2015 and he is playing with it. He drops it and then picks it up. The "Nadal clan," normally celebratory, is scattered in glum. Sebastián, his father, walks by with his gaze firmly focused on the ground, to avoid making eye contact with the reporters. Further back is Jordi Robert, nicknamed "Tuts," the man from Nike who travels the world with Nadal. Benito Pérez Barbadillo comes and goes, Toni talks with different groups, and Ángel Ruiz Cotorro, the ever-important doctor, paces from side to side with a nervous smile. Nadal spends the majority of his time in the changing room with Rafael Maymó, his physical therapist—and much more—as he always does after a match.

The players' area and changing rooms in Melbourne Park are a labyrinth of white walls and dozens of photos of the tournament champions, of the best Australians in history and their skills at tennis. There are multiple doors, and it's best to keep your eye on all of them if you want to find a particular someone and engage him in a chat. Any moment now, that someone is likely to show up.

"Damn, we're surrounded!" Maymó had just peeked through the back door of the changing room and, after seeing the group of reporters, lets loose that comment and closes the door. About twenty seconds later he goes out the main entrance, but the press is there, too. He can't do anything but smile as he hastens his step. Nadal himself seems uncomfortable when he emerges from the changing room and is confronted with countless faces that have been following him around the planet for years. The situation isn't the most relaxing for the reporters, either, but it's still a part of their job.

The Nadals don't have the will to talk, because they know that the question they'll be asked for the millionth time is about Nadal's physical problems after he had just lost to Berdych with clear issues with his right leg. The Czech played a great game, and, of course, he is a great player as well, but Nadal hadn't lost to him since 2006, and had beaten him the past seventeen times they faced each other.

The Nadals' reaction went beyond issues concerning image, and beyond the commercial implications; it was simply human: talking about an injury, again, was the last thing they wanted to do. The one on that day wasn't serious, it wasn't strictly even an injury, but it was a physical problem that had kept him from the doing the second thing he liked most: competing, which is just below the thing he most enjoys, which is winning. He had explained one afternoon in September in New York, during a US Open, "I love the sport and I view it in a specific light; a sport without a goal is stupid, that's my feeling. If I don't try to give my best, then I'm not doing a sport, and I should do something else. Sport is playing with your full passion and enjoying the sensation. Sport is competing, competing to win." Nadal is especially bothered by not being able to compete. That was the feeling he had in 2015 in Río de Janeiro, where he lost an impossible match against the fickle Italian, Fabio Fognini. Nadal would travel after every match in a minivan accompanied by his uncle, and his complaints were always the same. "Damn, I don't know what's wrong with me. I'm physically failing, my stamina is low, I'm having downturns." It was the beginning of his worst year, and Nadal, from one moment to the next, could no longer remember how good it felt to be in control and win on the court.

"Ha ha!" Roger Federer laughs happily. Dominating tennis for almost a year, and used to being labeled as the "best of all time," the Swiss player looks at the reporters while grasping his left arm. "It's enormous, impressive, it scares my rivals." The arm, quite lean, confirms that Federer is making fun of himself. This happened one afternoon in January of 2013 and also in Melbourne, during an Australian Open in which the absence of the player with the most famous and muscular left arm in the world was apparent: Rafael Nadal. Federer has an enormous amount of respect for the Spaniard, but that day in Australia it was obvious that he was comparing himself—jokingly, unfavorably—to Nadal, whose physique is impressive to spectators and rivals.

Federer had stuffed himself into a tight T-shirt with bright pink colors to defeat the Canadian Milos Raonic. The Swiss player, built as finely as a violin, doesn't have any extra weight, but he's not a waste of muscles either. He continues to make fun. "I put this on because my big muscles need to stay warm." In a hypercompetitive and extremely physically demanding sport—it helps to remember that 2013 saw four days in a row with temperatures of 111 degrees in Melbourne—having muscles is important, but even more important is stamina, the ability to explode forth, and above all, that your body doesn't break, that there are no chinks in your armor.

Nadal was the king of muscles for years on the circuit, but also at the front of the line in physical fragility, which might not even be a paradox. Nadal and his triumphs are a common topic of conversation, as are his problems with his powerful physique. His career had been as replete with victories as it was with injuries, although 99 percent of tennis players would sign on for that in exchange for just 10 percent of the Spaniard's success in sports: the sixteen Grand Slam titles that he had won and the possibility that he might surpass Federer's record of twenty (statistics through May 2018).

A ten-time Roland Garros champion, Nadal's arrival in the temple of French tennis had been late. He didn't play in 2003 nor in 2004, due to injuries. He was sixteen and seventeen years old, and his body was already giving him trouble, the kind that also showed up during the absurd final in Australia in 2014. Absurd because Nadal should have won. He faced off against Stanislas Wawrinka, the very talented Swiss who had lost his last twelve matches against the Spanish player without even winning a single set. Absurd, also, because while Wawrinka had played celestially in the first set, his victory in that match would always be accompanied by a small asterisk denoting: "Nadal played while physically diminished."

What happened that night? It's worth remembering. It's also a good way to understand the "Nadalian style" of tennis and the advantages and limits of his physique. It was a night during which, with the match already decided, the great Rod Laver took out his cellphone and, concentrating almost as much as he would on a match point, started taking pictures of the devastated Nadal. It was a dramatic night during which the Spaniard was cheered, but was also booed.

Just fifty minutes into the game Wawrinka was winning, 6–2 and 2–1, and it was as if the final was over. Serious, and with his left eyebrow raised, which only happens when something bothers him—the Spaniard went to his chair, and the physical therapist asked him two questions. There was no doubt. "Let's go to the changing room," the doctor said. The tunnel swallowed the Spaniard, who left without so much as a word to the chair umpire, the Portuguese Carlos Ramos. Wawrinka was left alone and disconcerted in the stadium, and the dialogue that was generated at that moment allowed for an unusual glimpse at the ghosts and weaknesses of the tennis stars. Tennis players live at the edge of an emotional precipice, more than one would think.

Wawrinka: "Why did he leave, what's wrong?"

Ramos: "I don't know . . . And the truth is, we don't have to tell you."

Wawrinka: "If he calls the physio, you have to tell me why."

Ramos: " . . ."

Wawrinka: "What's he being treated for?"

Ramos: "Stan, I don't know."

Wawrinka: "Ask! Or can you just walk off the field whenever you want . . ."

Ramos: "It's between him and the physio. You can either argue about it or you can accept it. I think you should accept it."

Wawrinka: "You have to tell me, you always have to tell me, in every match!"

While Wawrinka, clearly terrified, waited for Nadal to come back, the Spaniard was in the changing room dealing with a jammed back. The public didn't know what was happening, but among the fourteen thousand spectators at the Rod Laver Arena, there was a considerable number who knew one thing very clearly: whatever it was, they didn't like it.

The Australian night became definitively more confusing when Nadal, more serious than ever, emerged shirtless and bare-chested back onto the field, walking heavily, almost clumsily. He headed to his chair to keep playing, although he knew he couldn't. Wawrinka had already left his to go stretch on the court, worried about getting cold. And then something happened that is rarely seen in a tennis stadium: the great majority of the public started hissing at Nadal. "It was very strange," Wawrinka admitted later.

"I would never criticize the audience of this tournament," an almost self-flagellating Nadal said later. "They paid to see the best match possible, and at the time I couldn't offer them that."

The next hour and a half were proof for the Frenchman Fabrice Santoro, who swears that Nadal scares his rivals. Wawrinka just had to hit the ball within the lines and move Nadal, whose serve had fallen to the level of something like that from a Saturday match at the club, and he played only with his arm, because turning was impossible. That's how the third set of the final progressed, and Wawrinka ended up winning fairly in four partials, reflecting an inner struggle that also revealed something of the Swiss's good side: it was clear that he felt uncomfortable defeating such a physically inferior rival.

Inferior? Nadal is a tennis player, but first and foremost he is an athlete. He plays soccer with quality and power; he was a forward to be feared in his adolescence. One of his uncles, Miguel Ángel Nadal, was a midfielder and a center back for Barcelona and the Spanish team. He was so physically powerful that his teammates called him "Tarzan." His nephew could have easily inherited the nickname.

"When he walks on to the field, everyone is afraid of playing against Rafa. You could say that Djokovic is a great player, Federer another great player, Murray . . . but if it's Rafa, I'm scared." The phrase was Santoro's, who went on to explain that combination of physical-mental intimidation that the Spaniard inspires in his rivals. "It's not just the way he plays, but the way he fights, how strong he is. But at the same time, he's very humble on the court. He plays and fights; he'll never exert psychological pressure on his opponent or the chair umpire."

The intimidation that Nadal inspires in his rivals is spontaneous, natural, never purposeful, and never a trick. But there are few like him who are already winning the match before they've even arrived at the court. A common witness to what happens in the locker rooms of the great tournaments describes the minutes before the fight: "Before a match the players jump, they move, they flex their arms with a rubber they use to warm up their joints; they go to the shower, the bathroom, they look in the mirror. Rafa has earphones and listens to music, jumps, does small sprints, stretches. It generates a tension mixed with respect, admiration, and fear. He goes crazy for a few moments. Federer doesn't, he's much more calculating."

There is something, then, that seems hard to understand in Nadal: why is that physical exuberance accompanied by so many injuries? Why did Federer, over the course of his career, only have a twisted ankle, a bout of mononucleosis, and back problems (until 2016, when all calamities came together)? There are many explanations for that difference between the two protagonists in one of the historical rivalries of tennis. The main one is that Federer plays "easy;" he hits the ball flat on and moves lightly around the court, anticipating where it will be. Nadal, on the other hand, is an ode to physical erosion. This was perfectly summed up by Chris Evert, a great player from the '70s and '80s, who also starred in a historical rivalry with Martina Navrátilová. "Federer is an artist. And Nadal . . . Nadal is a warrior!" she explained.

Feliciano López, with his serve and net, one of the last remaining of a vanishing species, knows both of them very well. He is a close friend of Nadal's and deeply admires Federer. "If I had to choose one person's physique for playing tennis, I would choose Federer's. For every aspect: speed, coordination, stamina. You can see that in the five set matches that he's played, he almost never ends up exhausted. The other player wastes much more energy than he does. That all adds up in a career like his. By now he's won a thousand matches and has never had a serious injury. Other players, with many less, have suffered much more."

Federer never walked out on a match; he always played to the end. Nadal yelled at his uncle, "I won't stop even if I crap myself," during a match that he lost against his countryman, David Ferrer, in Australia 2011. He had already abandoned, a year ago, a match on the same stage against the British Andy Murray, one of six encounters throughout his entire career that he didn't see through. He wasn't willing to add another. Even more significant is what happened with Novak Djokovic.

By January of 2015, there had been ten matches during which the Serbian player left before the timer ran out.

"It's unreal, absolutely unreal, that the best tennis player in history has never left a match," López emphasizes while his eyes widen in amazement behind his smart-looking glasses, which he had started using a couple of years earlier. "Aside from taking care of yourself and leading a healthy life, not damaging or punishing your body, you also have to have a little bit of luck, to have a genetically strong body." López has been watching Federer play for almost two decades. "You see him, and he is very physically gifted, very coordinated. I've seen him play when he was fifteen, sixteen years old, and you could see then that he was physically fit for tennis. He's flexible, tall, coordinated, he's not lacking in any area; his movements on the court are perfect. That helps, too."

Ferrer smiles when he hears about the analysis by his countryman, López, who says that the Swiss player, rather than running, floats. "Federer is idolized a lot. But yes, he is the most coordinated player, he is always well supported, and his level of mobility is better." López explains further, "I've never seen anyone move around a court like he does. His technique is the best. And he floats around the tennis court. You always see him placed well, you never seem him move in a way that could injure him. You can see his body is always straight, he bends down low, you never see him in a bad position." Federer is so, so good, López says, that he even manages to look good in the pictures that are taken while he plays. "He's never in a bad position in the photographs, you never see him moving around in a way that could injure him. All of the players show up in pictures with our heads down, or a leg sticking out somewhere . . . He's always straight, his arm is always in the right place, the ball in front of him, and his legs flexing. And his serve is, technically, excellent."

He's superhuman. It's clear that, technically and physically, Federer is unbeatable. In mental strength, though, there are competitors at his level. "Roger has to win every day he's on a tennis court. He, Rafa,

Djokovic, every time they step onto a tennis court, they have to win. You have to be ready for that, ready to maintain that ambition every day. Only great players like them can do that, people who have a brutal amount of mental strength."

López's own game is as refined as his capacity for analyzing. *"Are Federer and Nadal so different as players?"* "They're very different, completely different. Rafa also has brutal mobility, but the way in which Rafa and Federer play is very different. Rafa has a different tactic for each point, which is something that very few are capable of. Federer always goes for the ball. They've grown up in different technical environments. Federer, on a covered court in Switzerland. Without wind and with a stable temperature, hitting the ball is different. Rafa, on a clay court, in the open air, and in Mallorca. It's absolutely different. Look at how the Czechs play, the Nordics, a good part of the French . . . They play with flat balls, always well supported. It's very different in Spain, a different kind of tennis. But Rafa, as far as mobility on a tennis court . . . be careful! I've seen few people who are faster. He puts in a lot more effort than Federer, of course, but Federer puts in the least amount of effort out of all."

When Federer is asked about "the years," the Swiss player smiles. "Let's do it, I love talking about that!" After the laughter in the press hall dies down, the man who, with four children, keeps fighting to be at the top spot in tennis finds an explanation that goes beyond the physical: his differences, now that he is fully in his thirties, are mostly mental, he says. "I feel good, I don't feel at all different from, say, four years ago. Really, I don't. I might pay more attention to the signals my body sends me, but I also know my body better than I did before. And as the years go on, I guess you want to try new things, although that isn't necessarily linked to age."

Yes and no, no and yes. When he enters into an analysis, Federer is extremely rational; he looks at all the variants and hypotheses. In a certain way, he does the reporters' job for them. "It's always about saying, 'Okay, you did such and such thing for this and that reason.' But maybe you did it because you wanted something different, something fresh, new, to try something else. That could be true for anything, but you should clearly listen to your body." And not just your body. "I think the mind becomes more important as well. How much willingness and passion do you have for being there? How much willingness and passion do you have for playing and winning? Why do you keep doing it? Are you doing it for the right reasons? I think that, in my opinion, that's more important than the whole physical debate that the world emphasizes."

Federer is an artist, and Nadal a warrior. It's enough to listen to Federer to realize once again that every generalization is a bit unfair, but no one can deny that Evert knows her tennis. On the other hand, as far as Nadal is concerned, without ceasing to be a warrior—which he couldn't do, which wouldn't be in his interest, nor would he want to change—he started to understand as the years went by that he couldn't continue to play throughout his entire career like he did during that final in Rome 2005, when he beat the Argentinian Guillermo Coria. A decade had passed, and very few matches on the circuit ever equaled that intensity, five sets of incredible physical exertion and adrenaline shooting through the roof.

That 2005 was the year of Nadal's explosion, when the world of tennis, and the player himself, felt that the Spaniard would always be able to play one more serve and win the point, no matter how far he was from the back line. "Everything is possible if you put in everything you've got," he had said with the confidence and simplicity that only youth can bring. And there was plenty of that: Nadal was superhuman, and had a level of physical strength that, together with a steel resolve, would in just a few months raise him out of the top fifty and into the second sport in the world ranking.

The first Roland Garros title was already in his pocket, and the question was how far this amazing Spaniard with the timid eyes and steel arm could go. The answer came toward the end of that same year: if it depended on his state of mind, Nadal's horizon was infinite. But the limits would come from elsewhere, from the same physique that frightened his rivals.

Shanghai waited for Nadal. It was his first Masters. He had won a place among the eight who are scheduled at the end of every year, and the Spaniard was there; not to play, but to explain to the Chinese public why he couldn't. If, just weeks before, the tendinitis in his knees had complicated his game, the problem in China was now a ligament in his left foot.

After declining to participate in that tournament he got to take part in others, but during 2005 and in the midst of his tennis explosion, Nadal was faced with a dilemma that was almost unthinkable for a nineteen-year-old athlete: retirement. He thought about it for some days, and even considered leaving tennis and challenging Tiger Woods. He thought about becoming a professional golfer in order to curb his competitive anxieties in some way. The biggest rival in Nadal's career was not Federer, nor was it Novak Djokovic; *it was his own body.* First, a delicate bone in his left foot, the navicular bone of the tarsus. Later, it was the degeneration of his knees, and also a malady with a strange name: hoffitis. The lesion is congenital, and after confounding several specialists, a doctor in Madrid who had written a thesis on the diminutive bone in question gave Nadal his diagnosis: it was possible that he might have to leave tennis forever and retire at nineteen years of age.

Nadal was devastated. He dragged himself around like a ghost, without any joy, motivation, or appetite. Just the idea of being forced to leave tennis tormented him. That was when his father, Sebastián, had an idea. "With all that talent and those balls you've got," he started to say, "I don't see any reason for you not to be a professional golfer." The possibility of Nadal becoming a golfer was revealed by the player himself, when he was with writer and reporter John Carlin, coauthor of *Rafa*, his autobiography. Carlin was annoyed at finding himself on a show by the American news agency, AP, on which that report was mentioned, which he branded as exaggerated, but you only need to understand Nadal to see that the thought had seriously crossed his and his team's mind. "That possibility, a distant one, will have to wait for now, and I hope forever," wrote Carlin.

In those days of uncertainty, comparable only to the period between June 2012 and February 2013, when Nadal once again thought that tennis would be over for him, the sports clothing company Nike was working on designing a tennis shoe with a special sole for that delicate left foot. But as time went on, Nadal's mood in Mallorca grew increasingly worse. He couldn't train. Nor did he know if it made sense to do so again. That was when his uncle and trainer, Toni Nadal, thought of a solution: Rafael would train forty-five minutes a day sitting on a chair. That way, at least, he would move his arms and work out energy and frustrations, even if he couldn't put weight on his foot.

Nadal, who is so exposed publicly and who generates so much interest that a blister on his left hand once became exaggeratedly famous, always prefers to downplay his physical problems. Even so, he always has to end up talking about them, which has been a central paradox of his life. "I think that if you asked the players, the great majority of them would say that they're playing or have played with pain through a season. That's how it is: the calendar doesn't take a break; you're forced to play a lot of tournaments, and hard court is bad for the joints. I won't see it happen, but hopefully new generations will have a healthier circuit," he says.

While the new generations are arriving, the Spaniard isn't the same as he was at the beginning. Whenever he can, he plays through matches standing at the baseline to try and get shorter points with less physical deployment. He serves a little bit better, and has more confidence and resources when it comes time to move up to the net. There are still heroic, agonizing, unthinkable shots, such as a spectacular parallel passing shot or a short crossed backhand when he seems to be beat. But it's impossible now for him to play a match like the one against Coria at the Foro Italico—in part because tennis has changed, and also because Nadal has changed.

With a more refined physique and a few pounds less, the passage of time is not indifferent to the Spaniard who, ever since he turned twenty-five years old, refers to his age more and more frequently. In that final stretch of his career, which was longer and much more successful than any expert had anticipated, the Spanish player's goal was to be no longer measured by the results nor the rankings. He tirelessly denies it, he turns attention away from the topic when he can, but at those heights his battle was with history, a 14–17 comparison with Federer (May 2016 figures), who wants to catch up and then surpass.

That's why the injuries and prolonged absences from the circuit frustrated him so much. He is perfectly capable of accepting a defeat, but what he can't wrap his head around is being unable to compete. Had he won the final in 2014 in Australia, and the one in 2012 against Djokovic, which he was so close to doing, his race against Federer to reach the pages of history would be neck and neck. The advantage that the Swiss player has is five years ahead and, although he is still playing a great game, at this point in time Nadal hasn't won a Grand Slam since July of 2012 in Wimbledon. He has a great opportunity, and the added motivation, of getting a second Olympic gold in Río 2016. (And he won that gold medal—not in singles, but in doubles alongside his friend Marc López.)

After the frequent betrayals of his body, the question is obvious, and Nadal responded in February 2015, in Río de Janeiro, his thousandth return after a period of injury. *"Is his physique becoming his worst rival, even over his opponents on the circuit?"* "I don't consider my physique as a rival. It has helped me a lot during my entire career; it helped me get where I am, and I'm confident that it will continue with me where possible so I can continue competing well and be in the condition to do what I like."

He's confident, but will it be possible? The answer is clear. Knees, foot, heel, abdominals, back . . . even his iron resolve, starting in 2015. Everything failed at some point, but Nadal keeps on.

CHAPTER 20

Unrepeatable

"I THINK FEDERER WILL CRACK open some beers tonight." Direct and graphic, Mats Wilander knew that on that last day of May in 2009, something very important had just happened. A week later, Wilander saw his intuitions confirmed. Robin Söderling was approaching the net on that cold, cloudy afternoon in Paris when something he saw on the other side threw him into an unusual situation. Instead of cursing his loss, a smile lit him up inside. He was happy for his rival's victory. He had just lost and he was smiling. "He was crying, he was so happy. And I was sad, but when I saw how happy he was, I was also a little happy for him. It was very strange . . . I told myself, 'But, what are you doing?!'"

When Söderling is talking about "him," he means Roger Federer, against whom he had just lost the Roland Garros final. What was he doing? Simple. Söderling had been the direct cause of, and witness to, a key event in tennis history. In the duel between Nadal and Federer for eternal glory, Nadal's earlier victory in the 2008 Wimbledon final had allowed him to overcome a formerly insurmountable barrier. Now, in this fourth round of the 2009 Roland Garros, something incredible was unfolding, which hadn't happened yet and would not happen again until 2015: Rafael Nadal being defeated in the French Open. In a way, the credit for defeating Nadal was Söderling's, and the credit for lifting Federer was his, as well.

History isn't always written during the finals. The fact that Söderling paved the way for him in that tournament is something for which Federer will be eternally grateful. He had lost to Nadal in the semifinals of 2005, and in the finals of 2006, 2007, and 2008. The latest defeat had been especially humiliating, a 6–0, 6–3, and 6–1 that made the Swiss player seem like a toy at Nadal's mercy at one of the most emblematic settings in tennis. "It was perhaps the best tennis that has been played on earth," Nadal admitted years later. But for Federer, it was a humiliation. The last thing the Swiss player wanted was to cross paths with the Spaniard again on that orange rectangle. And then Söderling showed up and played a perfect match against Nadal. He hit the ball from the baseline with incredible authority. The Spaniard's top spin couldn't hurt him; in fact, it seemed to give his own strikes more power. That was how the Spaniard spent his afternoon, running from side to side, disarmed as he had never been before on a clay court. Controlled. Dominated. Bested.

That's how it went, until 5:55 p.m. on May 31, 2009, when a wide volley from Nadal closed the match with a 6–2, 6–7 (2–7), 6–4, and 7–6 (7–2) for the Swede. Söderling raised his thumb in a sign of victory, but it was much more than that. He had broken the Spaniard's streak of four titles and thirty-one consecutive victories. Nadal left quickly, clearly bothered by the chant of "Robin, Robin!" still being sung by a stadium crowd that clearly was rooting for the Swede.

Sixty-four months after that unique day, Robin Söderling doesn't look like a tennis player, although he still is one at heart. It's an October afternoon in 2014, in a rainy autumnal Stockholm, and the man who changed the history of tennis looks more like an executive at some Swedish fashion firm. Thin and fit, at 6 feet 5 inches, he still weighs 192 pounds, maybe a bit less. But he's a different person. Impeccable in his dark blue detailed jacket and light blue shirt with no tie, the Swede's relaxed and happy smile doesn't quite hide the fact that he's missing something. He's sitting behind a mahogany desk in a dark office that has been on the second floor of the traditional club, Kungliga, for half a century. To his left, you can see through the window how the

Bulgarian Grigor Dimitrov, another powerful player, a great presence, is doing what he likes most: playing tennis. Now Soderling directs the Stockholm tournament, but he would trade it all to play again, like Dimitrov.

The smiling Swede is a key figure in the history books of his sport, a man who interrupted a huge streak of Nadal's, who prevented Federer from joining Pete Sampras, John McEnroe, Ivan Lendl, Mats Wilander, Stefan Edberg, Guillermo Vilas, and a few others on the list of men capable of winning three out of the four Grand Slams, and who all choked on the fourth. No, Söderling reset history, got Nadal out of Roland Garros through sheer will and who, after falling against Federer in the final, was happy for his rival, who in that instant became like Donald Budge, Fred Perry, Roy Emerson, Rod Laver, and Andre Agassi: a champion of each of the four greats. Six months later, Nadal joined the list after winning in Australia. Seven years later, Djokovic joined the list by winning Roland Garros.

Söderling challenged history, changed its path and two years later was unable to write his own anymore, that history in which he had been so well profiled. The "no" is forceful when you ask him if you are talking to a former tennis player, but the truth is by that time the Swede had spent more than three years without playing on the circuit due to mononucleosis.

"I will try to play again, and I hope it works." But it wouldn't work, and he retired in 2015. In 2011, Söderling was shaping up to be a serious threat to the Roger-Rafa-Nole trio. He was an angry player, with potential, talent, and cheek, a victory-seeking machine, a man who put success above almost everything and wasn't exactly loved by most of his colleagues on the circuit. "In 2011 I won four tournaments in six months. I always thought I would play until thirty-five, so I still have hope. When this happened, I was in the best years of my career . . ."

A grimace crosses his face when he hears that Federer is lucky even when it comes to contracting mononucleosis. When the Swiss player got it, it lasted some months and didn't affect his career at all. Söderling's case was completely different. "At the start it was horrible. The first six months I couldn't walk even thirty-three feet. I had to rest after sixteen. That lasted six months, but the first year was really bad . . ." Three years later, Söderling is going through what he calls "postviral fatigue." "Sometimes, if you're unlucky, the body can be tired for a very, very long time. Mario Ancic also had a lot of trouble, it took him years to return. The doctors tell me that everyone recovers 100 percent. It takes some two months. Others, three years."

The Söderling who has postviral fatigue sees things that he never used to. Sometimes he goes into the locker room or the players' room at the tournament he directs. "Small things . . . You see players that drink a little water and then throw the bottle. I did that when I played, too. I never thought about it. But now, from the tournament's perspective, you see two hundred bottles of water, and . . . There are other things too; for example, they take the towels. When you're on the other side, you think differently.

"As a player, you're spoiled a lot. You have everything, every week, and you take it for granted. You get used to it, you think it's normal. Although it's also a hard life, it's said that you have everything and that you win lots of money and travel around the world, but it's a hard life, especially physically, but also mentally. You have to perform every week, you have the pressure of the media, of the sponsors, the ranking, everything. Every week, and you don't get a lot of rest."

The tennis player who could no longer be a tennis player, is now dedicated to years of that sports "limbo" and to designing a ball that adapts itself to any surface. He traveled to Thailand to explain to the manufacturer in person how he wanted it to be. "I think that we players know tennis better than the machine that makes the balls. It's amazing; up until now there has never been a ball designed by a tennis player." That he named the ball RS provides a certain insight into the state of Söderling's thinking: if life will now condemn him to always see tennis from the outside, then at least he will leave his mark on the courts somehow.

Söderling's situation is, at the end of the day, unusually human. He reached the top of his professional life at twenty-five years of age. The greatest thing he achieved happened when he was barely starting to be an adult. "There is nothing in life that compares to walking into the Philippe Chatrier stadium, full of spectators, and knowing that millions of people are going to see you on television. And you play really well and defeat Federer, and you play really well and defeat Nadal. You can't get that from any other aspect in life." Söderling insists on one thing: his victory of Nadal in the eighth-finals of Roland Garros isn't what he most values when he looks back on his career. "I don't want to be remembered for winning a match against a player. I think that victory of mine says more about him than me, about how incredible his record was. I want to be remembered for having played two Grand Slam finals and winning ten titles. To me, that's bigger than having won that match."

That same month, Söderling had lost, 6–1 and 6–0, against Nadal in the Rome eighth-finals, although the results were tricky. "I hit ten point winning shots, and despite that I still lost," said the Swede, who five-and-a-half years later still remembers the match well, an eighty-four minute battle at the Foro Italico that, due to its length, contradicts the impression that he had been steamrolled. "I played well," he says, despite the results. "It was a good match. That's how it goes. Maybe in Paris I played 15 percent better and he 5 percent or 10 percent worse."

When his parents separated in 2009, which ended up being temporary, Nadal went through a personal rough patch. He was getting in every fight he could find: against the president of the Royal Spanish Tennis Federation (RFET), Pedro Muñoz; against the chief of the ATP, Etienne de Villiers; against the antidoping control system; and against the deal that the tournament in Madrid was giving him. Nadal was a kettle under too much pressure. It was no small thing that he was also going through something unprecedented after his explosion in 2005: losing two consecutive tournaments on clay, the Madrid final and the round of 16 at Paris. The Swede, without intending to, actually did the Spaniard a favor because it allowed Nadal to celebrate his birthday in Mallorca for the only time in years. June 3 had always been an away work day for Nadal, embroiled as he usually was in the refined symphony of conquering Roland Garros.

"I think that in, a certain way, losing helped him," ventures Söderling. "If you lose once, you never have to think 'I've never lost here.' It takes away all the pressure." There's no doubt that Nadal would have rather kept the pressure, but the Spaniard didn't make excuses. In fact, he said loud and clear that the defeat by Söderling was his own fault, unusual for him because he always tries, often unsuccessfully, to give the credit to his rival.

"I played short, very badly. I think the defeat was more my fault," Nadal said to a press room full of reporters who wanted to scrutinize every word, every gesture, of the man who had just lost his invincibility. "If we both play to our greatest abilities, I should win on this surface."

Although, objectively, the analysis was true, Söderling didn't like it at all. "If he says he played poorly, that's his problem, I would never say something like that." Five years later, he still thought the same. "When I lose a match, I could say that I didn't play very well, that I know I could play better, but I would never take merit away from my opponent. You don't do that. You can say it to your trainer, but not to the media. I don't think it's proper.

"Tennis isn't about that, it's not about who is the best when you're playing your best game. Tennis is about winning matches, and no one can play their best game in every match. Why are Nadal or Djokovic so good? Because they're not playing their best game. They play, maybe, four or five perfect matches a year, and player ranked one hundred plays three, four, or five really good games. But they manage to win matches when they're not playing their best games, they manage because they're so good. No, tennis isn't about when you play your best.

"And the truth is, I've been thinking about that, that if I had been a little more like Federer or Nadal, a bit more solid, I could have gotten even farther. Because when I played my best game I could beat anyone. I beat Federer, Nadal, Djokovic. I was, surely, one of the three best players in the world when I played my best game. But, I insist, that is not tennis."

Whatever tennis is, the exchange of words between the Spaniard and the Swede went beyond that match. Nadal, simply put, did not like Söderling. "Söderling is a strange guy," Nadal said after beating the Swede in Wimbledon, in 2007, by 7–5 in the fifth set of a match that lasted five days due to interruptions by rain. "I greet him and he never answers." Two years later, on the afternoon of May 31, 2009, Söderling got tired of being asked about that topic. "I'm fed up with this question. To me, he's just a player like any other on the circuit."

But, is it true that he wouldn't return greetings to any of his peers? Söderling searches for the words while he gets comfortable behind his desk in the Kungliga. "No . . . Well, maybe if I didn't see them. I noticed that sometimes people would wait for the other to say 'hello' first. If I run into you, I wait for you to say 'hello' to me, and if you don't say 'hello,' then I don't say 'hello' to you. And then they say, 'No, he's not greeting you.' You understand what I'm saying?" But Nadal was referring to something else: encounters in halls, players' lounges, training courts, and no response from the Swede when he greeted him. "I would never do that," a postmononucleosis Söderling insists. "Maybe if I didn't see him, maybe I didn't say 'hello' to all the players because you see them all the time."

Söderling, in his thirties, nevertheless has a critical opinion of the twenty-something. "I see myself in some matches and I don't seem like the most sympathetic of people. Maybe I wasn't on the court, but outside of it, it was different." It's likely, he adds, that he took tennis too seriously. "Maybe too seriously, because when I played I didn't do much else. I like to play golf, I like to hunt, I like to scuba dive, but I didn't do it because . . . No, no, I had to focus on tennis. I was in a bubble, my whole life was tennis."

But by the end, his obsession with tennis gave him success, it worked. "It worked, yeah, but maybe it works even a little better if you have something else." And then he returns to the memory of those two finals, the defeat against Federer in 2009 and the loss to Nadal in 2010, "They're two different players, so it's hard to say which of the two is better. To me, Federer is better. It was much harder for me to play against Federer than against Nadal. Because Nadal is one of the best players of all time; that's huge, of course, but each time he walked onto the court I knew what to expect. I knew what he could do and what he couldn't. I know that what he does he does very well, but I could always prepare a strategy, I knew what would happen. "I played against Federer, I don't know, fourteen, fifteen, sixteen times, and I think I can say I only played well maybe three times. I played so bad every time . . . And I would say, 'Why do I play so poorly against Federer?'"

Söderling, who only beat the Swiss player once, in the 2010 Roland Garros final, out of the sixteen times he faced him, knows exactly why he played so poorly. "He would make me play poorly. I could win or lose against Nadal, but there was much more of a rhythm. You know he can run for five hours, that all the balls are going to come back, that he's an incredible player. Out of the six times I played him, I probably played well four or five times, because it's not as hard to play against Nadal as it is against Federer." It was eight times, really, with six wins for the Spaniard and two for the Swede, who is still obsessed with how indecipherable the Swiss player's game is, and with his capacity to concentrate.

In that final on June 7, 2009, there was an intruder who could have changed history. Jaume Marquet Cuna, a Spaniard who tends to interrupt large sporting events, jumped onto the clay at Philippe Chatrier wearing a T-shirt from the Swiss team, a Barcelona flag, and a traditional Catalonian hat that, for a couple of seconds, he pulled down onto Federer's head.

Marquet Cuna has nicknamed himself "Jimmy Jump," a strangely appropriate name for someone who suddenly leaps onto the most sought-after courts of the sport and disrupts everything. That includes the final of the European championship soccer tournament, which he interrupted in Lisbon in 2004.

"I remember that guy when he ran onto the field. It was at the start of the second set. I didn't know what he was doing. I saw that he wanted to catch Federer. I didn't know what to do. It was kind of scary, because he could have had a knife or something like that." The security at Roland Garros was incredibly upset, because Jimmy Jump managed to avoid several of the six agents and even jumped over the net towards Söderling before being tackled. That moment, unheard of, could have thrown the Swiss player off balance. After all, it was the Roland Garros final; he wasn't playing just a normal match.

"It was mentally difficult; I was thinking about what it would mean to win this tournament," Federer admitted with the trophy by his side. "I was very nervous at the start of the third set, because I realized how close I was. The last game was almost impossible for me to play. I just wanted to come out good. It was a roller coaster of emotions."

The appearance of Jimmy Jump could have broken Federer's concentration, it also occurred to Söderling during those few minutes. "I told myself I needed to concentrate and win one or two points. And I thought that Roger might have lost his concentration a bit. But after a game, he was playing well again. He could forget about everything and play. That shows how strong he is, mentally." And then, at 5:12 p.m. on June 7, 2009, in Paris, Federer stopped caring about the 54 degrees and the heavy skies. Söderling smashed a right-handed hit against the net, and the Swiss player knelt and started to cry. When he stood up, his sobbing was replaced by a smile, and then Söderling understood that he should be happy as well. "It's like when you see a very sad person, or you watch television and get sad yourself. If you see a happy person, you also feel happy. And for me it was much, much easier to accept losing to Federer than to anyone else. Because he is so good, and to me he's the best player of all time."

Hundreds of miles from Paris, another man was excited for Federer: Rafael Nadal. "I cried when Roger Federer won Roland Garros," the Spaniard confessed in an interview with *L'Equipe*. Months later, Nadal told the Swiss *Tages Anzeiger* that he hadn't really cried. "I didn't cry, but it was very emotional for me. I felt that he deserved it after losing to me in 2005, 2006, 2007, and 2008 in Paris. I'm not the type of person who wants his rivals to always lose." Nadal watched the match on television at his home in Manacor. He doesn't tend to watch a lot of tennis when he leaves a tournament early, but he didn't want to miss that final. "I was excited. He deserved to win that tournament one day, after so many finals and semifinals. He deserved to win all four Grand Slams."

Five years after the unforgettable May 31, 2009, Söderling feels in hindsight that he distributed his wins poorly. "I think about that a lot. The first year, I beat Nadal and lost to Federer. The next year, I beat Federer and lost to Nadal. I found myself thinking, many times, couldn't I have done both things in the same year? Because I would rather have won the French Open once and lost the next year in the first round than to have gotten to two finals."

CHAPTER 21

Women

THE MIRROR DOESN'T LIE. IT's Martina Navrátilová, she's seated to my right; we're talking about tennis, and she has her hair in curlers. Curlers? Yes, Navrátilová is preparing for the television program she participates in during the US Open. She takes advantage of the forty minutes that she is given for putting on makeup and brushing her hair before standing in front of the camera to be interviewed. We talk, although she is always looking toward the mirror so that the makeup artist can do her job correctly. It's an unusual interview; we don't speak face to face but alongside each other. It doesn't matter; there's a mirror, so in a way I can face her as we speak.

Navrátilová is a legend who surpasses her sport and sports in general. Her life is marked by two of the great milestones of the twentieth century: the Cold War and the fight for civil rights. The player left what was, at the time, communist Czechoslovakia in the '70s. Then, in the United States she fought for gay and lesbian rights and, years after winning the fight, asked for her girlfriend's hand in marriage on television at the 2014 US Open. The connecting thread between the two decisions describes Navrátilová better than anything else: she is passionate about freedom.

So it is that on her Twitter account, her tag is simply @Martina. No other Martina could possibly compete; she expresses her opinions about everything, but mostly about politics. A regular reader of the *New York Times*, politically she is to the left of the Democratic Party and an ocean's distance from the Republicans. It would be very interesting to talk politics with her, but if Navrátilová is letting her interviewer see her putting on her makeup and with curlers in her hair on that New York summer afternoon, it's to talk about tennis. To talk about the two "R"s.

If it's fair to describe the rivalry between Nadal and Federer as epic, then the one between Navrátilová and Chris Evert was surreal. They played eighty times between 1973 and 1988, with forty-three victories for the offensive left-handed player and thirty-seven for the intelligent counter-striker.

In the case of Nadal and Federer, it's difficult to try to compare them with the women, says Navratilova, because the playing style that each matches—man to woman—doesn't fit the same matching player's personality. "Roger plays more like I do, and Rafa more like Chris, but Nadal is much more frank and talkative, while Federer is the diplomatic one. He never, ever smells bad. Which was, basically, the case with Chris. So it's a combination, but there are doubtless some similarities." They're all very kind, yes . . . " adds Navrátilová, who understands Jimmy Connors's criticisms in part. "There's no doubt that the clash of personalities was a lot greater during those times. There's no love between Djokovic and Federer, but no hate either. There's not a real conflict, compared to what would happen between Jimmy, John, and the others. Or the matches between Năstase and McEnroe, with everyone howling and yelling. And you ask yourself, what would happen today with players with that kind of personality. There's very little controversy these days. I think that the 'hawk's eye' prevents a lot of that, but even more I think that everyone is much more kind. There's also not a contrast of personality and style; everyone is controlled, both emotionally and when it comes to their style of play. You don't have what would happen between Connors and Borg, or McEnroe and

Becker. There's always tension; even if you liked the other player, you could feel more tension than there is today. And let's not forget Lendl. There was no love between Connors and Lendl nor between Lendl and McEnroe; there was a lot of tension between them."

The American, who believes that players today give "canned answers" in their press conferences ("they're very boring, they don't really say anything"), feels that her rivalry with Evert was superior to Nadal-Federer. "They're just behind us. You have to take into account quality as well as quantity, and we had both things. The quality of a rivalry is impactful, and that is what puts Chris and me in the stratosphere, because most of the time it was the number one against the number two, and mostly in the finals. And that isn't going to happen again."

Navrátilová is intrigued by how "Swiss" Federer is. "He's very diplomatic. He might be spontaneous, but he is Swiss, and you can't take that out of him. I don't know if it's his Swiss heritage or if Roger is just like that, but he's so nonconfrontational, so passive aggressive, but in a likable way . . . " The kind of tennis that is played today is also a factor that contributes to the players not having tension like there was in the '70s, the former number one thinks. "They don't go up to the net like we did, because they can't. The game on the court is also nonconfrontational, because they beat each other from the baseline. It's not that old 'I'm coming toward you, I'm going to the net, and you have to get by me.' They don't see each other's faces, they're not close. A lot of the time, we were at the net at the same time, and that doesn't happen much now. There's also less interaction with the spectators. I talked to them a lot. Some players do that; there's Fabio Fognini, for example. But Rafa never changes his expression; Roger doesn't either. Novak is much more emotive, but he doesn't relate to the spectators like we did."

Navrátilová isn't convinced by the notion that the world is different now, that you can't compare the lives of the current players to that of someone like her, who ran away from her country to avoid living under a communist dictatorship. "No, politics doesn't have anything to do with this . . . In fact, I think the fans have become more nationalistic. I once played in New York with Hana Mandlíková and they were supporting her even though I was American. They didn't want me to win because I won too much. There's no way that would happen to Federer, or to Andy Roddick, or to Pete Sampras."

As for another left-handed player like Nadal, Navrátilová never had the chance to sit down and talk to the Spaniard. "I would love to! He's not truly left-handed, but I'm sure that by now he thinks like someone who is." And what would she sit down to talk to Nadal about? "Just to talk, the same as with every top player. Compare experiences, philosophies, what motivates you, how we're different. I think we would find many more similarities among the champions than differences. I've talked to Roger, we've had dinner a few times. I spent some time with Roger, I would love to do the same with Rafa."

Days before the conversation with Navrátilová, a radiant Chris Evert also compares her rivalry with the Nadal-Federer duo. The slim, stylish dress she's wearing that afternoon in the New York summer highlights the figure of a woman who always knew how to be elegant, but it also serves to mark the contrast between her and Jimmy Connors, with whom she had exchanged some words on a television network. A couple in the '70s, Chris and Jimmy had even been engaged at one time. Four decades later Connor, pale, a bit hunched, and dressed in a wool cardigan, looks almost like Evert's father. He refers to her as "Marie Christine" in a reedy voice. Evert, proud, smiles just enough and sets her boundaries. A year later, it was confirmed that she was right not to lower her guard; Connors published an autobiography in which he hinted that in the '70s Evert had an abortion after becoming pregnant by him.

"I think the reason why the rivalry that I had with Martina was so fascinating," Evert explains, "was because of the contrasts. Had it been two Martinas or two Chrisses, I don't know that people would have followed with so much fascination. But she had come from Czechoslovakia, and I was American. She was emotive and I was cold. She was aggressive and I was a counter-striker. We were different in how we looked, in how we played, and our personalities. That made it possible for two different types of fans to form. Do I see that today between the men? Yes. Djokovic, Nadal, and Federer are different, they play differently depending on which surface it is, they have different personalities, and they have their followers. That's what makes tennis grow, the contrast."

Evert thinks that the business of tennis got so big, and television shows so many details, that the players "can't allow themselves" to be spontaneous. When she sees Federer play, what does she see? "Beauty," she responds, laughing. And when she sees Nadal? "A warrior. A soldier." And then she corrects herself, "I would say that I see Federer as an artist. And Nadal, a warrior."

"How does a rivalry work when you also admire your opponent?"

"If you have two good people you can have a good rivalry, if you have two people with good hearts. And I think that Roger and Rafa are good guys. If the person is bad, then the rivalry won't be good."

"Was the rivalry between Connors and McEnroe a good one?"

"No, they didn't care for each other. They didn't like each other at all. Maybe we should move to another topic . . ."

CHAPTER 22

Wood

PETE SAMPRAS HAD ROD LAVER on the other side of the net when an unexpected problem came up: Sampras had just broken his grip and he didn't have a replacement racket. "They gave him a wooden one," Laver remembers. "He told me he couldn't feel any speed, although he definitely had enough timing to hit the ball." That had been, many years back, a casual match without ambitions between two legendary tennis players, but Laver thinks that if you made one of today's players play on the circuit using wooden rackets from one day to the next, he would suffer a shock. Between the rackets that Laver used and the ones used today by Nadal and Federer, there is a world of difference.

The difference in speed between his era and the current one is huge, explains Laver, who remembered how his trainer, Charlie Hollis, insisted that he needed years to perfect each one of the strikes in tennis: two years for the right, two for the backhand, two for the serve. "It's not like that now," Laver maintains. "The players today can perfect that all in six months. When we would play, it was serve and volley, serve and volley. We picked up some balls and we would get back to playing, because we didn't have many ball boys at the time either."

The Australian Darren Cahill was a good singles and doubles player as well as Andre Agassi's trainer. A collector of rackets, he has more than two hundred in storage in Las Vegas and knows that there's nothing more important in the sport. "You have to understand your racket, trust in it. It's a part of your family. Those stories about people who take their rackets to bed and sleep with them . . . we live for that. We see our rackets more than any living person in our lives." Cahill confided one of Agassi's secrets to the *New York Times*: the former number one would buy the rackets that his rivals used to see why a certain strike was so good for them. It was part of his preparation when preparing for certain matches.

Tennis has changed, and not just because Rafael Nadal in 2015 introduced a racket with a microchip. Rather, the main thing is that rackets today allow for unimaginable strength and strikes that the old wooden rackets could not. A racket that weighs more than ten-and-a-half ounces is considered heavy today. Half a century ago, the wooden rackets weighed up to five ounces more. It's a new world filled with rackets that seem like catapults. Now, the players hit harder than ever before, and they also injure their wrists more than ever before. It makes sense; the human body, unlike the rackets, has limits.

The question has been circulating through tennis for years: who would suffer more with a wooden racket, Federer or Nadal? The Swiss Marc Rosset answers with a cruel irony, "The racket would suffer, with Nadal rackets always suffer."

Martina Navrátilová thinks that none of today's stars could play with one of those heavy wooden rackets from the '60s: "No one could. Roger couldn't play like he does, because he would miss a lot of balls; he would be forced to change his strike." Nevertheless, the technological setback would affect Nadal even more, according to Martina, "It would be a bigger deal due to the way he hits the ball."

Nadal's exaggerated top spin, which forces the ball to rotate at a speed unmatched on the circuit, is only possible with modern rackets. With the old ones, because of size, cords, materials, and weight, it would be impossible. "I think that Rafa took the game to a higher level," analyzed the Austrian Thomas Muster, who reached the top position in the world with a powerful play style using top spin from the back of the court, which categorizes him as a link between Guillermo Vilas from the '70s and '80s and Nadal in the modern game. "If you look at Guillermo Vilas and at Rafa, there's the evolution of tennis. They have similar styles, left-handed and with top spin."

Jimmy Connors, who, for the longest time clung to his legendary metallic T-2000 racket, prefers not to analyze the topic too much, "Opinions are like shoes, everyone has a pair."

It's been years since the spectators got used to seeing impossible shots, from supersonic serves to parallel passing-shots in which the ball clears the net with great height but then falls sharply into the limits of the court. But the kings of impossible shots in 2014 were the Bulgarian Grigor Dimitrov and the Australian Nick Kyrgios. The central court at Wimbledon was a key factor in Kyrgios's response becoming the shot of the year. Rafael Nadal launched a forehand that forced the Australian into a bad spot. Kyrgios's reaction, with no time to move and hit the ball, was to place the racket between his legs; the ball bounced and fell tamely on the other side, impossible for the Spaniard to respond to. It's one of those shots that you make during training, but is hard to pull off in the most famous tennis stadium in the world. It's also one of those shots that would have been impossible with a wooden racket.

The setting of Dimitrov's strikes was less massive, although not thereby less attractive: the Stockholm Kungliga Tennis Stadium, probably the most beautiful indoor tennis stadium in the world. On that October in 2014, Dimitrov scored two very unorthodox points consecutively against the American Jack Sock. The second point was a shot between the legs that became a winning strike, but the first was superior. Dimitrov was winning 30–0 and connected with a good open serve that Sock returned with a furious forehand straight to his rival's shoes. The ball landed to Dimitrov's left, next to his leg, and the Bulgarian did the same thing as Kyrgios: he had no time, the ball was coming in at supersonic speeds, he couldn't even set up a backhand attempt. Maria Sharapova's boyfriend at the time opted to transform into a wizard instead: Dimitrov moved the racket behind his back to the left, positioning it vertically to the floor, with his head pointed at the ground. The ball returned to the opposing side of the court at a speed spurred by all the violence of Sock's own shot and left Sock reaction-less. The Bulgarian didn't need to give the ball any acceleration at all, he just moved his racket. It was enough to put the ball in precisely the right spot.

Two shots that would be impossible with wooden rackets. Or not? Dimitrov answers honestly while we walk through Melbourne Park: "I think the first, yes, would have been impossible. The second, to be honest, I think would merit some discussion." The Bulgarian has no problem admitting his amazement at the wooden rackets that were used twenty-five years before he was born. "It's pretty incredible how they played with those rackets. It would be very interesting to try some shots with one!"

Stan Smith played and won two Grand Slam tournaments with wooden rackets, but he also experienced the jump to metal, to graphite, and to the modern compounds. He knows quite well what he's talking about. "Some of the shots you see today are only possible thanks to modern rackets," he says. "Rackets today are lighter than ever, but larger as well. The cord is completely different. All of that changed tennis dramatically." In his years, Smith remembers, everyone played with more or less the same kind of racket; there wasn't the variety of today. The American amuses himself imagining what the players of his era could have done with today's technology. "Laver would have loved these rackets, because they would have let him put as much spin on his right as on his backhand. For Rosewall it wouldn't have been much of a change, while I would have been able to give my shots some more spin. Or maybe not, but doubtless I would have had more control over my shots from the back; I could have hit the ball harder. Everyone would have been able to hit harder if they'd had these rackets. Just like they do today."

Manolo Santana was the most popular tennis player in Spain until Nadal showed up. His mother raised him, as his father died when he was thirteen years old, beaten by an illness he had contracted in prison, where he ended up during his country's Civil War. There was no money in his home, so his first racket was far from being a Dunlop Maxply. No, Santana, who Laver considers to be "a wizard," used the wooden backrest from a chair to make his own racket!

Smith believes that today's rackets would have benefited the Spaniard very much. "Manolo had spin and slice; with these rackets he would have served better and returned much more effectively. These rackets are made for a Santana, for a Laver." "And Vilas!" he adds. "Vilas would have been incredible. It also would have helped Borg; all those players would love these rackets. For Connors and McEnroe, however, it wouldn't have changed much. Maybe they would have helped improve Connors's serve, his control, although he played like he was crazy with his racket."

Aside from Kyrgios's and Dimitrov's two famous shots, which are clearly rarities, Smith also has a clear example of a shot that would be "impossible" with wooden rackets, but which has become one of the most habitual and important ones of the past decade: Rafael Nadal's backhand when he finds himself pinned against the corner, pressured by an opponent. "A strike which would be absolutely impossible with a wooden racket. In fact, it's a shot he hits from the back, when he's beaten; it doesn't work further ahead."

Smith employs a surgeon's precision when the question is reversed: wooden rackets for Federer, Nadal, and Djokovic. *Who would suffer most?*" "It would hurt Nadal. He would be the most affected, by a long shot. With all that spin he puts on his hits, he would hit the outside of the racket once out of every two strikes. He wouldn't have enough string surface. Federer plays a lot more old-fashioned, so he could play with them, although his forehand would also be affected. He wouldn't have the spin that he can put on that strike today. His serve wouldn't be very good either; it would be less effective, the ball would bounce less." And Djokovic? "It would hurt him, too, it would hurt anyone, but it wouldn't complicate his game as much as Nadal's. Federer would be the least affected, and it wouldn't complicate things too much for Murray or Del Potro, either, who hit the ball very cleanly. Their serves wouldn't be as powerful, nor their forehands, but they would still be stronger than everyone else's."

"Would you test yourself using a wooden racket?" Nadal thinks for a couple of seconds before answering: "It's complicated. Let's see. I would like to; it would be trying something different and it could be fun, but clearly we wouldn't be testing out how well we would have been in that era, because we're not accustomed to playing like that. Everyone who played then or has been in the top would be good in this era or any other. You're good, not because of how you hit the ball. You're good because you're good, and ultimately you adapt to the situation." On that he agrees with Connors. "If you were a great player in your era, you would be a great player in any era. Even with the change in technology."

CHAPTER 23

Tears

IT IS UNDENIABLE THAT FEDERER viewed the Davis Cup distantly and with a certain degree of discomfort during important phases of his career. Francesco Ricci Bitti, during his time as president of the ITF, tended to insist that "important things must be difficult." The phrase slips out of him every time someone suggests changing the format of the Davis Cup, about distilling it down to two weeks, turning it into a biennial tournament, and reducing the number of matches to the best of three sets.

The Grand Slams were always the most important for Federer, very much like his peers on the circuit, and he was conscious of the fact that he didn't have a partner of sufficient skills to generate the confidence for a victory at the Davis. That was most important and most difficult, even though he himself had won so much. He had to wait until his career was further along before Wawrinka could offer him a real opportunity to mount an assault on Dwight Davis's trophy.

The Davis was, for different reasons, more difficult than important for Federer, although it had certainly left a deep impression on the Swiss player from his beginnings on the circuit.

Federer's public weepings are well known, and three of the most intense and meaningful happened in Australia.

One of them, the second, occurred during the 2005 Australian Open final, when he received the champion's trophy from Rod Laver's hands.

The third also took place during an Australian Open tournament, after Roger lost in the final four years later against Nadal. The tears, which happened in 2009, gave way to a degree of confusion that has extended to the present.

"God, it's killing me!" Federer said an instant before bursting into tears like a child before fifteen thousand spectators in the Rod Laver Arena.

The phrase was clear, "God, it's killing me." The Swiss player was overcome by the situation, his emotions overflowing. It was understandable; he had arrived at that final with the expectation of matching the fourteen Grand Slam titles record of Pete Sampras. He came to Sunday's match with two-and-a-half days of rest after Thursday, whereas Nadal had himself been massacred on Friday in five hours and fourteen minutes of epic battle over five sets against his compatriot, Fernando Verdasco.

Nadal was exhausted and Federer, fresh and confident, should have won. But the Swiss player lost 6–2 in the fifth set, bested by a rival who, far from seeming exhausted, finished the match exultantly.

Federer lost, and his world came crashing down. It was hard for him to talk at the beginning of his speech during the awards ceremony. The public wouldn't stop yelling encouragements at him.

"Maybe I'll try again later," he said, almost babbling, referring to Sampras's fourteen Grand Slams.

A new shout of encouragement was heard in the Australian summer night, and Federer couldn't take it anymore.

"God, it's killing me!" he muttered. And he gave himself over to crying, really crying. His tears were thick and his sobbing was audible.

The giant screens in the stadium confirmed immediately to everyone what was happening. In the stands, Mirka covered her mouth, both concerned by what her boyfriend at the time was experiencing in front of millions and affected by her inability to comfort him in that instant. Nadal, serious and deeply moved, didn't stop applauding. Laver neither.

In his greatest moment of public weakness, Federer received one of the greatest ovations of his career.

For years, media from all over the world reinterpreted Federer's words from "God, it's killing me," which clearly referred to the painful feelings he experienced at that moment, into a "he's killing me," referring to Nadal.

You could argue that Nadal was "killing" him in the Grand Slam finals, but you could never picture Federer saying that openly at one of the four tennis capitals. No, what was "killing" Federer was his emotions, the disappointment following the anxiety, the unfulfilled desire to keep climbing through history. Additionally, and in great measure, there was the fact that an audience with vast tennis knowledge, as is the case in Australia, had made him feel their affection and respect.

That match in Australia was the third and last in a historic series, one that marked the highest point in the rivalry between the Swiss and the Spaniard.

Seven months before, Nadal had defeated Federer 6–1, 6–3, and 6–0 in the Roland Garros final. The result was humiliating, the worst beating the Swiss player had ever experienced. A month later, six days before the night of tears in Melbourne, Nadal reached the height of his career, again at Federer's cost. His 9–7 triumph in the fifth set of the Wimbledon final changed the development of the "R" years as well as a few other things.

"We might have to rethink the history of tennis," said a breathless commentator from the BBC once Nadal had sealed his victory.

"History held its breath. This was supposed to be the year that would close the debate and define Roger Federer as the best player of all time." That phrase from Jon Wertheim, which introduced his chronicle of the final in *Sports Illustrated*, is a perfect summary of what the Swiss player had brushed up against in those months, and then lost to Nadal, who in little more than half a year had earned the titles from Roland Garros, Wimbledon, the Olympic gold, and Australia.

Despite the pain and the tears that still clouded his vision, Federer had the presence of mind to give Nadal two congratulatory slaps when the Spaniard climbed onto the stage to pick up his trophy. The left-handed player, with the trophy in his arms, went back to Federer, wrapped his left arm around him to hug him, and said a couple of things in his ear while smiling.

"Another extraordinary final from Rafa, he deserves it," Federer praised when he could finally talk.

"Roger, sorry for today, I know how it feels. But remember that you are one of the best in history, and you will beat Sampras's fourteen soon," Nadal cheered him on.

On that night of February 1, 2009, Federer cried intensely and in public, but on the afternoon of September 21, 2003, everything had been much more discrete in the same stadium. Federer had locked himself in a small room in the catacombs of the Rod Laver Arena and had cried in a way that few people had ever seen or would ever see again.

The twenty-two-year-old Federer who let slip a two-sets-to-zero advantage and 5–3 in the Davis semifinal against Lleyton Hewitt had just won Wimbledon two months earlier and had his whole great career ahead of him. The thirty-three-year-old Federer who eleven years, two months, and two days later would shine at Lille to win the Davis for the first time had a notable career behind him, but still more to come (like the Melbourne tears in January 2018, but that's a different story).

CHAPTER 24

Argentina

ARGENTINA IS, WHERE TENNIS IS concerned, a special country. The first time he visited, the very Hispanic Rafael Nadal thought that maybe it would be best not to go back for a while. On the other hand, the first time the very Swiss Roger Federer stepped there, he asked himself why he hadn't gone there before. There is practically no other country where the live-ticker (a sort of bulletin of live results) for even a minor competition on the circuit appears on the front web pages of the country's main news outlets. Nor would a great media outlet headline announce that "the world is talking about Argentinian tennis" over a title at the Palermo tournament, a minor competition without stars. But that's how the tennis-focused Argentina played up the fact that Nadal arrived for the first time in February of 2005. He was talked about a lot, although he still wasn't big on the circuit, and had only won one title, in August of 2004 in Sopot. He had been, for sure, the hero of the Davis Cup, a decisive player in the victorious final three months earlier against the United States in Seville.

The explosion of fame was imminent; the tournament in Buenos Aires would be one of the last times for Nadal that failure might be acceptable. After Buenos Aires, Nadal started a string of successes that would take him to number one in the world and in the fight for being one of the greatest tennis players of all time.

But until then, he suffered. Gastón Gaudio took care of sending him off on that infernal Friday night saturated with humidity, mosquitoes, and backhand slices from the Argentinian who was, at the time, the reigning champion of Roland Garros. The result of the quarterfinals was bitter: 0–6, 6–0, and 6–1. As the years went on, Gaudio turned the match into a mythical event. According to him, when Nadal walked into the locker room after losing, he destroyed his seven rackets. That would be highly unusual, considering that Nadal was a player who always swore he had never broken one in his life, something which his uncle Toni confirms. "I think that Gastón is wrong," Nadal recalled between chuckles nine years later in London. "Well, he's lying! Besides, I never even have that many rackets."

What wasn't a joke was how he had felt after that encounter in Buenos Aires. Nadal was eighteen years old, his innocence and naive adolescence weren't very far in the past, and he had never run into an audience like the Argentinians. "When he came back from that tour, Rafa told me that he didn't much want to play in Argentina again," remembers the then mayor of Manacor, Toni Pastor, who is married to an Argentinian. "He didn't feel comfortable." Makes sense. Manacor is not Buenos Aires, and the Spanish do not "live for sports" in general, and tennis in particular, like the Argentinians, who take it to the limit and sometimes even further. Even after more than a decade of his playing for Barcelona, the fans at Camp Nou were unable to create a supporting chant for Lionel Messi, something that would go beyond the monotonous "Messi, Messi," with elongated vowels that they normally use. It's different in Real Madrid and, especially, in Atlético de Madrid, where the Argentine influence is much more noticeable.

But in 2005, it wasn't like that yet. In ten minutes of playing against Gaudio, Nadal, who has an internal radar and doesn't miss a detail of what happens around him, heard more jeering, booing, and nasty comments than ever in his life to that point. That reticence towards the Argentinian public faded as Nadal grew and better understood the character of a country that had been deeply fanaticized by tennis. Juan Mónaco, one of his best friends on the circuit, explained a lot to him, as did David Nalbandian. And Carlos Moyá, the most Argentinian of the Spanish tennis players, helped educate Nadal in the secrets of "Argentinism."

They were secrets that he did not have access to in April of 2006 in Monte Carlo. Nadal was in the semifinals, facing the most Argentine of the Argentinians: Gastón Gaudio. Again. It was a duel between the 2004 Roland Garros champion and his successor in 2005. Gaudio had won the first three clashes with Nadal, in 2003, 2004, and 2005, and had plainly lost the next two in 2005. Gaudio also had the memory of the 6–3 and 6–0 that he had been dealt by Nadal in the 2005 Monte Carlo quarterfinals. The duel in the semifinals, exactly a year later, was consequently very charged. So much so that Gaudio exploded during a side switch.

"Don't play dumb," said the Argentinian.

"I haven't done anything!" the Spaniard, then nineteen, answered.

"Seriously, don't try to get funny with me," Gaudio insisted at the same time that he did something unheard of in tennis: he lightly pushed his rival with his hand when they crossed while heading towards the chair. Sitting, now, with his towel in hand, Gaudio kept talking to his rival.

"Don't play dumb, don't make faces at me."

"But I haven't done anything to you!" Nadal insisted.

The dialogue can be heard if you look for the video on YouTube, although the sound is bad and of very low quality. Despite that, the conclusion is that the conversation in 2006 closed with a sharp comment from Nadal, "Shut up, sudaca." The expression "sudaca" that Nadal used was derogatory and offensive and not generally used in Spain. Those who do use it, though, use it to sum up all Latin Americans, because the Spanish have a concept of South America that is different from what is politically and geographically correct. To them, South Americans are any and all who were born or live south of the Río Grande, from Tijuana to Tierra del Fuego. That's how it was then, and still is now, that the Spanish joke around with their Latin American friends and call them "sudacas."

Between friends, anything goes and nothing is offensive if you stay within the preset bounds of the friendship. Nadal could, for example, joke around with Juan Mónaco and call him "sudaca" but doing so on the central court of Monte Carlo Country Club in front of television cameras was something else entirely. Did he do it? Nine years later and now retired, Gaudio tends to think not. "I didn't hear him, and I don't think he said it." The Argentinian found out later about the commotion that the supposed "sudaca" phrase had stirred in his country, but he insists that he can't confirm that Nadal said what so many believe he said. "They played me the audio, and I couldn't understand it either."

By January of 2008, everything had changed. Nadal fantasized about being Argentinian. He brought it up in Australia in an interview with *Clarín*, the newspaper with the most pull in Argentina. "I would love to be able to feel what it's like to be Argentinian sometime." Nadal's desire to experience "Argentinity" made many smile in Argentina and bothered many others in Spain. A month after that confession in Australia, during an interview in the Manacor Tennis Club he explained in detail what he had meant by that phrase. He repeated that in November of the same year, because Nadal would have to be in Mar del Plata a few weeks later to play the Davis Cup final against Argentina. Ultimately, he was absent due to an injury, but "Mary," his girlfriend, couldn't see what the problem was in that gray and cold players' lounge at the Paris-Bercy tournament when Nadal was explaining what he had meant, and she listened attentively although she seemed distracted. "I said what I did about wanting to feel what it's like, because the environment that the Davis Cup brings in Argentina is hard to find anywhere else. Someday, I would like to be able to feel that, even if it's clearly impossible to . . ." The "impossible" grated on Nadal's ears as soon as it left his mouth. He remembered the unconditional support he received at eighteen years old in the Davis final in Seville and tried to moderate the statement he had just made. "Of course, with our audience, you also feel incredible things," he clarified. But Argentina is "something else," he admitted again. "It's different there, the chanting and all that, it's a different thing. To live through something similar, to feel all that support behind you as a local, is something I'd like." An Argentinian website took advantage to run a headline, as undeniably logical as it was yellow, and to solidify their cold vengeance nearly two years later, "Nadal goes from 'South American simpleton' to wanting to be Argentinian."

Nadal, who by 2011 knew all the main Argentinian soccer chants by heart, realized that year that during the final at Seville—yes, again—the Spanish supporters would have to put in some extra effort. Ten years after the great crisis that struck their country in 2001, hundreds of thousands of Argentinians were installed in Spain. Quantifying them wasn't easy for the embassy in Madrid, because many of them were moving with a European passport instead of the Argentinian one. Although at the core, that didn't matter; they were all Argentinian. Their customs and some characteristics of their language found fertile ground in Spain, whose people always viewed them sympathetically, although they were at times overwhelmed by the extroversion and self-confidence that they are capable of displaying.

Nadal knew that ten Argentinians can make more noise than one hundred Spaniards. His message was clear: the visiting fans shouldn't be more noticeable than the locals. "What we need to achieve is that in this final, which will be attended by two thousand and something Argentinians, the twenty thousand Spaniards are heard much more than the non-Spanish. They are very imaginative with their chants, which is encouraging in a special way. The whole world knows that the Argentinian public is special and cheers heard," he explained. "Keeping in mind who we're against, the Spanish public has a clearly important task." It's impossible to establish whether Nadal's words were influential, but what is clear is that the Argentinian public did not drown out the Spanish fans in attendance at Seville. And Spain won the final.

Spain not only won the final. Nadal ended up winning over the Argentinians, just as the Argentinians had won him over after the discomfort he felt in 2005. At the beginning of his career he was viewed suspiciously in Argentina; after all, he had appeared during the years that Gaudio and Guillermo Coria were dominating on clay and wrapped that era up; but with time the feeling would change. The return of Nadal in 2015 to an official match in Buenos Aires, ten years after that mosquito-filled night against Gaudio, he received proof of the affection and admiration of the Argentinians. He won the tournament and, before doing so, he spoke a phrase that was met with ovation: "I once said that I would one day like to be Argentinian to feel what it's like to be supported by that audience. That is impossible, but even though I'm Spanish I have to say that it's exciting for me to feel this audience."

The organizers of the Argentinian Open were delighted with Nadal. A year earlier, he had told them "no" after suffering the jammed back that had affected him at the Australian Open, but a "no" received from Nadal is different than one received from other players. "Few players do that," explained Miguel Nido, the executive director of the tournament that is regularly played towards the end of the Argentinian summer. When Nido says "that," he's referring to the way in which Nadal handles matters, the most important of which was having personally called them to explain why he couldn't play in 2014, notifying them furthermore that he wouldn't be playing in 2015, and making his well in advance commitment for 2016. In short, he gave the Argentinians the courtesy of a full and respectful reply.

The series for the first round of the Davis Cup, which he was required to play in March of 2015, made it inadvisable for him to go to Buenos Aires, but Spain's defeat against Brazil in September 2014, for reclassification for the world team changed things; the Spanish would play in July for the Euro African zone. "We have to thank Brazil," Nido said. And Nadal. "When Rafa backed out of the 2014 tournament, he offered to call our principal sponsor to assure them that he would play in the future. Really, he didn't have to say anything, but he understood then, and understands now, like Federer, that when you make a commitment, you have to follow through. Another player withdraws from the tournament and he just says to call his agent."

"I was hoping you would say that." Roger Federer sighed, relieved. In the middle of the flurry that his visit to Argentina had caused, he finally found refuge, finally some hours of peace. It had been a good idea to call Gabriela Sabatini. Federer had never played professionally in South America and decided to pay a part of that debt in December 2012 by playing a series of exhibitions in Colombia, Brazil, and Argentina. Paying the debt and, in doing so, charging about $12 million for playing a total of six matches, according to estimates from several media sources at the time.

It was all very different from those juvenile tournaments in Mexico, Costa Rica, and Venezuela. He had arrived at those countries in the tourist class seats on commercial flights. During this exhibition tour he flew in a private plane and even gave himself a luxury far out of reach of mere mortals: his father, Robert, thought that instead of going directly from Brazil to Buenos Aires, the plane should make a stop at the Iguazú Falls. Said and done: the Federer clan spent a couple of hours by the incredible waterfalls on the border between Argentina and Brazil. "It's one of those places you have to visit at least once in your life," said Tony Godsick, Federer's agent.

The greatest display of commerce and matches in that exhibition tour occurred in Brazil, a much larger marketplace, and the home of the 2014 Soccer World Cup and 2016 Olympic Games. But the country that would impress Federer was Argentina. Upon landing at the Aeroparque—the local airport situated at the border of the La Plata river, the widest in the world—Federer signed autographs for ten minutes for dozens of fans who were waiting for him against a chain link fence. When it comes to tennis, there is no country in the world like Argentina. The Argentinians never won the Davis Cup, nor did they have a number one player (although Guillermo Vilas keeps fighting for the title retroactively), but they love tennis with a passion—often excessively. Federer arrived in that country for two exhibitions that drew forty thousand spectators at a cost of 150 to 400 dollars per ticket.

"This is bigger than I had expected," admitted the Swiss, who was the focus of limitless adoration during his ninety hours in Argentina.

"When are you thinking to return to your planet? Because it's clear you're not from this one," a reporter asked him. "I'm an Earthling," the Swiss man answered jokingly. Another television reporter had handed him some diapers so he could practice how to change them. "This is a country I've been wanted to come to for a while. I've played with Argentinians since I was fifteen years old. The Argentinians normally have to travel to come see me. This time I have traveled to come see the Argentinians," the Swiss player added, once again showing his perfect understanding of the situation. "That's why I want to go to the Boca Juniors stadium and play some soccer there with Juan Martín. I want to try the red wine. I've been told so much about Tigre and Buenos Aires. It's a short trip, but I'll make sure to somehow take some photos home."

Next to him was Del Potro, a frequent rival on the circuit. The memory of the 2009 US Open final which he lost to the Argentinian was evoked more than once, as well as the 19–17 win in the Swiss's third set over Del Potro in the semifinals of the 2012 London Olympics tournament. Del Potro admitted that Federer brings out the best and worst memories of his career. That final in New York still unsettled him, but the Olympic defeat in Wimbledon did, too, for other reasons. "I played the best match of my career against Federer, and I lost the most emotionally difficult match of my career against him," said Del Potro, who cried until four in the morning after the defeat in London. The understanding between the two of them was clear, and Del Potro was generous in his praise when he was asked if he would want to be trained by Federer someday. "Roger said that it is very simple to be number one (once you were number four). To him it's simple! I want him to give me a bit of his talent, and then, yes, I would hire him for life."

The Swiss had some fun and warmly wrapped his arm around the Argentinian's shoulders when he said that he didn't know if the former number one considered himself his friend. Federer not only talked about and played tennis for two consecutive nights; he also had two breakfasts with entrepreneurs, a barbecue, a chaotic gala dinner, and a visit to the Boca Juniors stadium where he showed that he wasn't just a great tennis player, but also a talented soccer player. This was experienced firsthand by the former Argentinian forward, Gabriel Batistuta, who played a match of soccer-tennis against the Swiss. Federer, like Del Potro, showed that he had the same control with his foot as with his racket. Diego Maradona, perhaps the best soccer player of all time, was generous when speaking about Federer, whom he described as the "most perfect machine who had ever been seen playing tennis."

Organized chaos, endless lines beneath the scorching sun, an unstable stadium, shouts, insults, and an hour delay before playing, all came together to create on that first night a dizzying situation that forced Federer to use all of his charisma to save the exhibition against Del Potro. "I felt like I was at a soccer stadium," said the man whom many consider to be the best of all time. So it was that, at the edge of midnight, Federer overcame—with a wide smile and an intelligently ambiguous comment—a few hours that he would never forget. Many things went wrong on the night Argentina was introduced to the seven-time Wimbledon champion.

The organizers were fortunate that Federer didn't understand Spanish, because someone would have explained to him that his match with Del Potro would start an hour late due to a section of the provisional precarious wooden and metal stage giving out with several people in the audience sitting on it! The spectators situated there hurriedly ran from their seats to over-fill the lower rows in a packed stadium for twenty thousand spectators. So the safety conditions were less than ideal. Nor was the stadium seating exactly comfortable. The forty thousand cushions with the inscription, "I saw Roger-Delpo" never arrived at Tigre, a neighborhood north of Buenos Aires.

Maybe in different circumstances the match would have been suspended, because the precariousness of the stadium angered many of the spectators, causing an uproar of shouting in the stands and entrances. Jorge Rial, a known variety show presenter on Argentinian television, was at the edge of a nervous breakdown due to his difficulty in handling the situation and the rain of insults pouring over him from a suddenly aggressive section of seats. And it's very likely that no one explained to Federer the reasons for the massive amount of shouted insults that filled the stadium just twenty minutes before he stepped out onto the court. On the receiving end was a controversial federal judge, Norberto Oyarbide, who abandoned the setting of the exhibition before the end. Many spectators had good reason to be upset: they had needed hours to arrive in their cars, find a place where they could park, enter the stadium, and endure a long wait under the beating sun.

The opening match, in which José Luis Clerc steamrolled Guillermo Vilas, started a half hour late. After another half hour wait, Del Potro's entrance was announced, but then a section of the stands gave out, the lack of control grew even worse, and everything kept getting more and more strange. On the stadium screens, which were small and of low resolution, videos were played of Sabatini, Diego Maradona, and Emanuel Ginóbili, but more than anything else were those promoting the omnipresent mayor of Tigre, Sergio Massa, who the day before had made Federer wait an hour for the start of his press conference, and who a couple of years later would be fighting unsuccessfully for the presidency of the country. Massa did not attend the first match, immersed as he was in the final of the South American Soccer Cup that Tigre would lose in San Pablo and that would end in violence in the changing rooms.

"I thank you, Roger, for traveling so many miles to come to Argentina," Maradona said from one of the videos made to celebrate Federer's South American tour. Before the chaos, the Swiss player's close friends and family had been pleased by their experience, in spite of the exhausting dinner for a thousand people, which the former number one left sooner than expected. The night had been a constant assault by photograph and autograph seekers. "This is fantastic, it's very different from Asia," said Tony Godsick, the Swiss player's agent and right hand. The American, who would also become Del Potro's agent months later, was happy: the intensity, the affection, and the passion with which the Argentinians followed each of Federer's shots had no equal. "I think that Roger must be asking himself why he didn't come to South America years ago."

Gabriela Sabatini's telephone rang at eleven at night. On the other end of the line was Mary Joe Fernández, an important figure in her career. An American of Dominican origin, Fernández was not only one of Sabatini's best friends during her career, but she was also the star of a match that sunk the Argentinian and probably precipitated her retirement: the Argentinian was winning 6–1 and 5–1 in the 1993 Roland Garros quarterfinals before losing 10–8 in the third.

When you tell Fernández that she might have accelerated the retirement that Sabatini announced in 1996 at only twenty-six years of age, the same age at which Björn Borg left tennis, the elegant American, married to Godsick, shudders lightly and genuinely, "Ooh, don't make me feel bad!" Sabatini isn't the type to hold grudges, especially not against a friend. That's why, during that exhaustively hot night, she was happy to get the call and was surprised by the question.

"Can I give Federer your phone number?" Sabatini was away from home when she got the call, dining at a restaurant.

"Of course!"

The phone rang again a bit later. On the other end of the line was Federer, with a proposal: moving up the start of that official dinner he wasn't too excited about, avoiding the food, and "escaping" to see Sabatini.

"And where would you like to eat? I can't think of a restaurant where we would be undisturbed. How about at my home?"

Sabitini knew that just the knowledge she and Federer were dining together in Buenos Aires would create a state of emergency in a ten-block radius. Federer was glad to hear the proposal from the Argentinian, who spends two or three months a year in Switzerland and would, sometime later, be invited by Mirka into their home as a way to return her kindness for the gesture in Buenos Aires.

"I was hoping you would say that!"

The dinner, which was also attended by former tennis player Paola Suárez, dragged on well into the morning hours. Federer slept little during those days in Buenos Aires, during which he also had a long talk with Gastón Gaudio, but he was plainly enjoying himself. The trip to Argentina was special; they treated him like a head of state. One reason why he met with the actual head of state!

The Federers knew little about Cristina Fernández de Kirchner, the president of Argentina between 2007 and 2015. Robert Federer, Roger's father, knew vaguely that she had been widowed by the previous president, who was of Swiss descent. Both father Federer and son Federer received comments in favor of, and against, the visit to the Quinta de Olivos, the private residence of the Argentine presidents. Del Potro made it clear to him that he himself wouldn't go, but that if Federer had made a commitment, then he must honor it with the Head of State. Mary Joe Fernández's mother, much closer to the Latin American politician, told Federer it was best not to go. But Federer had no reason to stick his nose into the turbulence of local politics. The invitation was an honor, and he would accept gracefully. Visiting an acting Head of State in her own home was something unusual in the life of the player, who days before had not had any contact with the Brazilian President Dilma Rousseff, although he had visited the "king" of Brazil, Edson Arantes do Nascimento ("Pele") in his home.

"It's not something that has happened to me often," he admitted, genuinely stunned, before the meeting with the Argentine president. "But I am very honored and pleasantly surprised. It will be very important for me to be able to visit the president of the country, someone so important." Some neighbors waved at Federer as his car went by on the streets of Olivos, an upper middle class area in the north of Buenos Aires, and several were waiting for him at the entrance to the president's villa.

"His grandfather was Swiss," the president told an impeccably dressed Federer. She was talking about her husband in a conversation that extended for a bit less than half an hour, and in which the head of state's official interpreter took care of translating to both sides. Federer gave her a racket, to which the president responded joyfully with a "Wow" of admiration while she displayed it for the camera. The visit was a success for the tennis player, who with one foot in the car and waving his hand in a gesture of last farewells, could see how his hostess, leaning on the frame of the glazed entryway to the setting of the meeting, sighed happily. Federer had won her over.

CHAPTER 25

Paris

ROGER FEDERER IS THE KING of Wimbledon, just as Rafael Nadal is the king of Paris. They are, however, different kingdoms. While the Swiss player receives nothing but encouragement every time he steps onto the court of the All England, the Spaniard is resigned to the fact that, every so often, some French wouldn't be bothered if he were to lose on the Roland Garros clay. "I am used to it, I know all my rivals' names here," said Nadal after the 2009 elimination against Robin Söderling. He was complaining about the cheering on of the Swede. "It's a shame that in a tournament that means so much for me, I'm never in the thoughts of the audience."

Hours later, his uncle Toni was considerably less diplomatic, "The Parisian public is pretty stupid. The French are bothered by the victory of a Spaniard." The argument, repeated for years throughout the Nadal clan but especially in many Spanish media outlets, especially state television, is false. The French, like many spectators in any part of the world, like to be a part of something large, something unusual, and then go back to their homes that night and to the office the next day to be able to say, "I was there, I saw Nadal lose." And Nadal, who never lost at the Bois de Boulogne and would never, until 2015, lose there again, showed himself to be human during that year of 2009 on the orange earth.

For the first time, after winning four consecutive titles. How could you not cheer on a player who was achieving the impossible?

"The French are bothered by the victory of a Spaniard," Toni Nadal insisted, who was perhaps afflicted by a similar attitude that some Portuguese feel toward the Spanish. The smaller country always thinks that the larger looks at it scornfully. The truth is sometimes much more cruel: the bigger is not even aware of what the smaller is doing. "When Rafa is training, he's one of the players who stirs up the most excitement," Toni Nadal points out. "But when he plays, what people want is for him to lose. Basing your happiness on the defeat of someone else seems to me a bad philosophy." The first part of that statement is the key; the French admire Nadal, they like to watch him play, hear him grunt when he trains, to be close to that incredible left arm. If they were anti-Spanish, it would take a lot for them to stand in long lines to find a seat in the secondary courts where he trains, and neither would they watch through the cracks in the wire fence or fight over an autograph. No, the French don't base their happiness on another's defeat. They are enthused by beauty, like everyone else, and also by the unusual, the surprising. Nadal's tennis is beautiful, although it is a different beauty than Federer's. It's beautiful because it is imposing. But even Toni Nadal, despite his love for his nephew, can understand that watching him win at Roland Garros is a habit. And habits, sometimes, are boring.

Söderling, empathetic for Nadal feeling poorly treated at the time, thinks that Nadal shouldn't worry about the issue. "I don't think there's any history with the spectators. They love him! It's true they don't care if he loses, but that doesn't have anything to do with them not loving him. They simply want a different winner. When you win too much, in any Grand Slam, there's a moment in which they'll want to see you lose. You want to see a new story."

A hero of French tennis, Guy Forget doesn't understand how it could be that the Roland Garros public hates Nadal. "When my kids were younger, they and all their friends preferred Rafa over Roger. That there are five spectators in a stadium of fifteen thousand people who yell something doesn't mean anything. Besides, Rafa never did anything that would justify people not liking him. The only thing that could bother Roger's fans is that he defeated him every time he played him there." "I adore Rafa," Forget insists. "And I know a lot of people," he says, emphasizing the 'lot' "who feel the same way."

Arnaud Di Pasquale is a former tennis player and by November 2014 he was the technical director of the French Federation of Tennis (FFT). When he is asked if there is a feeling of antipathy towards Nadal at the Roland Garros, he widens his eyes in surprise. "That's news to me; sounds like an urban legend." The Frenchman breaks down in praise for Nadal, but when pressed he searches for a reason why the public of the Bois de Boulogne might dislike him. "Maybe," and he emphasizes that word, "he doesn't show his feelings as much, his feelings during the speeches. Maybe he's seen as a machine. But let me tell you something: I want to be there when Nadal wins his tenth title. Although, since I adore Nadal, maybe I'm not the most appropriate person to talk about him. Maybe I'm not truly French, I don't know."

Di Pasquale has a great memory of the only match he played against Nadal as a professional. "You had to be securely situated, feet planted on the ground, because otherwise you ended up smashed against the wire fence at the back by his shots. I respect him a lot, he is such a kind person, so educated . . . He always greets you." And by the end, when he fantasized about a day that Nadal would be the ten-time Roland Garros champion, he made a joke. Or perhaps it wasn't really a joke. "We'll talk to the French in the stands, so they cheer him on. That will change starting from now."

CHAPTER 26

Nole

"Just good vibes, nothing more!" Novak Djokovic smiles while he hands out chocolates, and his words present a paradox: there is no one on the circuit who, while promoting "good vibes," unsettles or even irritates as many people. The chocolates are for the reporters, something that would never even occur to any other player, but which Djokovic had turned into a habit during the years of his career's greatest success: opening and closing the season with a box of sweets, the contents of which he would personally share among the journalists, in January in Melbourne and in November in London.

There are more than a few reporters who, forewarned of that tradition, prefer to follow the press conferences from their monitors rather than walk into a room and be faced with a situation where they had to dig around in the multichampion's chocolate box. How do you write about a man who gives you chocolate? It seems like a minor issue, because many in the media are fascinated by that opportunity for close contact, but the implication of a non-objective relationship between a journalist and the person being focused on is no small topic for many reporters.

Which doesn't mean that Djokovic isn't an extraordinary player and a very kind and fun person about whom very few have anything bad to say; the Serb has a prodigious memory and an innate capacity for public relations, and is capable of greeting by tossing out a few words in several languages depending on whom he runs into. He smiles, makes eye contact, always tries to empathize. There are very few number one players in the sport who act like that. Djokovic is so natural and popular that many see him as a future prime minister or president of Serbia, although that would be jumping ahead. He could start as the Minister of Foreign Affairs, since besides Serbian he speaks English, German, and Italian and can hold his own in French and Spanish. He would be a great positive example for the Serbians' image around the world. But while that moment has not yet arrived, the question remains, just who is Novak Djokovic?

Lauren Collins, who in September of 2013, in the *New Yorker*, wrote one of the best profiles ever published about Djokovic, gave some answers. She describes the Serbian as "the third man," an unexpected and often uncomfortable center of power in the era of the two "R"s. "He gives the impression that he would be the person in a magic show dying to be chosen to climb up on the stage," is how the reporter described him. Few on the circuit would disagree with that statement. Almost everything about Djokovic is just a bit excessive: his impossible tennis shots; his celebrations, including imitating his rivals; Serbian political concessions; promoting a gluten-free diet, or the unfortunate photo posted on social media in 2011, in which Djokovic was pictured with Janko Tipsarević, who is aiming a toy gun at him.

If you could accept that Federer is, within the microcosm of tennis, an impeccable gentleman and Nadal a happy adolescent, Djokovic would be a television show host, a movie star, a singer, and a soccer player, all in one. He always has to leave his mark; it's not enough for him to play tennis. He almost always is driven to perform. It's hard to forget one exhibition before Wimbledon in which he drove spectators crazy by slowly lifting his shirt while singing "I'm too sexy for my shirt" next to the Bulgarian Grigor Dimitrov.

Federer and Nadal are classic; they play a match at which there are spectators. For Djokovic, that is too restrictive: he plays a match *with* the spectators. Djokovic is very different from Nadal and Federer, two men much more devoted to the etiquette of tennis and who cannot understand the Serbian's sense of humor nor his love of putting on a show. The period during which he would, tournament after tournament, ridicule his rivals by imitating them did not last long. Djokovic got the message and the imitations became an exception instead of the norm, but if you ask those who were close to the two "R"s in those years, that was not the main issue. "Djokovic isn't well liked because of his arrogance in the locker room more than because of the problem with the imitations." Arrogant or not, the Serbian player is unique. "No, I'll leave that to him," Federer replied once when an Australian journalist commented that Djokovic had imitated the peculiar accent of the reporter's Oceanic country, and asked the Swiss player to do the same.

Federer and Nadal are very different from Djokovic in many ways, and also because neither of them spent seventy-eight consecutive nights when they were eleven years old in a bunker hiding from the bombings of the North Atlantic Treaty Organization (NATO). According to his biography, published five years earlier, the very young "Nole" had said that he wanted to be the number one tennis player. You can't deny the Serb's intelligence or sense of opportunism. The fact is that he would gain very little, as far as image goes, if he simply acted like Federer and Nadal do. His birthright as a Serbian, which he carries with overflowing pride while many others might see it as a burden, is no small factor within the context of a sport in which politics and antiquated traditions hold great weight.

Djokovic never forgets about Serbia, even though he lives in Monaco. There, on the Grimaldi's artificial ground, there was a time when you might run into him and grab a coffee. In 2009, for example. We were sitting at the table of a cafe, on the edge of the road—two journalists and Djokovic's press agent at the time—when a red Mini Cooper pulled up and parked a few feet away. Djokovic climbed out and sat down to join in the conversation. We were temporarily a group of four and talked about anything but tennis. The conversation went through the usual subjects: his Mini Cooper, how good the coffee at this bar was, how nice it was to be in so and so's house and not to be on the road, and then the talk turned to soccer. Djokovic set off on excited praise for Nemanja Vidić, a tough defender on Manchester United around those times . . . about whether Vidić is the best defender in the world, about whether Carles Puyol is better, and so on until, from one moment to the next, his facial expression suddenly transformed. The casual mention that, in the Louis II stadium, the traditional soccer match between Formula 1 drivers and the famous faces of Monaco was about to start changed everything. "Why didn't you tell me?!" Djokovic apologized and left almost instantly. He accelerated, and the red Mini was lost in the distance. He arrived in time to play a match at which he became a constant participant.

Almost four years later, however, he arrived at a stadium to which he would never want to return: La Bombonera. The mythical setting of the most popular team in Argentina, Boca Juniors, treated him unexpectedly poorly. It was November of 2013 and Djokovic was in Buenos Aires to play a serious of exhibitions with Nadal. They both wanted to get to know La Bombonera, and they quickly headed towards it as soon as they finished their match in the Sociedad Rural, in the center of the city. La Bombonera is in the south of Buenos Aires, in the middle of the La Boca neighborhood. It's one of the most special areas in the city due to its history with Italian immigrants and its proximity to the port and the Riachuelo, a waterway that is contaminated beyond imagining, separating the city from the province of Buenos Aires.

Djokovic and Nadal arrived just at the right moment, during the halftime, to greet Sebastián D'Angelo, the third goalie of the team and the costar of the brief series of penalty shots that took place before the start of the second half. "Nadal kicked really well, and Nole more or less. But they were in tennis shoes, they did what they could," the goalie explained. It's true; there wasn't even time enough to put on some cleats, only enough to wear the blue and yellow jersey of Boca and run onto the grass.

Entering the playing field impacted Djokovic. While Nadal couldn't stop smiling for an instant, fascinated by the spectacle and the soccer passion filling him with adrenaline, the Serbian seemed more pale than usual and barely smiled. Nadal offered to let him kick first, but Djokovic answered with a "no, no, no." The Spaniard scored first, kicking decisively to the left. Djokovic, immobilized, stood too close to the ball; he seemed to want to get the penalty over with and kicked the ball straight to D'Angelo's hands. From the second he stood in front of the ball, the crowd in the stands behind D'Angelo's goal didn't stop hissing at the Serbian. Nadal kicked again, another quality shot, and scored the second. Perhaps conscious of what was happening, D'Angelo seemed to let the second shot in, weakly kicked down the middle by Djokovic. From the stands, they kept hissing at him. Nadal they clapped for. Nadal let his third penalty be stopped, while Djokovic kicked his without force or will, making it inevitable for the goalie to be able to catch it. By that time, the Serbian was showing signs of wanting to depart as soon as possible from that inhospitable place.

D'Angelo had an explanation for the Boca spectators' antipathy towards Djokovic, although he evidently couldn't remember how many penalties he had caught, nor from whom. "Nole had a bad time, because they were booing him for saying he wanted the Pope's jersey [San Lorenzo's] and on top of that, I caught three of his shots . . . Nadal, who is more into soccer, was fascinated. I gave him the gloves and he promised to send me something signed," the goalie told the sports newspaper, *Olé*. Djokovic had effectively said in the press conference that his sympathies for Boca changed "in five minutes," and he became a supporter of San Lorenzo during a visit to a school. "The kids' reaction to the Boca jersey wasn't good, and I'm very grateful for the president of San Lorenzo's gesture of making me a partner," he explained.

A couple of days later, the Boca supporters made him realize that this type of statement would be paid for dearly on an Argentinian soccer field. A close witness remembers that Djokovic was seen in the stadium's exit tunnel with tears in his eyes, drained after what he had just gone through. His plan was to spend some days of vacation in the south of Argentina after the exhibitions; that's what he had told ESPN two months earlier, during the US Open. After the rejection at La Bombonera, the plans changed, and his vacation would no longer take place in Patagonia, or even in Argentina. Djokovic, this time, had not been able to get the fans to like him.

When that conversation over coffee took place in Monaco in 2009, the Serbian had won only Australia; he was still at the start of his growth as a formidable tennis player. There were, before and after that conversation, several victories in other parts of the world, but Monaco, now in 2013, again became the setting for a most interesting interview. On one hand, because the player in front of me was now much greater than he had been in 2009—a Wimbledon and US Open champion— he knew what it felt like to be number one in the world. On the other hand, on this new afternoon he dropped a few hints that enabled me to better understand his personality.

The question had been circling around my mind for years, since I began watching him in 2007 when he shone for the first time in a great tournament by winning Miami. No one would say that Djokovic isn't a nice guy; to the contrary. Ironically, while many think he's sponta- neous, others feel that even his spontaneity is calculated. What is clear, though, is that Djokovic always seeks to please. He has a *need* to. He wants to be liked. Fervently.

"Is there any extra pressure, a need to be more likable and sympathetic than you are, even normally, due to the fact that you're from Serbia?" The question made Djokovic rearrange his position on the sofa at the Monte Carlo Country Club, mostly due to nervousness. "To be honest, that's a good question, because I remember when I traveled with my father playing juvenile tournaments all over the world. Most of the time, when we said that we were from Serbia, people got very cautious and prudent about how to move forward with us."

The memory is painful for Djokovic. You can tell from his expres- sion that the experience had made him suffer. "The feeling was very ugly. First of all, because I don't think anyone should have preju- dices about others, be it over their origins or their religion. But I also understood, because most of the international media were writing negatively about Serbia. It started like that, but as time went on, people came to value me and my family, to understand that what we do, we do with our hearts and a clean conscience. People respected me for my success, and that was important, to allow people to see my true personality and that the Serbian populace is good and can be good."

The war in the former Yugoslavia was a very serious topic for Djokovic and his family. Surrounding it you can find stories that, as with any war, are not pleasant. The most well known is the one about the nights, when he was still a boy, of hiding in his aunt's bomb shelter, but there are many more. The reporter from the *New Yorker* asked him in her extensive profile if he was in agreement with the public apology made by the then Serbian president, Tomislav Nikolić, for the 1995 Srebrenica massacre in which Serbian troops ended the lives of eight thousand Muslims. "Let's not talk about that, please. I don't want to go into that topic, because everything I say could be taken in a very wrong way. The only thing I can say is that war is the worst thing a human being can live through."

When asked less specific questions, though, Djokovic has no problem elaborating. He did so enthusiastically during that conversation in Monte Carlo. "It took me a while to understand, when I was young, what the situation in our country was, especially after the war. I was twelve years old in '99, and in '92 I was five. There were many political and economic problems in Serbia over the last ten years. Standards are very low, and people suffer. As in any country in the world, but there especially, because it is a country marked by the war. The experience of overcoming that suffering made me even closer to my people and made me appreciate the true values in life. In a certain way, it motivated me to represent my country in the best possible way and to take advantage of the opportunity to show that Serbia has many positive aspects, not just negative. It's a process, and I can't influence our image just by myself, there has to be more people. As an athlete, I do all I can to win matches, and if I have the time and the opportunity, to represent my country in the Davis Cup, which is also a means to talk about the positive values of Serbia. What I've seen in the media about Serbia over the last twenty years is very bad. The focus of the press each time they talk about Serbia is negative. The violence, the crime, all that. And that is something that I definitely oppose and want to change."

Five years before that interview in Monaco, Djokovic had had to confront politics after receiving a direct question. *"What do you think about the independence of Kosovo?"* Djokovic was in Dubai, the conversation took place in a huge garden at the Aviation Club in the city of the emirates. A few feet away was an artificial lake; some palm trees protected him from the sun. Djokovic, who had won his first Grand Slam title in Australia three weeks earlier, didn't hesitate to answer: "They're taking away everything we have. Kosovo is Serbia and will continue being Serbia. Kosovo is the heart of the country. Can you imagine a country in which a majority of the population wants to be independent and does so? How would they feel? They take away something that is our history, our religion, everything we have."

The face of the then number three player in the world hardened when asked if he could put himself in the Kosovans' shoes, whether he would be able to understand their reasons, the desire to cut ties with Serbia after a war that shook Europe's conscience. "I don't want to think in that sense. I know the history, it's talked about a lot. But, like I said, it was Serbia and will continue to be Serbia, forever. My father was born there, my uncle was born there, most of my family lived there for thirty years. I was there often visiting the churches. You can't imagine the number of churches, monuments, and historic sites that are there. I can't think of Kosovo as a different country." He added, "I know that, as a professional, I have to keep playing and winning. I've never known much about politics, but this isn't just politics, it's very serious."

If the figures of the '70s were interested in poetry, music, and literature, then Djokovic is, as a star, perhaps the closest thing to years which saw such characters as Ilie Năstase, Björn Borg, Guillermo Vilas, Jimmy Connors, or Vitas Gerulaitis. The Serbian is interested not only in politics but also in the religious phenomenon, meditation, and culture. He might not always understand or guess correctly, but he always has his eyes open so that nothing of what the world offers slips by him. Which, when you're young, famous, and a millionaire, is a great deal. "I learned a lot from many of the people who I've been able to talk to. One of those was Santana, the musician. I ran into him a few years ago in Monaco, and we had a great half hour conversation. I always try to keep my mind open and learn new things. We can't be so obtuse that we don't listen to others." The fact that Djokovic wants to take advantage of everything that his fame and the world brings him is undeniable. That he may not always be able to do so is equally likely. At times, so much activity overwhelms him, such as that time he left Prince Albert of Monaco waiting for forty minutes for a meeting that they had agreed on.

When a book is written about ten of the great finals in the history of tennis, Djokovic can be sure to have at least one place in it, thanks to the incredible five hours and fifty-three minutes in the 2012 Australian Open that he ended up winning against Nadal: the longest Grand Slam final of all time.

Months later, Djokovic was at Arthur Ashe stadium in New York, explaining to the journalists from American television how to correctly pronounce his name. The Serbian did all he could, and it wasn't his fault that the North Americans could not get the pronunciation correct. At the heart of it he didn't really care, because he had already cemented his place in the history books with what happened in January in Australia.

That final at Melbourne was very painful for Nadal, who made a mistake when he had it cinched. He was 4–2 and 30–15 in the fifth set, then rushed to hit a strong backhand when he only needed to place the ball on the other side because the exhausted Serbian couldn't reach it. Nadal went too fast and hit the shot into the net. A while later he was spread out on a chair during one of the strangest trophy award ceremonies ever witnessed at a Grand Slam. Neither Nadal nor Djokovic could stay on their feet. Physically drained and with the beginnings of cramps, the two colossi of the final went through it while sitting.

It was the seventh consecutive final that Nadal lost against Djokovic, a player against whom he would measure up more than forty times, even more than against Federer, and whom he was always afraid of. It was August of 2007 in Montreal, and Nadal had fallen in the semifinals against the Serbian. The Spaniard's conclusion after the match? "I can't beat that dude, he's better than I am."

A bit of an exaggeration, you would think, considering that it was only his second loss in seven matches against Djokovic. But Nadal had an intuition about the future in which the balance between victories and defeats eventually became unfavorable, and about a man who would make him suffer more than Federer: between July of 2011 and January of 2012, Djokovic defeated Nadal during three Grand Slam finals in a row. Federer never did that to him.

When matches are heroic and the victories epic, the players tend to stay longer in the locker rooms. They get massaged, rehydrate, shower, and lower their elevated adrenaline. Twenty reporters were waiting in front of the locker room on that Australian morning. They watched the door, of course, because any moment it would open and offer something, even if it wasn't necessarily the appearance of the champion. And they were watching, just next to the door, seated perfectly on a bench, slender, elegant, and serenely proud, Jelena Ristic, who was at the time Djokovic's girlfriend—later to be his wife, then mother of Stefan, the firstborn son of the tennis star.

The celebration of the Serbian clan was a long one that night. So long that it ended at eight in the morning. Djokovic didn't get a wink of sleep, and a couple of hours later he was on his feet again for a photo session and several meetings with the news media. "I'm full of happiness, but I think I'm still not totally conscious of what happened," admitted the Serbian, who in 2011 had won ten titles, three of them at Grand Slams, and who at the time was thinking that it wasn't crazy to dream of repeating Rod Laver's feat of conquering the four great titles during the same season, and liven up the Grand Slams in a way that hadn't happened since 1969. "One player already did it, so it's possible, yes. It would be the greatest challenge to win the four Grand Slams in the same year, but with how I'm playing now I think that my game is good enough to win titles on every surface."

Djokovic didn't win the Grand Slam and neither did Nadal nor Federer, who both also won three in a year but never four. To dream of that you have to win in Australia, and during the year 2012 Nadal could no longer dream of emulating Laver. The Spaniard arrived in Madrid at midday on the last day of January, after a flight with a lay-over in Doha. The times during which his uncle made him travel in economy were behind him; the routine now was to wait for every-one to board and so avoid the sessions of photos and autographs. It was the same when disembarking. The whole group—Toni Nadal, Miguel Ángel Nadal, Carlos Costa, Rafael Maymó, and Ángel Ruiz Cotorro—all walked with their heads down across the conveyor belts of the gigantic Barajas airport. Nadal, somewhat ahead, walked alone, carrying on one shoulder a black and fluorescent green racket bag. Wrapped up in his thoughts, he suddenly felt someone tapping his shoulder. A traveler in a soft jacket was tapping him and showing him a phone. Curiously, he didn't want a photo with Nadal, he just wanted a photo *of* Nadal. Serious, Nadal posed for the picture. One. And one more. And Nadal just as serious.

There is almost no flight home as long as one from Melbourne to Mallorca, with three planes and two layovers. Once free of the inter-rupting traveler, Nadal approached one of the information screens, found the gate for his flight to Palma de Mallorca, and kept walking firmly, quietly, and, above all, alone. All said and done, he had again clashed with Djokovic, as in July of 2011 in the Wimbledon final, when he took from him the title and his position as number one in the world, and in September during that same year in the setting of the US Open.

In September of 2011 in New York, the "R" years were teetering. New York was tensing up for the arrival of Irene, a "hurricane that turned out not to be such," but above all for the tenth anniversary of the September 11 attacks. The tension was also building in Federer and Nadal, because no matter how much effort they put into their games a replacement for the once impenetrable "duopoly" had finally appeared.

The Swiss player's sixteen Grand Slam titles, the Spaniard's ten and his Olympic gold, the shared dominion of the number one spot, the fact that they had starred in the perfect rivalry . . . it was all becoming a part of the past. A recent past but threatened by a new and unsettling present. Glory is never forever, but few things must hurt a sports star more than knowing at the instant it happens that the glory is fleeing treacherously toward the body of a different young, ambitious, and talented player. Future years would show that it wasn't exactly the case, that glory would continue to be a close ally of Nadal and Federer, but during September of 2011, the feeling was of nearing a certain end to the cycle.

Not content to just take Nadal's place at the top of the ranking at Wimbledon, the young Djokovic was seeking in New York to cement his spot as the "number one" for the whole season. This was no small achievement of Djokovic's: you had to go back to February 2004, when Federer replaced the American Andy Roddick, to find the last time that the number one player was neither the Swiss nor the Spaniard.

Those key moments in the history of the sport, those instances that symbolize a turn of the page, take place on great stages and are televised directly to millions of people, but they are celebrated or suffered in quiet hallways or humid changing rooms, in the interiors of those stadiums, and in the eyes of very few, such as occurred on the September 10, 2011. A whole period had come to an end, although not an era, and the two stars, the two men who gave shape to the "R" years, crossed each other in the locker room. "A lot of bad luck," Nadal managed to say to a devastated Federer, who had lost in the semifinals to Djokovic. "Cheer up," the Spaniard added. Again, as six years earlier in Basel, there was not enough time for more. That's how the greatest stories begin and end sometimes, in front of a hotel room door, or in the corner of a locker room. Moments as brief as they are intense.

After hearing Nadal's heartfelt words, Federer walked down a 150-foot hallway, aware that the weight of history is not a joke. There he saw photographs of Arthur Ashe, Rod Laver, Ken Rosewall, Stan Smith, Ilie Năstase, John Newcombe, Jimmy Connors, Manuel Orantes, Guillermo Vilas, John McEnroe, Ivan Lendl, Mats Wilander, Boris

Becker, Pete Sampras, Stefan Edberg, Andre Agassi, Patrick Rafter, Marat Safin, Lleyton Hewitt, Andy Roddick, Juan Martín del Potro, and Nadal himself. A succession of great photos, they begin in black and white, and as the years go by become colorful. All the champions of the US Open's professional era, forty-three versions. He had been the champion for five of them.

But that was no comfort at the time, because Federer was heading toward the moment that so many athletes hate: to tell dozens of reporters why he lost. "This is the reason why we watch sports, because the unexpected can happen." The phrase, surprisingly cold and analytical, escaped the lips of a pale Federer. Something very strange had just happened. For two years in a row, he had fallen in the semifinals of the US Open, a tournament that he conquered five years in a row between 2004 and 2008. As remarkable as it had been, what was most notable wasn't the loss, but the way in which it had happened. He lost to Djokovic after having the chance to win at two match points. Exactly what had happened to him a year before in 2010.

With an advantage of 5–3 and 40–15, Federer didn't wait for the public's screams to die down, which is really the natural state at Arthur Ashe stadium; he hit the first open serve that Djokovic returned with a powerful and adjusted crosscourt shot that was impossible to stop. Djokovic then behaved more Djokovic than ever and started to lift his arms to request more support from an audience that was clearly in favor of Federer throughout the entire match. He was asking almost angrily, nearly defiant. Neither he nor Federer nor the New York audience had forgotten certain events of previous years on those same cement courts.

In 2005, the Serbian had asked for five timeouts—he was given four—to be attended by the medic during a match that he won, 7–5, in the fifth set against the Frenchman Gaël Monfils. The New York audience on court 10 booed him. Djokovic admitted the obvious, "Those timeouts really helped me, because he's in better physical condition than I am. I know that it's irritating for a lot of the people watching the match, but it was the only way that I could win."

It would be five years before Djokovic would swear to the world that a gluten-free diet was responsible for ending his respiratory difficulties, for his noticeable physical change, and for his transformation into a gladiator who reaches unthinkable shots and can always run more than his rivals.

Normally diplomatic, Federer surprised everyone in 2007 when he was asked about the frequent injuries of the greatly fragile Djokovic in those years, "I think that it's not serious." He would repeat that again two years later in Australia. "It's a bit deceiving." But the height of his criticisms of Djokovic came in 2008, in the preview of the quarter-finals clash with Roddick and during the game itself. Roddick, master of a corrosive sense of irony, had Djokovic in his cross hairs. A reporter asked the American about the ankle injury that was affecting the Serbian. Roddick leapt to the attack without holding back:

"Yeah, I know. Both ankles? And his back?"

"And his back."

"And a hip?"

"And a hip."

"And the cramps [in a mocking tone]."

The reporter tried to steer the conversation elsewhere, but Roddick was delighted with the chance to settle scores with Djokovic, whom Federer had pegged as a fake. "Bird flu," added the American, who had been number one five years before. "Anthrax, bird flu, the common flu." The reporter finally slipped in a question: *"Do you think he's making it up? That seems to be what you're suggesting."* Roddick's answer was devastating, "No, if it's there, it's there. It just seems like a lot. He's either very quick to ask for the medic's help, or he's the bravest man of all time. It's your call, guys."

The next day, Djokovic defeated Roddick in five sets and, when the interviewer asked him in the middle of the court about the game, his answer amazed all. "Well, Andy said I had like sixteen injuries, that's obviously not the case. And the spectators think I make everything up, so I don't know . . . "The booing of the Serb from the stadium crowd was one of the most deafening ever heard on a Grand Slam court, comparable to the one the Swiss Martina Hingis received in the 1999 Roland Garros final that she lost to the German Steffi Graf, but Djokovic seemed to be in his element. He looked defiantly toward the stands while his mother and father euphorically celebrated his words. You can't deny the Serbian's bravery; others would not have done the same in his place.

It was no coincidence that three years later, again victorious over the public's favorite—Federer this time—Djokovic requested, practically demanded, that the spectators give him recognition for once. They still didn't all like him; they only halfheartedly cheered. But the Serbian was saving a surprise for the end. Those match points that Federer didn't take advantage of in 2010 and 2011 helped to maintain a curious statistic at the US Open: it is the only one of the four Grand Slams that didn't see a match between the Swiss and Nadal.

While the stadium roared after Djokovic's unexpected return of Federer's too-hurried serve in the 2011 US Open semifinals, some commentators were asking themselves if that swing by Djokovic to save the first match point was the best return of all time. It was not, clearly, although the circumstances did make it one of the most important. With all the spectacle involved in that strike, the return wasn't an impossible shot, not even excessively difficult for Djokovic. Federer possesses so much talent that he sometimes becomes blind and wants to win on his own terms. If you look at his career it makes sense, but he made a mistake: he wanted to hurry the match with a spectacular serve, but it probably would have been better to lower the speed of the serve and change the angle to work against his rival's body. The fact is that Federer's serve ended up at an ideal height and a comfortable distance for Djokovic, who only had to react instinctively, lightly adjust, and look for the hit. It's a shot that is tested a lot in training and that came out perfectly for the Serbian. His shouts and his euphoria lifted him at the same time that they sank Federer, who still asks himself today how he could have missed that opportunity.

With the match concluded, the Federer who stepped into the press conference room wearing a white shirt and a black cap with the initials "RF" in red could obviously not have been feeling great. He started the press conference analyzing, as if it had nothing to do with him, the enjoyment of the spectators upon seeing the unexpected turns of the sport, which is something few could have done so objectively. Despite his calm presentation, Federer was devastated. While speaking he passed his hands over his eyes, and though there were no tears his sadness was almost palpable. It was also obvious when his gaze drifted for a few long seconds to the semifinal between Nadal and the Brit Andy Murray that was playing on the press conference room monitor. His father, Robert, also devastated, was watching from the fifth row. "I don't want to talk; it was a very hard match." He knew that on that hot and humid afternoon on the Queens cement, his son had let slip too many things: the possibility of cutting Djokovic's journey short, as he had done in the Roland Garros final three months earlier, and the dream of adding a ninth year in a row of winning at least one Grand Slam title, which he achieved between 2003 and 2010, and Nadal between 2005 and 2014.

"What I have isn't arrogance, it's confidence," explained the Serb to the *New Yorker*. Djokovic, that man who is "so different" from the two "R"s, in Nadal's own words, had become a true demon in the year of 2011. Not in vain had he beaten the Spaniard in the last five finals in which they played each other: the cement at the Indian Wells and Miami; the clay of Madrid and Rome, and the grass at Wimbledon. New York, during an enormously intense final, had been no exception.

In 2011, after winning his first Wimbledon, Djokovic bested Martina Navrátilová, who after losing in the final against the Spaniard Conchita Martínez, had ripped up some blades of grass to take as a memento. In the midst of celebrating, Djokovic also ripped a bit of the sacred grass . . . and ate it. "I felt like an animal. I wanted to see what it tasted like, and it was really good," he explained. "It just happened, it was spontaneous, truthfully. I didn't plan on doing it. I didn't know what to do with all my joy today." Spontaneous or calculated? Three years later the question was reasonably evident. Djokovic defeated Federer in the final and again ate some blades of grass at the tennis cathedral. "It didn't have much flavor, to be honest. It was shorter than a few years before, so I also swallowed a bit of dirt. But it was the best meal of my life." Envisioning Federer or Nadal chewing the grass at Wimbledon would require a powerful imagination.

Beyond his extravagances, Djokovic had justifiably become *the* rival for Nadal in 2011. After the Indian Wells final, Djokovic and his group loudly sang the "champions, champions, oe, oe, oe" that Spanish athletes, and Nadal of course, tend to chant after a great victory. That deeply bothered the Nadals, who considered it an unnecessary mockery. Two months later, defeated by Djokovic in Madrid, his own home, Nadal didn't hide his disgust at the shouts of the Djokovic clan in the Magic Box complex while he was giving his press conference after losing the final.

During that season, Nadal felt in a certain way that the landscape had changed for him. Djokovic, who, ever since he entered the circuit had a high profile and level of aplomb that never endeared him to the Swiss or the Spaniard, didn't just play and win at tennis. He also did it off the court. How else could you interpret what happened in the hours surrounding the tenth anniversary of 9/11?

After defeating Murray on Saturday the 10th in the semifinals, a sweaty Nadal with his pulse still beating went straight to the heart of the spectators at Arthur Ashe stadium and expressed his support during America's national anniversary of that tragic event. "It is the most impacting image I have seen in my life," declared the Spaniard, who was fifteen years old at the time of the attacks. Djokovic hadn't spoken about that after his victory against Federer, but he resolved to correct that mistake on the day of the final. He wanted, if not the affection, then at least the respect of the uncontrollable and wild New York audience.

"Nice hat," said Mary Joe Fernández, a former tennis player and a years-long interviewer for ESPN, at 4:02 on Monday, September 12. Djokovic thanked her and walked onto the court, savoring beforehand the ovation that wearing the blue cap with the acronym "FDNY" would guarantee him. It stood for the Fire Department of the City of New

York, the most appreciated institution in the city that remembered its heroism during those days in 2001. Nadal avoided that gesture. It was the tournament organization itself that proposed that the finalists wear symbolic hats when walking onto the field to play, offering either the Fire Department's or the Police Department's. "I don't think so," said the Spaniard, who tends to avoid excess. The Serbian, on the other hand, loves to go as far and as hard as he can. While Nadal answered Mary Joe Fernández's questions seriously and with a knot in his throat before entering a final which he was afraid of losing (and he would), Djokovic was enjoying a public that loved him. And the number one player had even fallen short of his true objective. He wanted something more than the hat; he had proposed walking out with an authentic metal fireman's helmet. "It was a gesture of respect, a tribute," Djokovic said a year and a half later during the interview in Monte Carlo. "I know what it is to know someone close to you, to see how your country is destroyed. I felt that it was the right moment to do something like that." But, did he ask for the metal helmet? Djokovic makes a fleeting grimace before laughing: "They didn't give it to me, so it was better to do it with the hat." For once, during that unrepeatable year of 2011, one of his desires had been denied.

CHAPTER 27

Fight

THE TRADITION WORKED FOR YEARS: days before the start of the Australian Open, Nadal and Federer would share a relaxed and hearty breakfast with the director of the tournament and other high-level individuals. The start of a new season always brought plenty of topics for conversation and the occasional pending score to settle. Craig Tiley, the director of the Australian Open, is also a jovial man, perhaps the most popular among the players out of all those who have similar responsibilities on the circuit. Anyone would enjoy a chat with him. That includes Nadal and Federer.

Nevertheless, in 2012 it was different; there was no breakfast, no encounter. There were, instead, pending grudges. Roger and Rafa didn't want to see each other because the tension between the two had been growing for months and was nearly at the bursting point in public. It burst due to an error, as with so many things in life. It was Sunday, in the summer, well into the afternoon in Melbourne, and Rafael Nadal was chewing over his anger with Federer. So angry was he that for five minutes and before a cluster of reporters, he ignored the name of his friend and rival, something which no one could remember ever before happening in public. Federer stopped being referred to as "Roger," nor was he even "Federer." Nadal simply referred to him as "he." And all due to a question from the sharp Christopher Clarey, a journalist for the *New York Times* and the *International Herald Tribune* (it was still called that at the time and had not yet become the *International New York Times*). Clarey had lived for several years in Andalusia and spoke very good Spanish. *"Friends, can I ask something?"* he said in a friendly tone to his colleagues in the Spanish media, who were talking to Nadal after the press conference in English was finished. The green light was obvious to Clarey, and the American got down to it. This is the exact dialogue, translated from the Spanish:

Clarey: Rafa, I talked to Roger in the month of December about the circuit and all that, and he told me that he doesn't like when the top-level players talk negatively about the circuit.

Nadal: The players who . . .?

Clarey: Who talk pessimistically.

Nadal: Who? Who are the players? Who are talking negatively . . .

Clarey: People like Murray . . .

Nadal: Or like me.

Clarey: Top-level, who talk negatively. Do you agree?

At that point, Nadal wasn't in control. The "like me" had shown that he thought Federer had attacked him. And then, without thinking about it too much, he attacked back. "No. Not at all. I completely disagree," he said before laughing bitterly. "Besides . . . What he does is very easy, 'I don't say anything, only good things, I look like a gentleman, and everyone else can burn.' It isn't like that." The phrase was brutal and unexpected, although Nadal was only doing what he had done so many times throughout his career: talking too much. The "I'm not going to lie to you" is a habitual crutch of the Spaniard's, but the truth is that on more than one occasion he was sorry for being so sincere, or he was made to regret it by his close associates. In that aspect, nephew Rafa and uncle Toni are very alike. They believe in something, they jump to the offensive and don't think of the consequences until later. That's what they do.

"We all have our opinions about things, each of us is free to have a different vision of how things are. Maybe he likes the circuit . . . I also like the circuit, I think that we have a fantastic circuit, and much better than in most sports, so I can only talk positively about tennis. That doesn't mean that there isn't room for improvement. Is the circuit good? Yes, but there are bad things in the circuit, and when things are bad, you have to try to change them." What Nadal was doing was cathartic, he was finally saying in public what he had confided so many times to others. But the issue didn't end there. Nadal kept talking dryly about "him," referring to Federer. Of the warm and respectful "Roger" that he normally uses, there was no hint.

"That's all that we say, and the vast majority of players have the same opinion. If he has a different opinion, then . . . If the majority think one thing and very few think something else, maybe they're the ones who are wrong then." It was three hundred seconds during which the Spaniard spit out his truths, his vision of the circuit, and his anger with Federer for not going down that path with him. Five minutes, in short, that returned tennis to its usual state, because what had been happening lately had been unusual: the number one and two players in the world working side by side in the Players' Council.

Only under the effects of acid could you imagine John McEnroe, Jimmy Connors, Boris Becker, Ivan Lendl, Pete Sampras, or Andre Agassi going through a similar experience, sharing hours and hours of debate and decision-making with their toughest rivals. Sampras himself admitted it in an interview in September of 2012 with the *New York Times* when justifying why players in his and Agassi's era did not act like Federer and Nadal, "It's hard to get the top ten into the same room, not to mention getting them to all agree. It isn't the NBA, there's no syndicate, it's about individuals. There were a lot of differing opinions and, to be honest with you, I didn't have the energy to get involved."

And it wasn't just the two "R"s. The leadership of the stars was total during the years that Djokovic added himself to the duo to give form to an unprecedented trident. An executive at the ATP with access to those meetings explained it simply, "Could you imagine Messi and Cristiano Ronaldo getting together to talk for hours about the problems of their colleagues and what affects the players of the second division?" Another higher-up on the circuit also present at the meetings expanded on the point, "Seeing Rafa, Federer, or Djokovic talk passionately about who has the right to play the qualifying rounds, about whether the doubles registration should close on Friday or Saturday morning . . . It's simply incredible." He added, "You see Federer, a day before the start of the US Open, locked up in a hotel room at ten and a quarter at night. He eats a sandwich or snacks and debates about quality control of the qualifying rounds before a 250 tournament or whether the Sunrise Challenger should be played the same week as the Indian Wells Masters 1000 and how much money should be awarded."

Australia 2012 was the setting of a turbulent players' reunion in which Nikolái Davydenko was especially caustic toward Federer, of whom the Ukrainian Sergiy Stajovsky also spoke ill. "I thought the comments by Stajovski and Davydenko were very unfair, when they say that Federer does not represent the players. I go to the Players' Council meetings, and I can assure you that Federer is incredible," insists one of the sources with access to the meetings. "When a decision is being considered that affects the players in the spots between fifty and two hundred, Federer always asks, 'Is this good for you, are you in agreement?' Even during the meeting in 2011 a very minor topic was brought up about the conditions of the entrance of the doubles pairs to the main draw—one of those topics that anyone would yawn at and sit with a blank mind. But not Federer. 'Guys, here we're going to do what you say, we'll back up whatever position you take,' he told one of the doubles players."

The Australian Peter Luczak shared the Players' Council with Nadal and Federer, and his admiration for both is obvious "I think it's incredible the way that they respect tennis, and how they try to find what's best for all the players. We're very lucky we can count on those two guys at the front of the sport." Why is the Players' Council important? Basically, because the circuit is shaped during those meetings, decisions are made that can benefit or be harmful to many players. There are eleven players of different skill levels and specializations, doubles and singles players, debating topics that, as a last resort, would be decided by the ATP board. In attendance at those players' meetings are three men who, in turn, represent them on the council, which includes representatives from the tournaments and the ATP president.

Brad Drewett, a former tennis player who reached thirty-four on the ranking in singles and eighteen in doubles, had just made his debut as the executive director of the ATP, and found himself in his first big tournament and in his country, Australia, facing that bomb of a comment from Nadal about Federer. The whole circuit knew that Nadal had backed the Dutchman Richard Krajicek, a 1996 Wimbledon champion, as chief of the ATP, but that Federer had seen his own candidate win: Drewett.

The Australian died less than a year and a half after taking the post due to an incurable illness, Lou Gehrig's disease. The tragedy was not foreseen in January of 2012. Drewett, an amicable mediator, was not a man of strong gestures or words. In Melbourne, where the first press conference under his charge took place, no one asked him about the differences between Nadal and Federer, even though the ATP communications department had prepared an answer for him, "Eh, guys, I played in an era during which the players would say anything to each other; I even saw fist fights break out in the locker rooms during the '80s. Compared to that, this is all extremely educated and smooth." It's true. Different times, different players, something summed up concisely by Jimmy Connors on a torrid afternoon in September 2012, in Flushing Meadows, "In my time, there were no hugs or smiles."

Nine months earlier, in Melbourne, Nadal wasn't smiling either while he laid out the reasons behind his disagreement with Federer. "I say a lot of positive things now about tennis. I can't complain about tennis, it has given me the opportunity to experience things that I might never have even dreamed of. However, is ending your career with pain in every part of your body positive? No, it's not positive. Maybe he just has such a great physique that he'll finish his career like a rose. Neither I, nor Murray, nor Djokovic will end our careers like roses; we will finish physically affected. Tennis is an important period in our lives, yes, but with how focused the game is, and how it's spread out on the calendar . . . how old will we be when we finish playing? Unless you're super privileged like him, who has an ease, and I don't doubt his efforts, but for him the game comes easy. The rest of us all have to put in just a bit more effort than he does and we physically wear our bodies out more than he does. And at what age do you finish your tennis career if you start young? At twenty-eight, thirty, thirty-one? You still have a lot of your life ahead of you. It's also important how you end your career, because when I retire I want to be able to play a soccer game with my friends, I want to be able to ski if I feel like it. I'm afraid that I won't be able to. Is it logical to complain about that or not?"

Nadal was really getting into gear at that point. He scrutinized the problems caused to the players' physique by the hard surfaces, the calendar, and the annual ranking, which he would rather see as biennial. But at the end of his five minutes of Australian fury he went back to pointing out the object of his anger, "Maybe sometime he could also support us . . ." The astonishment in Australia was huge. For the first few moments, no one could believe that Nadal, costar of the most friendly rivalry in the history of tennis, had said something like that. The incredulity was also justifiable due to the format in which the relationship between players and reporters usually works: first a press conference in English, then one in the native language of the tennis player, in the event that the first is not English. The players tend to expand more and be more precise when they speak in their own language, but they generally don't drop "bombs" as powerful as Nadal had just done. And on that Sunday, Nadal hadn't said one critical thing about Federer in English. What's more, just minutes before attacking Federer Nadal had said that one of his goals for the year would be to keep his mouth in check. "I'm going to be more careful with what I say during the press conferences," he assured, still bothered by the consequences of another fit of honesty two months earlier at the London Masters, when he said that he had lost "a bit of the passion."

The night before, nearly a hundred players had held a fairly agitated meeting in which there was even mention of a strike. It became known that Nadal, vice president of the Players' Council, had been one of the most vehement. Federer, the president, hadn't opened his mouth.

The press wanted to know more, but the Spaniard, well instructed, offered no details. "I'm here to support what the majority of players are thinking, but I'm not going to be the one who speaks about it, especially because I'm always the one talking, and I'm tired."

Shortly after his tough criticism of Federer in Spanish, Nadal ran across the Swiss in the players' lounge. "I saw him after he made those comments, on Sunday afternoon," Federer recalls. "I asked him how the press conference had gone, I didn't know that he had talked to the press. He said, 'Yeah, it was good.' He mentioned a few things, and I said 'Okay.' Later I read what he had said." Federer, with an enviable level of self-control and in a relaxed tone, disarmed the situation. "Things are good between us, I don't have any hard feelings towards him." Months later, during an interview with the Spanish newspaper *El País*, he was more specific. "What Nadal said didn't hurt at all."

Both Nadal and Federer always agreed that there was no reason for the rivalry to include harsh words, angry looks, and disrespecting your counterpart. For that reason, the Swiss star, although he had every right to strike back, opted instead to lower the decibels. Despite that, the topic would turn out to be one of the news items of the year in tennis, because after the years of peace and love something was changing.

Nadal didn't have the excuse of his lack of fluency in English this time, which has on more than one occasion led him to choose an inappropriate, or not altogether, precise word with which to express himself. No, this time his tirade had been in Spanish. Moreover, the famous nerve of the Nadal clan had gotten the better of Rafael to such a point that the player made another mistake: when he was asked by journalists the next day, after he won the first round, whether he had seen Federer after his intemperate statements, he said he had not. But the Swiss, minutes later relating the story of his encounter with the Spaniard, made it clear that they had seen each other. "Don't exaggerate those crazy stories," Nadal asked of the reporters. "I said what I said. I regret saying it, especially in front of you all. Because when I say things like that, I should say them to him directly," Nadal emphasized, thus bringing to an end the "damage control" that he had begun many hours before through mediators on both sides, basically between Tony Godsick, Federer's agent, and Carlos Costa, the Spaniard's representative.

To understand the reasons behind the frustrated breakfast in Melbourne and Nadal's verbal explosion, you have to go back two months and fly over nine thousand miles. To London, at the edge of midnight on Friday November 25, 2011, the place and time of the last attempt at an agreement between the two. A failed attempt, as would be seen later.

Nadal moved through London with his eyebrows furrowed. That the O2 Arena might be the most extraordinary indoor stadium that tennis has ever been played in mattered little to him in those days. Neither would he be moved by the fact that that stage had been shaken by the best pop and rock and roll (British and worldwide). The Spaniard's musical tastes don't quite follow that path. And even less important to him was the fact that his days in London were spent in a luxurious suite at a hotel, the Marriott County Hall, one of the best that you can find in the British capital. Opening your window and seeing the Thames, Big Ben, or Westminster is something anyone would appreciate, but Nadal, who enjoys the big cities and their small historical corners, cares little about luxury. It embarrasses him, in fact.

Nadal wasn't angry about the 6–3 and 6–0 loss that he had been dealt by Federer in the group phase of the Masters that closed the 2011 season, although that result served to confirm that all his arguments were valid. The Spaniard barely mentions it in public, but he believes that the tour would be more fair if the end-of-year Masters, a tournament he could never manage to win, changed its surface. Why not on clay and in the open air sometime? Or at least open air cement, as in 2003 and 2004 in Houston. Why always surfaces that are fast and very fast? Why always a covered tournament, which favors players like Federer, Djokovic, Juan Martín del Potro, or Jo-Wilfried Tsonga? It was the Frenchman, specifically, who knocked him out of that Masters.

The next day, a sleepy-faced Nadal with a hoarse voice answered a question, during an interview in a private room in his hotel, with a comment that revealed the truth about what was going through his head. Two days later, Federer conquered his sixth Masters, an unequaled record. Nadal was angry about the issue of the court surface, and it was a novel sort of anger. At any rate, during November of 2006, both had shared hours of conversation flying on the Swiss player's private plane between Shanghai and Seoul. And a year before, his mother and his sister had congratulated Federer with affectionate kisses after the Swiss star's victory over the Spaniard in the 2010 Masters final. A couple of weeks later, Federer was waiting for Nadal at his arrival gate in the Zurich airport to personally take him into the city, and to serve as his tour guide during the hours preceding the exhibition being held to benefit Africa that they both played in Spain and Switzerland in the days before Christmas. "It's good for us to chat, to talk about the problems on the tour," Federer had said excitedly at the beginning of 2007.

Five years later, they no longer played for the same team. There was no more duo; they weren't on the same side of the net. Federer, Nadal's great ally in getting the South African Etienne de Villiers out of his position of power in the ATP, no longer thought like him. That *coup d'état* of 2007–2008 against De Villiers showed who truly was in charge after all. In the words of an ATP insider with close ties to them both, "Roger and Rafa decided to get rid of De Villiers and lead the sport."

They were successful and installed a successor, but once they had reached that goal Nadal and Federer were now thinking along very different lines. If Nadal proposed a biennial ranking, Federer insisted on the annual. If the Spaniard wanted to shorten the schedule even more, the Swiss would say that everything has its limit. If the left-handed player wanted to promote Krajicek as the new chief of the ATP, the right-handed player came back with Drewett's name. If Nadal played around in public with the idea of a tennis players' strike, Federer would invalidate him. "That whole business of a boycott came up a few months ago, but it doesn't make sense," the Swiss said during a press conference in London, recalling the turbulent 2011 US Open.

"Now I'm getting angry, I really am!" The angry man was Andy Roddick, an American who was number one in the world during the 2003 season and who, as the US Open champion that year, had a certain right to be furious at what was happening on the cement of Flushing Meadows. It was September of 2011, the tournament was in the final stretch, but the rain had completely mixed up the schedule . . . and revealed the weakness of the New York cement after an hour and a half of going back and forth, the tournament organization had confirmed their powerlessness to solve the defects in the paint on the surface of Louis Armstrong stadium, in which Roddick and the Spaniard David Ferrer had started to play. Their match would eventually have to be moved to court 13, with a capacity for 580 spectators, instead of the ten thousand at the Armstrong.

A couple of days earlier, Flushing Meadows had had its "day of fury" when Nadal, Roddick, and the Brit Andy Murray had gone to protest together at the office of Brian Earley, the main umpire of the tournament. That three top ten players would go, at the same time, to the office of the highest sporting authority of the tournament is something that has happened very few times in tennis history. Nadal, Murray, and Roddick were angry about being forced to play on a wet court before the rain had stopped coming down. Minutes earlier, the Spaniard had forced the delay of the match that he was losing, 3–0, against the Luxembourger, Giller Müller. "Always the same, you only care about the money!" Nadal yelled angrily in the middle of the court.

The dissatisfaction of the players with the US Open is historic. It was the only tournament in the Grand Slam in which the men must play in the semifinals and the final on consecutive days, the "blame" for which lies with the "Super Saturday" that pools the male and female semifinals into the same day, excluding the period between 2012 to 2014, when the problem was dealt with eccentrically by holding the final on Monday. That tennis binge was born in 1984, during a twelve-hour day that started with an exhibition between Stan Smith and John Newcombe, and closed with a victory by McEnroe over

Connors in five sets. In between, Ivan Lendl defeated Pat Cash in five sets, and Martina Navrátilová achieved victory over Chris Evert in the final. A perfect plateful for television, which is, after all, what pays a significant part of the millions that Nadal and company take in year after year.

But nothing is forever: the organization opened the 2012 edition convinced that the "Super Saturday" wasn't sustainable, and later, when a chair flew onto the court in the middle of the semifinal between Djokovic and Ferrer, the concept was ended. A small tornado had turned that Saturday afternoon into a never before seen spectacle, and there was no more room for experimentation. The players, as they would in any high-level tournament, would again be able to count on a day of rest between semifinals and finals.

But during that year, 2011, Roddick wasn't thinking that a part of what was happening had to do with the always turbulent and unpredictable final stretch of the New York summer; his fury was directed straight at the tournament hierarchy. The 2003 champion had found that in the Louis Armstrong stadium just around one of the baselines, there were small trickles of water coming up. They were minute little New York geysers, something you could hardly expect in a tournament of that magnitude. "Brian! What is this, what is this?" Roddick practically yelled at a distressed Earley, who couldn't come up with any answers. It was the second time that Roddick and Ferrer tried to play in the second most important stage of the tournament. Ferrer, a man who is calm during press conferences but hyper excited in matches, also pointed at Earley. "When you stepped on it, water came out. You would slip on that part. And the ref . . .what's with that guy. When we went in for the second time, he was asking us 'How's it look?' I swear I can't understand it."

Up to eight higher-ups, technical experts, and tournament assistants gathered next to the defective areas. Towels, electrical tape, a shop vacuum, stomping and stamping, and other "techniques" were used, without success, to try and flatten the surface. In a previously sent communication, the tournament organization had attributed to the "unusual amount of rain in August and the first days of September" the fact that the water saturated the play surfaces of the National Tennis Center.

It could rain a lot in New York in those days, but the water wasn't enough to lower the heat in the locker room. It was so bad that Nadal said he would do "anything" to force a change. "We have to try to change things, because I think the moment has come. It will be hard to change things nicely, because they're in a fairly comfortable position. We'll have to look for a solution," Nadal added, before bringing up, for what seemed the millionth time, his endless quest to shorten the duration of the season. "I think they have to change things, you can't play from the 1st of January to the 5th of December, year after year after year, because you can't take it. This is increasingly demanding, both physically and mentally. There's a point where you have to say enough. You have to have a little bit of tranquility to be able to play." Ferrer, who is more than discrete and usually stays behind the scenes, did not hold back that time with his criticism, "The treatment of the players in the Grand Slams is ridiculous. You go to a normal ATP tournament and things are done much better."

They asked him if the players wanted more money. Ferrer swore they didn't. "It's not about money. I'm happy and I get have much more than I deserve. But they play you for a fool with the topic of money, in the only sport where the event takes more than twice as much as the players. I don't know how far to go. Strike, lockout, whatever you want to do . . ."

It is about money, of course, as with so many human activities. Roddick confirmed, "We have 13 percent of all the money that the tournament generates. I'll let you write the story," he told a journalist. Roddick had just been preaching to his colleagues during a tournament in Cincinnati. Extroverted, sharp, and fearless when talking, the former number one player in the world had fired up emotions in the locker room. At the heart of it, it made certain sense that everything would come to a head in a country like the US, where money is a sport in itself.

Between the 13 percent given to the men and the remaining amount that goes to the women, the US Open gives the players 26 percent of what it makes. In American football, whose season starts usually during the US Open, the stars receive 52 percent of the winnings, and in the NBA the number is similar. Around those days, basketball fans were carefully following the lockout of the NBA, the result of which showed that the model wasn't as workable as the players thought. And it's also not possible to apply the business model of a sport with a hyper commercialized and centralized structure, like American football and basketball in the United States, to one like tennis that's based worldwide and in which one key problem is that there is no single clear leader. The ATP isn't, which is powerless to force the Grand Slams or the Davis Cup to do anything. The WTA isn't either; it's in the same situation. Neither is the International Tennis Federation (ITF), nor the Grand Slam tournaments.

The director of one of the four great competitions once precisely described the sort of schizophrenia that affected the workings of the circuit. "I had a meeting with Brad Drewett and, in the middle of a discussion about the tournament, he said, 'Listen, at this moment I'm speaking to you as the players' representative.' And I said no, that wasn't possible, you can't be one thing and something completely opposite according to the circumstances." The answer would be simple from the players' point of view: create a tennis players' syndicate. But for some reason, as Sampras explained, the players of the third millennium aren't capable of, or aren't interested in, improving on something that others had managed to live with.

Flushing Meadows in 1972 was the setting of the gathering that gave origin to the Association of Tennis Professionals, the ATP, whose first president was Cliff Drysdale; Jack Kramer was designated the executive director. You needed the cooperation of the tennis players on the male circuit to effect any improvements to the situation. Sixteen years later, in 1988, Flushing Meadows again saw a change: eighty-five of the top one hundred players in the world gathered in the parking lot of the complex and signed a letter that resulted in the creation of a new circuit, the ATP Tour, in 1990. The Grand Slams and the Davis Cup would continue under the leadership of the ITF, but a great step had been taken on behalf of the players. Mark Miles was the first president of the new ATP, which slowly changed from being focused on the tennis *players* and instead became more and more focused on supervising, administrating, and even finance.

By 2011 the tennis players still had no syndicate. Nothing and no one was preventing them from creating one, and just watching what happened with the flooding at the US Open should have provided enough motivation: nearly a score of drop-outs due to physical injuries. But even that wasn't enough of a motivator. Getting three hundred people from every corner of the planet to all agree on something is not easy. "Everyone has their own agenda," wrote the American doubles players, Mike and Bob Bryan, in the Australian newspaper, *The Age*. "When you're talking about shortening the schedule, the clay special-ists don't want to lose any of their tournaments. And the same goes for the hard-court specialists as well."

The best one hundred in the world don't lead a hard life at all. Nadal, for example, won more than $10 million in 2010, a year in which he finished as the number one, and more than $14 million three years later when he, again, reached the top of the ranking. The Belgian Xavier Malisse, fiftieth in the world during the tense days of September 2011, took home about $390,000, and the Frenchman Nicolas Mahut, ninety-ninth, accumulated $192,000. To that you have to add the advertising contracts, and the fact that during tournaments the play-ers have all their meals and lodging tour paid for, although you do need to subtract a player's taxes, the cost of flights, the trainer's salary, and other expenses. It's estimated that a tennis player spends between 20 percent and 30 percent of what he or she wins from official prize money, although many of them receive extra payments (guarantees) to secure their presence at tournaments.

The numbers are very good, although they don't quite reach the $15 million that an NBA star officially takes home, or the $26 mil-lion that soccer players like Leo Messi or Cristiano Ronaldo earn just from salary. At any rate, many of the tennis players pad their accounts with exhibitions during those few weeks that they are given time off to rest, for which they are generously compensated. That is another of the regular contradictions allowed many of the stars: they ask for more resting time (less from the Davis Cup), but as soon as they have a free week they rush off to play lucrative exhibitions. Life is different for someone in the 150th or 200th spot in the ranks: they do suffer.

Craig Tiley, who after the turbulent 2012 Australian Open instituted a notable prize increase that dragged the other three Grand Slams along with it, compared tennis to another sport of worldwide reach and big sponsors. "The best 250 tennis players in the world earn a quarter of what golfers in similar positions earn." It's no wonder that players love Tiley.

A historical perspective of tennis helps to understand that progress has in fact been enormous as far as the financial comfort of the players is concerned: The 1984 US Open champion, John McEnroe, earned $160,000. The 1994 champ, Pete Sampras, earned $550,000. Marin Cilic, in 2014, pocketed a check for $3 million. The problem isn't for the champions, but for the third or fourth line of tennis players for whom winning a first round is big news. That's where money is lacking.

Eric Butorac, who has a degree in psychology and is a good doubles player, but unknown to the great majority of fans, assumed the position in August 2014, of president of the Players' Council; he had previously been Federer's vice president. The little money earned by those who are lower than the 100th spot on the ranking is a topic of priority for the American. "The prizes increased in recent years, but the gap was so big. The question is, how many players should be able to make a living from tennis, 200, 250, 300? Let's say it's 250. Then we look at how much the 250th player is making, and we try to improve that number. Some money is being diverted to the first rounds, and that's good, but I think there needs to be a plan, to see what our objectives are and how quickly we can reach them."

A good example of the difficulties faced by the lesser known players is Samuel Groth, an Australian whose ranking hovered around

250th for most of his career, an irony for a player whose serve, at 163.5 miles per hour, is the fastest of all time. A devastating serve is not always a guarantee of success in tennis. The most interesting thing about Groth, however, was what he wrote in August of 2012 for the *Sydney Morning Herald* an article that exposes the dark side of tennis, in which reside the players who are so far from the top, "From the 13 tournaments I played this year, I gathered a total of 20,343 Australian dollars. Flights, hotels, food, grips, clothes, and any other expenditure you could think of resulted in me spending approximately the same. You share rooms, or if you're lucky you stay with family, you take flights with more stops because they're cheaper and you eat when you can, which isn't ideal for peak performance, but you still need to do it to survive."

Groth, who years later would finally make the jump in doubles and singles, wrote those few lines of text in the midst of an endless worldwide economic crisis in 2012. Neither then, nor previously, could any high level tennis player say that they lived poorly. There's no doubt that the Indian Mahesh Bhupathi couldn't, an exemplary doubles players from one of the most economically unbalanced countries in the world. Or couldn't he? In 2011, Bhupathi complained on his Twitter account of an inconvenient "change": having to get on a tournament bus to be transported to his hotel in Manhattan. For the first time in his seventeen appearances at the US Open, the Indian man found that there weren't enough Mercedes-Benz autos available. Federer, Nadal, Groth, and Bhupathi: the same sport, but very different lives.

The German auto maker is one of Federer's sponsors, another thing that differentiates him from Nadal, who is linked to Kia, a South Korean manufacturer of automobiles very far removed from the German luxury cars. During the days of November 2011 in London, with the two "R"s so far apart in their thinking, Federer expressed himself clearly during a press conference in which he was not even directly asked about the subject: he would not back a boycott, nor any change in the design of the world ranking system, nor any renewed request to reduce the duration of the season.

Nadal responded days later during an interview with the DPA agency, "He has his ideas as president of the council, and I as the vice president have others, apparently." Among the exchanged messages was a text message that Nadal sent to Federer, and which the Swiss delayed two days in answering, despite the fact that they were at the same tournament. The Spaniard wanted to talk to his, still, partner, but the Swiss made him wait. While Federer was qualifying for the semifinals of a Masters, with a final on Monday, Nadal was dining in London with his girlfriend, María Francisca. After concluding both appointments, at midnight of that Saturday on November 25, Rafa got into a car and went to see Roger. He wanted to find common ground, but especially to convince him to accept a world ranking that would govern for two seasons, instead of the historical annual system. He carried a letter that was signed by the overwhelming majority of the top twenty who backed the idea. It was his thousandth attempt at winning Federer over to the cause. He'd already spoken with him at length about the topic during a dinner held to pay homage to Tim Phillips, former director of Wimbledon. It was his thousandth attempt, and it would be the last. "It was just a matter of hearing him out, and him listening to what I had to say on the matter," Federer said a few days later to the *New York Times*.

There wasn't much more than that; it was a meeting so they could tell each other their positions without either of them changing his own. That's why on Saturday the 14th of January, without any successful agreement between the two circuit leaders, things boiled over during a meeting of players in Melbourne two days before the start of the Australian Open. In a heated environment, Nadal took the microphone and said that the players were "united," "ready," and that they would look for "what they deserved." Other players had already spoken, some of them critical of the way money was being shared, particularly with the amounts that are given to those who aren't stars. Federer didn't open his mouth to speak, he just listened. Nevertheless, in the midst of all the chaos, a vote was called on whether or not to strike. The players who were present remember that Tiley, the director of the tournament, joked a bit nervously, saying that whatever happened, just not to do it at his tournament. The overwhelming majority voted in favor and a few hands remained without being raised, Federer's among them. There would be no strike.

A couple of days later, the Croatian Ivan Ljubičić, former president of the Players' Council and a good friend of Federer's, recalled the tortuous meeting, "In my opinion, it was completely nonsensical. The guys were fired up, excited, but fortunately some of the cooler heads there calmed the rest. It's like a circus, you can't take something like that seriously, it's shameful. You don't achieve anything in that way, I've already seen one war, and I would rather talk than fight." Djokovic spoke along the same lines and, despite agreeing with the concerns of many players, was clearly on a different page than Nadal, "I would rather talk about the issue in detail behind closed doors."

Tony Godsick, Federer's agent, knew what every reporter who approached him would be asking for the time being. His answer, always given with a smile, gave nothing away, "They're both fantastic guys. The circuit is going through some great moments." Then, with a little more frankness, and laughing the whole time, he tossed a little jab at the reporter, "Nice try!" It would be better for Federer to talk. With elegance, the Swiss star closed Pandora's box, which had been opened hours before by Nadal. "We can't always agree on everything. [Nadal] used to say that whatever Roger said was good for him. Today he's much more grown up, he has strong opinions, which I think is wonderful. It's what we need."

Nadal shifted attention from the matter in his own way. After his victory during the first round, he left the journalists open-mouthed with the strange revelation that the day before his knee had made a "clack." It happened, he said, outside the tournament. "It's the strangest thing that has ever happened to me. I heard a 'clack' in my knee. That has never happened to me sitting down like that. I tried to bend my leg a couple of times, but by the third I couldn't bend it. The pain was incredible; I needed help to get up to my room. I went through a very difficult afternoon. By around six-something in the afternoon yesterday, I couldn't bend my knee, and today I was playing. I'm happy to be able to continue in the tournament."

By that time, nobody remembered his criticisms of Federer. For once, Nadal's knee had, in a certain way, done him a favor. The same knee that would, months later, prevent him from competing in Wimbledon, and from all playing until 2013. But despite the "clack," the Spaniard defeated Federer in the semifinals of the Australian Open in a match during which the Swiss player wasted too many opportunities. He later arrived at the historic final won by Djokovic after five hours and 53 minutes of battle that ended at dawn. The knee held up, and the sport was on the front page, although there would soon be new lashes in the "divorce" between the two protagonists of a "romance" that had astonished and impressed observers for such a long time.

"I think that the judges could be a bit stricter with the time." It was March in the California desert and Federer was throwing a curve ball at Nadal weeks after the encounter in Australia. Not without reason, since the Swiss plays tennis at a quick pace when compared to his rivals. The list of the "guilty" was topped by Nadal, number two in the world ranking, following closely by Djokovic, who can bounce the ball up to twenty or thirty times before serving, a habit that sometimes drives both rivals and spectators crazy, a tic that presents itself often during key moments in his matches.

"A lack of respect for the spectators," according to the former president of the International Tennis Federation (ITF), Francesco Ricci Bitti, who doesn't understand how players need to be given their towels after every point that they play. The Italian—who by "lack of respect" is not referring to any one player in particular, but to tennis in—has a recipe for accelerating tennis: taking away the second serve and shortening the sets. The question is whether you could affect such changes in such a deeply conservative sport.

Nadal is probably known as the slowest player on the circuit between every point due to his numerous tics. The Spaniard also begins matches by making his rivals wait at the net, which is something to which his rivals have resigned themselves. According to Federer, the time that goes by between points is much longer in practice than what the ATP rules set out. "I don't understand how, throughout the length of a four-hour match with Rafa, he never receives any warnings for wasting time," stressed the Swiss who, during the semifinals of the Indian Wells, defeated Nadal forcefully. "It's natural, and even I take too much time, but no one ever says anything. There are times in which [the judges] could be a bit stricter. Because at the end of the day, I don't know if the fans aren't feeling frustrated after seeing five points that are going to take five minutes. We can't be losing fans over this." Two months after the players' meeting explosion at Australia, the tension between the two "R"s was still there.

Miami considered itself, at times, as the "fifth Grand Slam." There was a lot of good marketing behind that tag line, a lot of truth, too, because the tournament that is played at Crandon Park on the island of Key Biscayne not only gathers the best tennis players in the world, but it is also a small jewel of the circuit. It's central stadium approaches perfection, as much for the players and the spectators as for the journalists, who work in one of the few press conference rooms in the world that allows you to watch games directly by just taking a couple of steps to approach the wide window that provides access to the stands. A white sand beach just five minutes' walk away; the lush palms that provide respite from the impious sun; the wide blue gates to the Caribbean, and a tireless nightlife all make the tournament at Miami one that everyone wants to attend.

With time, however, Miami would lose importance in the circuit. When Butch Buchholz, its founder, sold the tournament, it was a strike against its international appeal because the tournament, controlled by the agency IMG, began to think more and more along local lines. There are few today who remember the tag line of "fifth Grand Slam," even though Miami continues to be an important and coveted competition. It is, also, one of the few that Nadal never won, although it is still a place that brings the Spaniard pleasant memories: there, in 2004, he served up a 6–3 and 6–3 in the third round against Federer in the first clash of an extensive series between the two. There was no Nadal-Federer in

2012 in Miami, but there was the validation of a separation. This city in Florida is, along with Wimbledon, the US Open, and the season-closing Masters, one of the four in which the Players' Council of the ATP officially gathers year after year. There might be a meeting in another city, but in these four the appointment is traditional.

Everything seemed to be going well during that meeting in Miami. The members of the council were talking and Federer, in his capacity as president, was organizing the schedule. But Nadal had a surprise in store. In a press conference afterward, he explained that he was leaving his post because he no longer felt he was an appropriate person to be on the council. He said it diplomatically, though he didn't deprive himself of shooting a last message at Federer: "I think we did some good things for the sport, but not enough. I'm not the best option to continue working there. Another person could do a better job than I could these days. I think we could do many more things than what we've done." A little while before, during the council meeting, the farewell had been clean and quick: "I want to thank you all for these years of working together," said the Spaniard, who barely gave his colleagues a chance to react. "Rafa stood up, shook everyone's hand, and left," described one of those present at the meeting in Miami. "Roger was very surprised."

Two and a half years later, Butorac reconstructed the Nadal of the, at times, effervescent council meetings. A former psychology major after all, the American had carefully studied the differences between the Spaniard and the Swiss. According to Butorac, Nadal was volcanic. "Yes . . . and just like his tennis is very passionate, so too does he get passionate about certain topics, while others didn't seem to interest him as much. He went into some of the meetings very hard, but we wanted to have him all the time so he could be with us, it was grandiose that he was there."

The "obsessions" of Nadal included reducing the mandatory tournaments on the calendar and the proposal of a two-year ranking. Neither came to fruition. "I think he was a little frustrated by the end, and maybe he didn't have enough time either; some of the injuries came back . . ." suggested Butorac, who remembers perfectly well the day that Nadal told them he was leaving. "He gave us a good explanation, 'Guys, I'm very frustrated with some of the things that are happening. And that frustration that I have is turning into aggressive conversation with some players, or here in the group. Instead of continuing to pour out my frustrations here, I would rather resign.'" Two years after that resignation, Federer, now the father of four children, also left the council. That marked the end of the unprecedented years of peace and love; tennis went back to normal.

CHAPTER 28

Face to Face

MAYBE ROGER FEDERER AND RAFAEL Nadal aren't exactly who they're believed to be. Or *what* they're believed to be. The roles of both have been assigned forever: Federer is the intelligent, reserved, meticulous Swiss who would never hurt a fly, while Nadal is the spontaneous, sociable, and passionate Spaniard who lays waste to everything. Those roles are anchored in an undeniable reality, but they're also touted by their agents and by Nike, in order to give shape to a commercial strategy and images that would ultimately result in better business and more money for both.

At first glance you might think otherwise, that Federer's image was meticulously controlled from the very beginning. But the reality is different; Anna Wintour of *Vogue* wasn't always there, and you just have to look at the successive photos of the thirty-one Grand Slam trophies that the two held up between them (as of May 2016).

On the first day of the saga, in July 2003, Federer is visibly excited about conquering his first Wimbledon. His excitement is as apparent as his lack of style and image strategy. The Federer in that picture has long, messy hair tied up in a little pony tail. His shirt is excessively baggy and there is generally no statement in the way he dresses. You could say the same about the photos that show him after he won in

Australia and Wimbledon in 2004. The US Open that year marks the beginning of the change in his image, because the hair is shorter (though not as short as it would later be) and the shirt fits a little better. At the 2005 Wimbledon you see Federer for the first time as he would become firmly planted in memory: short, carefully combed hair, smart attire. Everything under control.

It was different with Nadal, at least in part because his and Nike's strategies had the advantage of having observed Federer's experiences before Nadal was really in the public eye. And partly, also, because the Spaniard was always accompanied by the same team in every dimension of his career, while Federer made significant changes. When his moment came, Nadal was perfectly dressed for the occasion. He arrived at the Roland Garros final in 2005 emphasizing his impulsive young attitude in contrast to the established persona of Federer, number one in the world for the prior year and a half. A sleeveless shirt and capri pants, muscles and sweat both on generous display.

When Nadal burst onto the circuit full of adrenaline and testosterone, Federer was already very close to achieving the image of a gentleman that ended up being his distinctive mark. That contrast was present for both of them during the early years of the rivalry. Nadal's image remained the same until he won the 2008 Wimbledon title, the last final he would play with a sleeveless shirt. After conquering Australia in 2009, he left behind his image as a teenager to adopt that of an established young man. It was a decision made by his manager and his family before Australia, and the title confirmed what was already guessed: he was now one of the very few players in history to have won each of the four great tournaments at least one time. A legend. It was time to stop being a teenager.

Lost somewhere in the midst of all this is the memory of Federer's *faux pas* at the 2006 edition of the Wimbledon, which was played on the same day as the Soccer World Cup in Germany between Italy and France. Hours before Zinedine Zidane would perform what is perhaps the most memorable head butt of all time, Federer stepped onto the faded grass of the All England Club wearing a white linen blazer that many thought to be "a touch too much." He wore it when he entered, and put it back on during the awards ceremony. Three years later, Nike made him go to Wimbledon with a white and gold bag combined with a military-style white jacket. He was also not seen on that occasion as a fashion front runner. The line that divides success and failure in public perception is, at times, perhaps much too thin.

During that final in 2006, Federer almost seemed like Nadal's uncle, for the Spaniard still had a boyish face and was crammed into a sleeveless T-shirt, more appropriate for a beach than for Wimbledon, although the color served as a letter of safe-passage. Between Anne White's tights in 1985 and the sleeveless T-shirts worn by Nadal to his first two finals, there is no doubt that the only mandatory dress code at the All England is the color white. Outside of that, you are free to dress however you please.

Chris Evert, who doesn't hesitate to describe Federer as an "artist" and Nadal as a "warrior," subscribes in a certain way to that cliché, although she has more than enough reason to do so. Novak Djokovic, who knows them pretty well, thought about it for a few seconds when asked about the topic during the interview in Monte Carlo:

"*Three words to describe Federer, three to describe Nadal.*"

"Very, very responsible, very competitive, and . . . professional."

"*And Nadal?*"

"Passionate, hot-blooded, and very humble."

The six words chosen by Djokovic, who doesn't extemporize when it comes to those things, are significant. It's not too much of a stretch to say that he feels humanly closer to Nadal than to Federer. The chain of responsible plus competitive plus professional speaks of a much lesser empathy than he has with someone whom he sees as passionate plus hot-blooded plus very humble. The Czech Tomáš Berdych, another man who knows the two "R"s well, doesn't have any trouble describing them. Federer is "a tennis genius." Nadal? "A bull."

There are some aspects, however, in which Nadal is more "Swiss" than Federer. One of them is his trainers. While the Swiss player has alternated through several over the course of his career, and went through a period of time in which he explicitly and implicitly said that he did not need a full-time trainer, Nadal only had one: his uncle Toni. The cliché of the Spaniard would indicate otherwise, a rebellious player who occasionally exhibits a lack of discipline and should, therefore, be expected to keep switching trainers.

Their musical tastes also don't exactly fit in with the stereotypes. Federer would like to be Angus Young, or at least Lenny Kravitz. Nadal, when he turns the key in his ignition, is frequently and happily carried away by the voice of the eternal romantic, Julio Iglesias.

When speaking about Nadal and Federer, it is important to keep in mind that both of their personalities are much too rich and complex to be defined by the clichés. They are clearly a Swiss and a Spaniard, with all that is implied there, but they are also much more than that. Nadal is extremely Spanish, sure, but he also has Prussian tendencies, a level of discipline and self-criticism that is not usual in his country. He tends to blame himself for his problems instead of searching for some exterior cause, which is one of the favorite pastimes of many of his compatriots.

Federer, on the other hand is much more truly Swiss than Nadal is Spanish. As Navrátilová says: he can't separate himself from his "Swissism," although Marco Chiudinelli, one of his best friends, confirms that the very Swiss Federer dreams of something that the Hispanic Nadal would go to any lengths to avoid. "We've been friends since we were six," says Chiudinelli. "We trained together, played together, we rode our bikes . . . Yes, I can see Federer wanting to be Lenny Kravitz. But speaking of musical tastes, I definitely was further out there. He was always a softie."

Softie or not, Federer revealed in 2007 in Dubai that when he lets his imagination soar, he sees himself with an electric guitar, riffing in front of thousands of people. He told Bruno Ziauddin, the reporter from the Swiss magazine *Weltwoche,* that he wanted to be Angus Young, the legendary guitarist and leader of AC/DC. To the journalist from the DPA agency, he offered during that same week a lightly retouched version: he dreamed of being Lenny Kravitz.

"I don't want to be next to Angus Young, I want to be in his place!" When the reporter for the Swiss magazine asked him why he couldn't see himself in a secondary position, Federer laughed. "Somehow, in my case, it seems pretty obvious."

That comment would be unthinkable coming from Nadal, who is convincingly humble, if at times excessively so. As he continued to play against Federer until February of 2016, with a total of twenty-three triumphs and only eleven defeats in the duel between them, his insistence that Federer was a superior player to him started to become even irritating to others. During the later years of rivalry, Nadal modified those statements; the reality forced him to.

Reality also dawned on Federer who, after getting married and having children, gave up his dreams of playing guitar in front of multitudes, his dreams of being Lenny Kravitz. "I saw him live in Paris, and I was so moved by way of connecting to the audience, how they were cheering for him, how I was screaming myself! I would really love to be Lenny Kravitz . . . ! I have to admit: it's something I would love to experience. I would love to play the guitar. But . . . I don't have time."

There is one thing that is very sacred to both Federer and Nadal: respect. To varying degrees, they both believe in respecting and being respected. Formal respect is very important to Federer, in the way that you approach him, the way that you speak to him. Beyond that, you can later build a more spontaneous relationship; but first you have to go through certain steps.

Nadal, the player who was heard uttering the words, "Thank you," more than anyone in the history of tennis, thinks that respect in everyday life is essential, but he obsesses over it most of all in athletic relationships. That's why he was often bothered by Djokovic's jokes or reactions; that's why he didn't like Nick Kyrgios's celebration in the eighth-finals of the 2014 Wimbledon after scoring a point with a shot from between his legs. In that sort of situation, Nadal would have asked for his rival's forgiveness. And not only him.

This is one detail that is worth noticing in the Federer-Nadal duels. Before starting to play and after the greeting at the net, they both give each other a couple of quick slaps on the back. That is respect. The two "R"s are also joined by their ability to manipulate, something that is easy to notice during their press conferences after each match. While Federer makes jokes with subtle details and speaks in very well-rounded phrases, Nadal gets everyone to laugh because he's doing so himself, and manages to disguise the importance of a lot of what he says, even if he's being serious. In their own individual ways, each of them manipulates well. A kind of manipulation that doesn't generally carry a negative connotation. What they're both trying to do is win over their audience, and they do it masterfully.

There are other times, however, other situations that happen behind the scenes in which the two show off just what they're made of. This was apparent in March 2013, at Indian Wells, one of the players' favorite tournaments. Federer had just lost, 6–2 and 6–4, against Nadal in the semifinals, and was suffering from back pains. After a defeat like that, the players quickly wrap up their press conferences and other appointments. But Federer is different. The seven-time Wimbledon champion had postponed an engagement that called for him to answer on video a series of questions from children for a tennis promotional program in Switzerland. The kids sent in the questions, and Federer would answer them in front of a camera. "Okay, come with me," he told the two reporters, Marco Keller and Doris Henkel. The three of them ended up seated on some traditional bar stools around a round table. "Marco read the questions and Federer answered with unmatched sympathy and caring," Henkel remembers. "It would have occurred to no one that his back was hurting, and that he had just lost. Not a trace of that. One of the children's questions put Federer in a tight spot, *"What's your favorite joke?"* "Uh . . . I'm very bad at jokes! I can't remember a single one . . . Oh yeah, here's one: why do the Swiss police always carry a pair of scissors when chasing thieves? To cut off their retreat!"

It is also easier to get to know Nadal through his interactions away from the spotlights. Once, in Viña del Mar, during a training session, a woman sat her two-year, nine-month old daughter, who was about to start treatment for a brain tumor, on Nadal's lap. Nadal played with her for a few minutes and posed for pictures. On more than one occasion, Nadal has found himself in a situation where someone wanted his autograph for someone with a serious illness. What many would deal with using a quick signature and a standard phrase, the Spaniard makes into something special: he asks for the person's name, age, the illness and the state of the situation, and writes a few unforgettable lines for the recipient. He's not the only one: Andy Murray even made a small video for an American in Portland whose life was being eaten away by cancer. It wasn't a marketing ploy; he simply agreed to the spontaneous request.

But every rule has its exceptions there were times in which Federer wasn't exactly respectful. "Don't tell me to calm down, okay? When I want to talk, I will. I don't give a shit what you say," he spat at Jake Garner, the chair umpire during the US Open final in 2009, which he lost to the Argentinian Juan Martín del Potro. Three months later, on the night of his fourth title at the Australian Open, the Swiss player gave an answer that wasn't exactly laden with modesty. The question was, how did he manage to win so often. "It's not a secret: I am definitely a very talented player. I always knew that I had something special, but I never thought it would be as crazy as all this. I always knew I had the skill in my hands, the question was whether I had it in my mind and in my legs." The journalists also occasionally annoy the Swiss player, who, in January of 2016 after falling to Djokovic in the semifinals at Australia, made an ill-tempered remark and labeled a question as "stupid," that absolutely was not.

From a very young age, Federer felt destined for success. Nadal, on the other hand, when he was young felt that success does *not* belong to him, that instead he has to earn it in every match. The Spaniard Àlex Corretja had the opportunity to meet and play against the early versions of Nadal and Federer as professionals. It has been years since then, but his memory of that time is very clear, and he is still impressed by what he saw back then. The last match was on a fast surface in Madrid, with Federer having already won Wimbledon. "I remember the five minutes of passing the ball around before the match. I tossed him the first ball and he tossed back a missile with zero effort. I fired the next shot, and he answered with a slice that hit me right at my feet and buried me. I was shocked. I have the memory of that really fast ball. It surprised me. I noted that it was going to be impossible, and I was impressed how he rotated shoulders, just like Sampras did. Impossible to read his serve."

During that year of 2003 in Madrid, Corretja got a perfect look at both players, because he defeated a seventeen-year-old Nadal in the first round and fell against Federer in the second. It had been three years since he first saw Nadal, but much less time had passed since he managed to actually talk to him. "The first time I saw him was when he carried our flag at the 2000 Davis Cup final. We couldn't get a single word out of him, he wouldn't talk! They introduced him to us before we left. 'Hey man, what's up!' we said. Nothing, he wouldn't open his mouth. Not a word.

"My second memory at the professional level was during a winter training in 2003. Monday, nine in the morning, I arrive in my jacket, scarf, hat, gloves. It was December! It was 35 or 40 degrees out. I got there and I found Rafa in short sleeves, shorts, and with a racket, waiting for me. 'You're going to get a cold!' I told him. 'No, no, I'm ready when you are,' he answered. 'I have to take a few laps around the track, warm up,' I explained. I started to run laps, to get warmed up. I kept going. He was waiting for me. When I shot the first ball at him, he tossed back a heavy forehand at 9:15 in the morning that made me say, 'Where did this kid come from!' You can't imagine how hard it was . . . I stopped it and asked him if he always starts off that hard. I told him he was going to break. 'No, no, I always play like this . . .' This kid was raised to be such a killer that he has to do everything right on the very first try. In training, he played at a speed and a rhythm at just fifteen years old that you could barely keep up with. I've never felt anything like that with anyone. It was like when you would toss the ball around with Agassi during a training, you would go up the net and have to put on a helmet. Or with [Gustavo] Kuerten. Missiles, clubs."

Months after that training, Corretja, in the last stretch of his career, ran into Nadal in the Polish city of Sopot. It was 2004. "Rafa was there, and I remember him studying the list of the rankings and the tournament bracket, the points being assigned, all that. He looked and said, 'If I win here, I'd get two hundred points and would enter in such and such tournament, I would be prequalified here . . . ' I thought he was being really bold, how could he already be talking about winning the tournament? On Sunday, when he won, I understood that he felt he was ready for it. That is something special, he is unique, different."

Corretja, who was also the captain of Nadal's Davis Cup team, thinks that the left-handed player's humility is key to his success. "He takes every match with the same humility and discipline as if it were the hardest one all year. If he finds out, once started, that it's easy, then all the better. If he needs to give it his all, then he's ready too." As the years went on, Nadal realized that spending hours and hours on the court wasn't good for him. "The Rafa of these later years is different. He knew that by using an established system he could win 90 percent of his matches, but his game today is much more aggressive than five or six years ago. Then there are people who say that Nadal is a pusher, but how is he a pusher? Nadal is a rock, a boulder that can hit a thousand balls with colossal intensity that only the best prepared can withstand!

"When you see Rafa train, he hits the ball much harder and moves his arm forward more than he does in matches. After his last injury that changed as well, he's much more aggressive. If he has to miss, he misses, but he doesn't think along the lines that he'll still win if he only plays with 80 percent of his effort. But he still will if he needs to, and take four hours to win against the 170th in the world. He has one play style that he can adapt, and another that he uses to steamroll you. Not many can do that."

Nadal and Federer, of course, attract women. Including Martina Hingis, a child tennis prodigy who reached number one in the world at sixteen years and ten months of age, and who admits to feeling privileged that she was able to closely experience the "R"s rivalry. "It's the best there's been. Agassi versus Sampras was a great rivalry, too, but I didn't live through it as much. And of McEnroe versus Connors I only have memories from television. For me it was very nice to see the Nadal and Federer era, the contrast between the power and muscles of Nadal with the lightness and grace of Roger." Another female observer of the circuit took that comparison down a different route, "If I imagine having an affair with them, I think I would rather have Roger in the bedroom; he seems smoother. And Nadal, in the kitchen. He's so wild!"

Tennis isn't like the other great American professional sports leagues, like basketball, American football, baseball, and ice hockey, where the reporters are used to walking into the locker rooms and talking to the stars. But those who do frequently move around the locker rooms of the male circuit notice another fundamental difference between the two "R"s. "Federer always has a towel on. Nadal doesn't seem to be aware of the need for one."

In tennis there are observers in discreet places, people who aren't on television but who see and hear many things. This is true of Jaime Morrocco, who has been traveling to tournaments since 1995 to provide a product that is very much appreciated by journalists, agents, and even the players: the transcripts from the press conferences. Morrocco is part of a team that offers extremely quick and highly reliable logs of the questions and answers of the main players and stars on the circuit. From his corner, he has gotten to know the players as few others have.

"As always in life, you run into people you like and, sometimes, with others you don't so much. The same thing happens in tennis. Sometimes you connect, sometimes you don't." Morrocco says he and his colleagues tend to classify the players into three categories: the kind of person he is; the difficulties involved in transcribing his words (such as how fast he talks, the quality of his English, and his accent are three key factors), and finally, what kind of tennis player he is. "Some people like Rafa, who I love as well. I love his tennis, I love him as a human being, although transcribing him is not easy due to his strong accent. But despite all that, we love him. As far as Novak, his game is incredible. In my opinion, he's very good during the press conferences, not only because it's easy to type what he says, since his English is very good, but also because he's clever and he can play with the reporters a bit. I also think he's a good person, contrary to what many people may say. I think he matured and learned from his earlier mistakes."

"And Federer?" "For some reason I could never connect with him. I sometimes think that he seems too perfect to be real. Although probably no one can deny that he's the best player that has ever held a racket, my experience in his press conferences isn't the best." *"Why?"* "I'm not a big fan of dynasties, and he's been the king for almost a decade now. I would like to see more variety. And another thing about Roger is that he's never said thank you to me, which is curious. He definitely knows who we are, but he never says 'hello.' It just strikes me as strange in someone who people consider to be generous with his time for the media. And Serena Williams is another player I don't connect with, she also has never greeted us. I've heard her talk in interviews about 'checking the transcript,' so she definitely knows that someone is doing it. I also didn't connect with Justine Henin; she seemed cold and distant. But at the end of her career, when she retired, she came to your desk after the last press conference and thanked us for all the hard work during the years. It was something that I found really moving and it changed my opinion of her."

Although Nadal's communication skill is one of the most professional on the circuit, and although the Spaniard's image is one of the best on the circuit, things don't always turn out the way the player and Benito Pérez Barbadillo would like. The clearest example was his interview with Lynn Barber in 2011 for the British newspaper the *Sunday Times*. Known for her strict prose when interviewing, and for her sometimes overly-caustic style, Barber condensed into 3,500 words something that had never been read about the Spaniard. It was clear that she did not like Nadal. The paradox of that case is that the interview was part of a contract: the Queen's tournament paid Nadal a large sum to have him as a star that year, which is something that happens in the rest of the tournaments. One of the clauses of the contract was the obligation of offering an extensive interview to one of the big British media outlets. Barber isn't just some nobody; in fact, she is a winner of several journalistic awards, among them the prestigious British Press Award. She wrote for such media as *Penthouse*, the *Independent on Sunday*, *Vanity Fair*, the *Sunday Times*, the *Daily Telegraph*, and the *Observer*. Her first book is titled, *How to Improve Your Man In Bed*.

An excerpt from their interview includes: "If someone tells me how pleasant that boy Rafael Nadal is, I might scream. He's not a boy, he just turned 25, which is certainly young, but he's been in the circuit for nine years, he won nine Grand Slam tournaments, and has already earned 68 million pounds. And I didn't find him pleasant at all. When we finally met at the suite of his hotel in Rome, where he was playing the Masters, he was lying on a massage table with his pants unbuttoned, allowing me a good view of his Armani underwear, which is one of his many sponsors. Makes sense.

"There's no doubt that in that situation, millions of his fans would be screaming, jealous, and bent on killing me, but honestly, boys, it was a bit rude. He was laying there watching me with his eyebrows wrinkled while I situated myself however I could on a nearby table until his press agent, Benito Pérez Barbadillo, brought me a chair. Benito sat in the back, and every time Nadal didn't like a question (which was basically every time one was asked), he asked Benito to "translate," which meant that they would talk in Spanish until the press agent came up with a very public relations answer. Nadal's mastery of the English language seems highly variable, but never very good." The article clearly wasn't what Pérez Barbadillo and Queen's expected.

The permanent staff at Roland Garros have a very different opinion from Barber's. All the men there, and especially the women, are Nadal's fans. "He always says 'hello,' he always says 'thank you,' and he always smiles at you," explains one person who deals with the stars year after year. "Federer is proper, that's the best way to describe him. Novak, on the other hand, hardly looks at us when he talks, he's not very empathetic."

There is another anecdote that reflects the degree of respect and care that Nadal has always had in his relationship with Federer.

A fan of golf, Nadal had been an admirer of Tiger Woods from the time he was very young, but he kept that admiration and contact in check, because the relationship between Federer and the American golfer was very widely known and promoted. By 2015 Nadal and Woods both spoke over the phone easily and familiarly, but ten years before, when they first met face to face, the situation overwhelmed the young Nadal.

Woods was playing a tournament in Shanghai, and Nadal and a couple of others in his group had been invited to follow the game from inside the rope. Tiger Woods took a big bite out of an apple, approached the tee, hit a good drive and approached the Nadals. "Hi, Rafa!" "Hi, Tiger . . ." "Rafa was shaking," his companions at the time smilingly recalled a decade later. "Hello, nice to meet you," they added, joking about Nadal's thick accent when he said "hello."

Nadal has a dream he would like to achieve someday: playing eighteen holes with Tiger Woods. Now, without exaggerating: even though Àlex Corretja thinks that Nadal could be a professional golfer once he leaves tennis, and even though his own father fantasized about the idea, the tennis player assures that he's not really considering it. "It would be hugely arrogant to think that once I retire I could focus on golf. Those who have seen me play know that's not a possibility," he said in 2013 to the Spanish reporter Ana Pastor. But he would love to . . . he would love to.

Ever since he turned twenty-five, the topic of age and the passage of time started to become a recurring theme in Nadal's conversations, although there is one thing about him that never changes: there is always something boyish about Nadal. In Federer's case it's different; you often see an older man reflected in his face.

Flushing Meadows, during the first minutes of September 6, 2011. Federer is massacring the Argentinian Juan Mónaco, and he wants to change rackets. He pulls one out of his racket bag and, without saying anything, points the end at one of the ball boys, who already knows what to do: pull on the plastic bag that is wrapped around the racket. And later, throw it away.

Federer doesn't always have a lot of time, and Eric Butorac, when he was the vice president of the Players' Council, knew it well. To talk to the Swiss, you had to look for any opportunity. "He's so busy that you have to find the proper moment to talk to him. For example, he was in the locker room tying up his tennis shoes and I would say, 'Okay, this, this, and this are all happening.' And he's so intelligent that he picked up on it all so fast!" "I think I was a very good vice president for him. I would investigate and study topics, things he asked me," added Butorac, who has no history as a singles player, but is a reasonable doubles.

When Federer left the presidency of the council, which Nadal had left earlier, the American Butorac knew he could count on Federer, whom he admired unreservedly.

"We have a good relationship, and he knows how passionate I am about it. And I know that when there is some negotiation or important topic, I can rely on him. He called me before and after being elected and really supported me. We've talked a lot in the past two years. He knows so much about this sport . . .!"

The question was repeated for years in different press conference rooms around the world. They both heard it, but Federer did most of all. *"Did Nadal make you a better player than you were?"* Federer likes to talk about the fairness of it, because it gives way to an excessively ample debate. The question came to him again in January of 2015 in Australia. "It's hard to define exactly what makes you a better player. I think that maybe your work ethic, being more professional, trying different things, your mental attitude . . . Those kinds of things, for me, are more important than a specific shot that I work on before facing Rafa. The thing is that you can't just work on your game for the purpose of playing Rafa, because we were number one and two for a long time, and now we are again. So we're only playing in the finals. To get there we have to beat four, five, or six other players. No one plays like Rafa does, and the same is true for him about me. That's why it's not adequate to focus on facing just one other player."

"But did he make you a better player?"

"I've already answered that several times, and so has he."

278 • ROGER FEDERER AND RAFAEL NADAL

Are Federer and Nadal friends? No, they're not, according to Nadal. "We understand each other well, but we're not friends. Not because we're rivals, but because my friends are those friends from Mallorca. Friends are those people who are a part of your life day after day, the ones who you are always in contact with. But I've always had a good relationship with Roger," Nadal explained to *Tages Anzeiger* towards the end of 2014. "I always had great respect for him and he for me. Besides that, we did a lot of positive things together, for example the exhibitions all over the world for our foundations. I hope we can maintain that good relationship after our careers."

They're not friends, but they can have a lot of fun together. There is a video in which both are seen rehearsing some phrases for a television promotion of the exhibitions in 2010. It was material that was not meant to be public, but ended up a bit hit on YouTube. Sitting shoulder to shoulder, Federer recalls an interview on CNN in which he couldn't stop laughing, and he mentions the interviewer. "A fun guy, Pedro Pinto. He plays golf well, right?" Nadal's face makes it clear that the Portuguese is not exactly a splendid golfer, "Well, more or less . . ." Federer keeps cracking up over and over, starts laughing and can't string together more than two phrases of the dialogue they are supposed to have. "Can you imagine if we had to make a movie together? It would take five years," he says at one point. Nadal, who feels he is at a disadvantage against the Swiss when speaking English, puffs and tries to lessen the tension, "Man, I'm sweating like a beast." Federer interrupts the recording for the thousandth time and breaks out in laughter. Nadal seems genuinely surprised.

"I said 'Switzerland,' did I say it wrong?" "No, no, it was perfect. It's me, this situation is so crazy," answers Federer. By the end, the Swiss even manages a phrase in Spanish. The announcement is a wrap. Nadal gives the Swiss star a smack on the leg, who offers up the last joke, "And tomorrow, more."

The Spaniard can also be very serious if the situation calls for it. During that September in 2010 when he won his first US Open, Nadal hadn't yet read *Open*, Andre Agassi's autobiography, but he was surprised to hear that the American had written about coming to "hate" tennis. *Could you hate tennis?* "No . . . Hate it, I couldn't hate, because tennis has given me so much. There are other things in life, sure, but tennis has given me a lot of things, I can't hate a sport that has given me what it gave me. And I can't believe that Agassi hated tennis when he played until he was thirty-five. If you hate tennis, and you start at sixteen, you would probably leave a lot sooner, as soon as you had the chance."

Feliciano López isn't just a great tennis player. At six feet and two inches, with blue eyes and an imposing physique, he is also handsome, something which gave him many advantages and the occasional problems throughout a career in which he played his best tennis in his thirties. And not just because of Andy Murray's mother's insistence on calling him "Deliciano," or because of the reporter who made him blush during a press conference in Madrid. "Maybe you'd like to know that there's one journalist who thinks you're more handsome than David Beckham," she started to say, to the player's confusion. "And I am that journalist," she concluded. Stunned, López limited himself to just thanking her. He did not, however, thank Justin Gimelstob, a lesser known former American player who reached number 64 on the world ranking after only ever playing one final in a major circuit, at Newport in 2006. He was more successful in a doubles role after his retirement, as a television commentator and a political player in the ATP; that's when he was at his best. Gimelstob liked to talk and make jokes, but at the 2011 Wimbledon, his joke didn't go over so well. During a presentation prior to a lunch in the Wimbledon VIP zone, Gimelstob analyzed the matches of the day on the central court, among them the one between López and his compatriot and close friend, Andy Roddick. The American praised López's game, but commented on two occasions that "if he looked at himself in the mirror less," the Spaniard would "be a better tennis player."

Hours later, López defeated Roddick on the central court, which didn't prevent Gimelstob from going even deeper into his sarcastic analysis. "I think Feliciano is a great player, but he definitely loves looking at himself in the mirror. And that's okay, he is a very attractive man. You always hear about the women, but he's tall, good-looking, with a good body. Very metrosexual, yes. But not only him, his tennis is also attractive, very stylish." López did not like his comments at all, and reacted with a sharp tweet: "It's fun when people like Justin Gimelstob say foolish things without knowing me at all. He wasn't taught about respect when he was a child." Gimelstob apologized while speaking of a "misunderstanding" and, without a shred of legitimacy, said that he had been "taken completely out of context."

López is, apart from a successful tennis player, a solid analyst of the circuit. A great friend of Nadal's, he also admired Federer's tennis. "It's that Federer doesn't sweat, he doesn't sweat! The day that he retires is going to be very impressive.

"If anyone has merit it's him, because the demand for him to keep playing every year is very different from what the rest of us at his age get. Aside from the fact that he doesn't get tired and that his tennis game is incredible, on top of it all he is authentically super-gifted, because no one in his situation would be playing tennis. Not only because of the four kids, but everything: because he has been the best in history, because he has won everything possible, and more. There are a lot of reasons he could have for saying farewell and leaving the sport, but he loves to play. The fact that Federer is still playing is a gift to tennis."

López can't believe the things Federer is capable of doing. "He plays and wins, with four kids . . . It's brilliant! I see him every day, and I can't believe the display of logistics that he puts on. He has the grandparents, the nannies, the transportation . . . And sure, his wife is there, but he's the father. He's here with his four kids, that's not something that has happened in tennis history."

Federer has never left a match. Never. And only three times did he not show up to a match and give his opponent a walkover. Nadal, on the other hand, didn't make it to the end of six matches, and gave a walkover to another two. That statistic doesn't reflect their attitudes towards the sport, because they are identical in that respect: they give their all, always. Nadal, in addition, hates leaving. What the statistic does confirm, however, is the great difference between their tennis game and physical constitution. Very little fatigue in Federer's case, and much more in Nadal's.

American television presented an interesting fact in January 2015, during the Australian Open. Federer had just lost the first set against the Italian Simone Bolelli and was being attended to for a problem in one finger. It was only the third time in his career that a medic walked onto the court to look at the Swiss. In Nadal's case, the number of times that has happened is innumerable. Could it have something to do with the savage effort that the Spaniard puts in during training? When it comes to playing tournaments, Nadal squares away about 30 percent or 40 percent of that potential; his priority is winning. "Toni says that because he hates losing so much he's more conservative, he doesn't want to miss," points out Carlos Moyá, Nadal's friend and mentor. "I've trained with him many times, and his rhythm is intolerable. He hits harder than Federer, than Djokovic. Harder than anyone."

Nadal was, during his first years as a player, a man with two personalities. "When I started playing at sixteen, I was very shy. Very shy. But I wasn't when I was on the court," the Spaniard admits. At the same age, Federer was throwing rackets and was happy to be kicked out of a training class. Moyá also remembers those first years with Nadal. "He was the kind of person who barely looked you in the eyes, because he was shy. But then he would get on the court and there he was comfortable. He had the same self-confidence as McEnroe, to face down whatever he needed to, that winner's mentality. And he had Borg's coldness. His attitude was 'until you finish me off and have me pinned on the ground, I'll keep fighting.'"

CHAPTER 29

Unbelievable

IT IS FEBRUARY 2016 IN Buenos Aires, and all eyes are fixed on Rafael Nadal, no different from anywhere else in the world. The difference is that this time, the crowds watching him don't know who this player is anymore.

Yes, Nadal's gestures are the same as ever, and he has the same nasal Spanish accent with remnants of the Catalan-Manacori that he speaks at home. It seems like him, because his eyebrow keeps going up and down at inhuman angles, and because the verbal tics—"evidently," "I'm not going to lie," "and what do you think?"—are the same as ever.

But this is not Rafael Nadal. If before his faith helped him win games, now it consoled him after defeats that seemed out of character, to fool himself about what was happening.

It's a Saturday afternoon. Summer. The night before, the sky fell on the Argentine capital with an electrical storm as apocalyptic as the question that fans and journalists were asking over and over.

"Is Rafa finished?"

Even those who no longer watched him on TV called him "Rafa," so familiar was the left-hander that plays tennis like no one ever played before and probably like no one will ever play again.

"Is he finished?" The question had been circulating for a while on the circuit.

On that humid and oppressive Saturday ("one day there's going to be a tragedy," Nadal, red as a tomato from the heat, had said the day before), the best Spanish athlete of all time became a photocopy of himself. And the printer was out of ink.

He had come to have a match point in his favor against the Austrian Dominic Thiem, a talented and promising player, but in that moment it was no more than that. The match point came with Nadal up 5-4 in the third set of the semifinals of the Argentina Open, and as it came it went, as it often does, with the player set to serve saving the game. Normal.

What's not normal is the way in which Nadal ultimately lost the match, by a score of 6-4, 4-6, and 7-6 (7-4), against the man who was then the youngest of the 20 best players in the world. When it came to the tiebreaker in the third set, that moment in which experience is everything, Rafael Nadal was crude: double fault on the first point.

Anyone can double-fault, although not all double faults bear the same weight. Depending on the moment in which they fail to hit the rectangle, erring two consecutive times is either an anecdote or a category. In the first moments of 2016, double faults and tiebreakers left a mark on Nadal, who lost the two tiebreakers in his surprising defeat against Fernando Verdasco in the first round of the Australian Open, a game in which there were also double faults at key moments. It was also a tiebreaker that caused his defeat in the semifinals in Rio de Janeiro against a player, the Uruguayan Pablo Cuevas, that previously would not have frightened him.

There was no longer any doubt: Nadal, about to celebrate his thirtieth birthday that June, was feeling the pressure. He was afraid, a healthy human fear, of not being able to be as good as he had been. This fear took hold of him when the pressure to win the point rose, and it weighed in his legs until he no longer had his historic strength: agility.

Nevertheless, he can't feel bad with what he's done. After all, he's still one of those born with that "something special" that he's convinced is necessary to win. He was, among many other achievements, the best in the world in 2008, 2010, and 2013. Whether experiencing a period of success or failure on the court, though, Nadal rarely made excuses: "The maker of all success and all bad moments is the player."

He went far, clearly farther than he or others expected, although in those afternoons of unbearable heat in Buenos Aires, Nadal would utter a phrase that said a lot, coming from him: "No one wins eternally."

No one. But what stood out about Nadal wasn't that he didn't win. What was surprising was that his level of play was deteriorating. Through history, many players slow down without losing who they are. Nadal, on the other hand, was fading and seemed less and less himself. He was still himself when it was time to play the hero, resisting and recovering an impossible point, but he stopped being himself when it was time to finish off a match from a vantage point.

Loss by loss, Nadal pulled rabbits from his hat. But one couldn't ask him for the regularity or consistency in 2016 which he had had in the past. It was all lost in his labyrinth of emotions. The Argentine Open is not—"evidently," according to Nadal—one of the top tournaments of the circuit. It is a small event, though full of passion and fans. Because of that and for other reasons, focusing on Buenos Aires to explain Nadal's situation in such a strange season makes a lot of sense. Almost every Nadal went through the Argentine summer tournament, except the explosive eighteen-year-old one and the despondent thirty-year-old one.

He came from the worst year in his career, 2015, which was the first time he failed to get a Grand Slam title since his break at the top. The same would happen in 2016. However, he did not know that when, in February of the same year, he would arrive at Buenos Aires looking for an emotional bandage: a title that would help him to recall who he was and to keep believing he still was that person.

Not only did he leave without either of those beliefs, but he also carried with him the memory of Toni—his uncle and coach—performing one of his periodic honest rants.

Surrounded by hundreds of Argentines, already nightfall in the port city, the nine-times Roland Garros champion's coach gave an open and spontaneous talk. The question that came from the crowd was whether his nephew shouldn't hire a different coach to relaunch his career. Toni did not avoid the topic, although by what he said, avoiding it might have been wiser: "I have been lucky to be his uncle so that it has been difficult for him to change coaches. This has been easier for me because if I were not his uncle he probably would have already replaced me".

He added that his nephew "had always liked football much more than tennis" and confessed that he wished Nadal's mythic, devastating right topspin never existed. He would have liked to see him hit like Federer: "I would have loved to see him hit the drive out front, which is how we always practiced it when he was little."

Toni recalls when Nadal's approach originated. "I still remember the moment, against [Guillermo] Coria in Monte Carlo, when Rafael was sixteen. Up until then, Rafael was a player who always tended to hit forward, but once he started to play the professional circuit he began to hit the ball a little later, and began to lift his hand more."

Ultimately, barely a year after that tournament in Argentina, a change was reportedly underway:

Toni would tell an Italian journalist that he would no longer train his nephew at the end of the year. The catch was that his nephew didn't know about the decision: he found out through the press.

Yet even harder than determining the future of uncle and nephew was to answer the other question. Was Nadal finished? Not even he knew. However, before losing in Buenos Aires he commented: "The saying that winning is learned by winning is very true."

It was. And Nadal was forgetting how to win. Although not forever, because tennis was still awaiting what would end up as arguably one of the most astonishing comeback stories of all time.

• • • •

How is it possible? The question ran through the tennis world with growing astonishment and volume throughout 2017. One would think that the future would be coming, but what returned, stronger than ever, was the past. Roger Federer and Rafael Nadal were once again the dominant names, on the heels of several seasons that saw them both overshadowed, worn out, and hesitant.

They were so dominant, in fact, that the 2017 season ended with a balance that seemed out of a previous decade: Federer, champion in Australia and Wimbledon and number two at the end of the year in the ATP rankings; Nadal, owner of Roland Garros, the US Open, and number one for the season. The last time that the two Rs had owned the first two positions in the ranking was 2010. Seven years later, the veterans were back in charge, accompanied by young players like Grigor Dimitrov, Alexander Zverev, and Dominic Thiem to round out the top five. How is it possible? If we listen to Mats Wilander, ex-number one in the world and now one of the sharpest and most scathing analysts in tennis, January 29, 2017 is one of the most important days in the history of tennis. It's the day in which Federer beat Nadal in the final of the Australian Open after coming back from 3-1 down in the fifth set, when the Spaniard could have made set point at 4-2. Federer won 6-4, 3-6, 6-1, 3-6, and 6-3, and his history of inferiority to Nadal would never be the same. As Wilander noted, "He beat Nadal last year four times in a row. He's the best."

Wilander, who has a journalist's soul as well as that of a tennis player, likes a strong headline, and in this chat at the end of the year in the hallways of Flushing Meadows, he was blunt: "Nadal's 3-1 in the fifth set of the Australian Open was the defining moment of the year, because it changed everything, everything that we knew about the two of them, everything we knew about what the duel between them historically is. The fifth set of the Australian Open changed the next five years of professional tennis . . . or say the next three or four. It changed them completely."

Slightly excessive, perhaps (the next 3 or 4 years?), but the Swede's theory is based in something simple: If Federer had fallen to Nadal in that final—as had happened 23 of the 34 times that they had played before then—his spirits would have been crushed. Nadal was, throughout his career, Federer's Kryptonite. The Swiss found the way to counteract its effects in that Australian duel, and that gave him the formula to do the same in Indian Wells, Miami, and Shanghai. The events of 2017 have no precedent in the long history that the two players share: they faced each other four times, and Federer won all four. Breaking this psychological dependency was key for the Swiss to also win Wimbledon and finish the year with seven titles in total, coming within striking distance of number one in the world. He would recover that title in 2018 to become the most veteran leader of the ranking in history.

Wilander, in trying to analyze what had happened during this magical year, had his eyes wide open. Pure and simple astonishment. Were two simultaneous and successful comebacks possible?

"No, no it wasn't possible. I never could have imagined this . . . People ask me why it happened. It's simple: because they are the two best players in history. Period. And by a mile . . . It also so happens that both of them love to play tennis, and when you love tennis you also continue learning. When Nadal is playing, you see the love that he has for tennis. It's visible, almost palpable."

According to the Swede, these men that he defines as the two best players of all time continued learning new things in 2017. "What did they learn this year? Well, Federer learned to come up more on the backhand, to attack it more. Which he does now, really, almost all the time. He also learned to be a better volleyer and to cover the net. Strategically he's much better than he ever was. And exactly the same happened with Nadal. They both have a much bigger variety of strokes than before.

"If Federer improved his backhand so notably, I should say that Nadal changed his serve completely. It's much, much better than before. The first serve is much flatter than before, he doesn't rely on the slice as much. Now it's evident that he controls the play much better."

It was true: in those six months of 2016 during which Federer was off the circuit preparing for his big return, his coach, Severin Lüthi, told trusted friends to prepare to "see some new things."

One of these novelties was the backhand. Lüthi worked a lot on that; it was his idea to change the stroke. And it was Ivan Ljubicic who gave Federer decisive technical advice to transform his backhand into a fearsome weapon.

Beyond the technical aspects, Wilander believes that there's something in the hearts of both champions that allows them to go farther than all their predecessors: "The key is that they both respect their rivals a lot. Why? Because they love this sport. They play simply to compete against whoever is on the other side. And they don't want to lose. They don't play to win Grand Slams; if they keep playing it's to beat the other guy in the battle on the court. Every point, every game is important to them."

Wilander's observation is no small thing. These days, when so many young, talented tennis players throw their careers in the trash and openly say that they're only interested in earning a lot of money and spending it, the two "Rs" still see their sport the way it was a century ago: a gentlemen's game, in which respect for the rival is fundamental and not giving your all on the court, a sin.

This is enough and more to revive an extraordinary history and make it even more extraordinary.

• • • •

It was 5:05 in Paris on June 11, 2017 and Rafael Nadal was demonstrating, once again, that devastating enormity of skill. Stanislas Wawrinka went up to the net because, well, with a two-set disadvantage at zero, he had to do something. But the truth is, he nearly went for a stroll. The Swiss deserved it then when Nadal hit him with a passing drive and celebrated with a bestial grunt.

"This is mine!" the play made it clear. Mine. Mine. Mine. And so on, six more times, ten in total. Many times Nadal had broken, but not this time. This time, he reached the unthinkable number of ten Roland Garros titles and everyone was wondering if he would stop at twelve or fifteen. All of this, after a hard psychological start to the year, after the losses to Federer. Now he was playing on the clay at the best level of his career, and with a more stylized and "intelligent" physicality than ever. The "Incredible Hulk" from Mallorca was just a memory. He reinvented himself to win at thirty-one years of age, with fifteen years on the circuit under his belt. He even had the luxury of replacing Toni, his uncle-coach, from the center of decision-making and still had the elegance to keep him in the center of the photo when he received the trophy. Nadal knew that his uncle hadn't taken the addition of Carlos Moyá as trainer so well.

Those days in Paris, in which Federer was absent to prepare for Wimbledon, were crazy. The final was played under oppressive humid heat, simply atrocious conditions. Having a front-row seat in the official box wasn't a privilege, but torture. Nevertheless, Nadal had a perfect afternoon and his rival melted right away. The Spaniard was so anxious to start playing that historic final that for the first time he didn't make his rival wait at the pre-game ceremony by the net. It was Wawrinka who was late.

The final can be summed up simply: Nadal scored the first point at 3:15 and sealed his victory at 5:20. After collapsing on his back, overcome by happiness, in the orange dust of Paris, Nadal went up to the dais in Philippe Chatrier Court to receive his trophy, while strains of tango filled the stadium.

It was uncle Toni who went up to give him the trophy after a video display of Nadal's ten titles on the stadium's big screen. The images gave goosebumps. There you could see young Nadal, almost a kid, the Tarzanesque Nadal, the Nadal who grew and suffered . . . and the Nadal who won, because he (almost) always won. Who says the Parisian crowd doesn't love Nadal? The ovation was long and thunderous. Everyone present was witness to something unprecedented. They enjoyed it and reveled in it together in tennis's *terra incognita*.

Two days later, the sports daily *L'Equipe* launched a 40-page special edition on the Spaniard's ten titles. Forty pages—an entire edition—dedicated to Nadal!

His compatriot Alex Corretja, defeated by Moyá in the final in 1998, interviewed the champion's coach for Eurosport and couldn't hide his astonishment. "You've won it, you know what it feels like. And now Rafa's won it 10 times!"

"Yes, it's incredible," Moyá admitted. "We thought that we'd never see it in our lives." But there it is: life is like that: Nadal x 10.

• • • •

When Wilander analyzed the astonishing year Nadal and Federer had in 2017, he already intuited that the Spaniard would end the season in the number-one spot, but he couldn't have known that the Swiss would return to this position on February 19, 2018. Thirty-six years, six months, and eleven days to become the most veteran leader of the ranking in the history of professional tennis. And to confirm that "fairy tale" is a good descriptor for Federer's revival.

Curiously, it was Federer himself who used "fairy tale" to describe his road to Melbourne and his 20th Grand Slam title, essential for his leap to number one. What's interesting is that months before, he had asserted that this idea of "fairy tales" was something that journalists obsessed over, but which did not interest him.

It was during an interview with Peter de Jonge, journalist for the *New York Times*, in August of 2016 in the lobby of the Le Mount Stephen hotel in Montreal. De Jonge asked him if it was a shame to see Usain Bolt with the bronze instead of the gold in the hundred-meter at the World Championship in London.

"Well, you know, it was maybe a pity that he didn't win," said Federer, stressing the "maybe." "But at the same time, it doesn't change anything in my opinion if he won the last race or not. I'm long past the thing that you have to end your career in a fairy tale. Everybody kind of wants this—mostly the press—and if you don't win, it's: 'Ohhh, my God! The fairy tale didn't happen!' So for me, yes, it would have been nice, but this way is okay, too."

Federer can say what he wants, but those two weeks in 2018 when he defended his Australian title (which he'd won the previous year against Nadal), against the Croatian Marin Čilić was basically a fairy tale. His tears at the award ceremony moved everyone.

While they celebrated his success, a certainty passed through the minds of many spectators: in Federer, there was something that went beyond his celestial tennis. More than that? Yes, the man had superpowers, or at least, influences of a higher power. For those who doubted it, two images from that Australian night suffice to confirm it.

It was the unusual emission, in the middle of the men's final, of images of the Romanian Simona Halep asleep and with an IV in her arm. Halep was recovering from the severe dehydration she suffered the night before during the final lost against the Dane Caroline Wozniacki. It was the first time that a Grand Slam final connected to a hospital room in the middle of a game.

The other image was the closed roof of the Rod Laver Arena, a highly questionable decision: beyond the intense heat, the game was played at night. Closing the roof when the sun was no longer hitting? It was clear that the organizers didn't want Federer to end up like Halep.

The Swiss took full advantage of the conditions that most benefited him—fast surface and covered court—in order to, without the stress of the sun or the complications of win, overpower Čilić and conquer the Grand Slam at which he'd been historically disadvantaged (compared to the other three major tournaments) for the sixth time. Australia was thus the major landmark in tennis for the second year in a row. In 2017, it had been the emotional final in which Federer beat Nadal. This time, with "Roger XX," which coincidentally sounds like the name of a king.

Does Federer get special treatment at tournaments? The answer is that everyone knows full well what it means to have a man capable of winning a Grand Slam at 36 years and 173 days of age. You have to take care of him. And they do.

Blessed almost always with nocturnal sessions, Federer didn't waste away under the sun during the tournament, and in the final he played at a comfortable 23 degrees, when the night before Wozniacki and Halep had been condemned to play in the middle of the extreme heat wave that the "Outback," the desert in the center of the country, occasionally throws at the coast.

If Federer surprised everyone in 2017 playing a type of "tennis ping pong" to drive Nadal crazy, a year later he was demonstrating remarkable force in the backhand at shoulder level, a position from which he hit winning strikes that he never could have dreamed of in his youth. The moral? Talent alone is not enough; you have to work. Or perhaps it's that not everyone has the talent to want to work. Federer has an excess of both: technical talent and talent for hard work.

So the Swiss started out 2018 in a parallel dimension. He played something different: he hadn't won a Grand Slam since 2012 at the All England Club, but after winning Australia and Wimbledon in 2017, he got the twentieth in Melbourne right at the beginning of the following year. What more could Federer want? He wants more: he wants, for example, to reach 22 Grand Slams like Steffi Graf, whose photo he touched in the halls of the Rod Laver Arena when he left with the trophy in hand.

Federer's parallel dimension is so special that in the moment he made history in a stadium named for Rod Laver, Laver himself wanted to take photos to immortalize it. The legendary Australian will have time to keep trying out his cameraphone, because Wilander and Andre Agassi see the Swiss playing until he hits forty.

Pete Sampras had already predicted it in 2009: "Federer's going to win twenty Grand Slams."

It sounded like science fiction, but it was possible because Federer has the exact mentality that an elite athlete needs. When he is moved to tears by every great triumph he proves that the sport can't be won with the mind alone; it requires a lot of heart.

And just as those who were around in the 1960s were moved to see *The Post* in theaters in 2017, it's likely that in a few decades young spectators will be similarly moved to see a movie about the Swiss tennis star. Of course, they couldn't be more different, because a war has a real and symbolic dimension (and a sadness) impossible to compare to sports. But still, the Vietnam War and the athletic triumphs of Federer have something in common: they are powerful stories that mark the minds and hearts of a generation. An entire generation with the senseless horror of Vietnam burned in the consciousness, the memory of the tears spilled. And another generation, half a century later, that proved that sometimes, fortunately, tears come from joy: it's the generation that will remember those years in which we cried with Federer. And him with us, as he already said to his fans after the final: "You make me nervous."

This coming, of course, from a worldwide idol who still is excited every time he rediscovers himself and isn't afraid to show the emotions via tears. Paradoxical for someone who loves the pure joy of the sport? Perhaps not: the healing and revitalizing power of tears is well known. And in 2018, for millions of fans, there was no greater joy than to imagine themselves crying alongside Roger Federer for many more years.

• • • •

Paul Dorochenko is a name that means nothing to the majority of tennis fans, but the man is qualified to talk about Federer more than most. Born in Algeria, Dorochenko is an osteopath, physical therapist, and physical trainer, although many prefer to call him a tennis "guru." His specialty is the study of laterality.

Laterality? Dorochenko explains it: "In tennis, the hand-eye relationship is the decisive factor; it's how we classify players as homogenous, if the dominant eye and hand are on the same side of the body, or crossed, if the dominant eye and hand are on different sides. In addition to saying a player is right- or left-handed, we can distinguish between right-handed homogenous and crossed, and between left-handed homogenous and crossed."

Both Federer and Nadal are "crossed": in the case of the Swiss, the right hand and left eye are dominant; in the Spaniard, the left hand and the right eye.

"Both of them also have a natural right and struggle with the backhand."

What does it mean that both the Rs are "crossed"?

"'Crossed' individuals tend to be poorly disciplined, inconsistent, and exhibitionist, but also more creative, intuitive, and better at making decisions. On the other hand, homogeneous players are hard-working, ordered, analytical, and cerebral, but pressure takes a greater toll on them and affects them negatively when it comes to decision-making."

Poorly disciplined, inconsistent, and exhibitionist . . . Who would say that about Nadal and Federer? For the Swiss, there are reasons in his past you might say that. For Nadal, never.

Dorochenko emphasizes that seven of every ten tennis players in the top 100 in the world are "crossed." "If we think about it, it's not a coincidence, since their best stroke is also the one they perform the most, and they also are better suited to handle the pressure of competition."

Laterality was not Dorochenko's professional focus when, in the '90s, he first crossed paths with Federer—a Federer that few people now remember.

"In the three years I worked with him, he burnt me out. He threw games away, broke racquets, and was not punctual. . . . He touched me every ten minutes to provoke me. And I used to be a boxer; I came pretty close to hitting him."

"One day I got a very good offer from Sergi Bruguera to live in Barcelona. Young Federer had burned me out so much that I left him and went with Bruguera. I never thought Federer would get where he is now."

Dorochenko remembers something that, two decades later, now seems prophetic.

"In '98, Federer told me he was inventing the tennis of the year 2000: he played me volleying from the back of the court, a tennis ping pong like he showed in 2017 in Australia. And he beat me playing with the left hand."

So much youthful arrogance from the Swiss doesn't mean that Dorochenko and Federer don't get along. In fact, their friendship remains frozen in time sometime in the late '90s. "Every time I run into him, he says 'Meehh', like a sheep. It's as if we're still the young kids we were two decades ago."

Dorochenko has studied Federer closely and cites three reasons that he overcame his youthful disrespect and irresponsibility to become one of the greatest athletes of all time.

"One reason is that [soon afterward] he started to work with a sports psychologist. The other, is that Nike forced him to play a role: if Agassi was the pirate and Nadal the bullfighter, Federer should be the gentleman of tennis, with impeccable conduct on and off the court. The third reason is Mirka, who changed him completely. She's ambitious; she likes power and money. She created a bubble around Federer, and is totally loyal to him. Federer doesn't like to change things.

"When we talk about his natural talent, it's true but it's not the whole truth. Roger is very natural because he has a vision quality and superior coordination, but it's a product of hard work as well. He lifts a lot of weights in the gym, more than one hundred kilograms on the bench press. He's strong, quick, flexible, and resilient.

"They ask me, also, about players comparable to Federer. I would have mentioned Sampras and Dimitrov, who have an exact same laterality. But Dimitrov doesn't have Federer's head, and Sampras is less complete."

Dorochenko agrees with Wilander that Federer's backhand is in a much higher dimension than it was for most of his career. "Because Ljubicic gave him a parallel backhand that he never had; Federer, before, pushed the ball when he hit the backhand. Now he hits it fully, same as the right."

And, without knowing what the Swede had said, he repeats Wilander's theory: "Federer's victory in Australia 2017 changed the history of tennis. If Nadal had won, Federer would not have won Indian Wells or Miami."

Dorochenko sums up that incredible 2017 very efficiently: "Federer and Nadal had similar physical problems and they both came back at the highest level at the same time. Remarkable!"

The "guru" from Algeria is convinced that the Swiss is a lucky man: "[H]e had some luck in his career. Those who were giving him problems, like Agassi, [Marat] Safin, and [David] Nalbandian, left the circuit quickly, and [David] Ferrer and [Nikolay] Davydenko couldn't beat him; you could say that in his early career, Federer took advantage of a gap in the tennis world."

But that's the past, and what matters is the future. "If Roger takes care of himself physically, I see him playing until he's forty. He could surpass 20 Grand Slams. He doesn't smoke; he doesn't drink; he takes care of himself."

And then, Dorochenko makes his most controversial claim: the Grand Slams won by Nadal are worth more than Federer's.

"I think Nadal is stronger than Federer, because he came into a tremendous generation. To win his sixteen Grand Slams he's had to fight against some incredible players. His sixteen are worth more than Federer's twenty. His record is more complete, and he's dominated Federer enormously, in a way no one else has."

What can happen to Federer when he retires?

"I don't see him starting an academy like Nadal did. I see him in tennis in the political sphere, maybe president of the International Tennis Federation or the ATP, which is like his second home. His advantage is he speaks perfect English."

CHAPTER 30

Eternals

IT'S INEVITABLE FOR A CERTAIN icy feeling to run down your backbone when Serena Williams stabs you with her eyes, and maintains contact for a few seconds with the implication that she wants to kill you. Figuratively, of course. And that's how we all felt during the early dawn of February 1, 2015, hoping for a break from the murderous gaze of the top player in the world. A couple of hours earlier, Serena had won her sixth Australian Open and her nineteenth Grand Slam title. She was tired and happy, but the question caught her off guard. Just for a few seconds, it's true, because the younger Williams sister has a successful future in front of cameras on the day she hangs up her racket. Serena reacted with all the presence of a star.

"I don't know whether to answer you or kill you," said the gaze that, fortunately, we journalists get to see every once in a while. Without it, everything would be much more boring. We were eight reporters with a few minutes alone with her after the multitudinous postmatch press conference, and the younger of the two Williams tennis stars wanted to be absolutely clear. "I am definitely not better than Roger. There's not even the slightest chance." The numbers could contest that statement of Serena's. Since she and Federer won Wimbledon in 2012, the American has added another nine Grand Slam titles, compared to

Federer's three. Federer has twenty of the Majors, Serena three more, surpassing the record of twenty-two held by the German, Steffi Graf (statistics through May 2018). To the American, it doesn't make any sense for them to be compared. "He's a great player, a great champion. He made a great effort; I know that he was injured for a while and came back playing his best tennis. He played a couple of finals, he's been playing really, really well, so I think he'll win another Grand Slam very soon."

But nineteen against seventeen, why is it clear that he's so much better? Serena Williams dissolved the fierce glare and turned it into a lightly sardonic smile before giving the most American answer, the statistic that sealed the discussion for her, "I think he's already won $83 million. I think I'm at $64 million, or something like that . . . Well, $67 million after today." And she laughed, even though she was being serious.

The concept of "living history" is very much overused, but it's not a terrible way to describe those two men leaning against a white wall who, during a night full of tension and expectations, are chatting without being disturbed. Leaning on that white wall in Melbourne are the holders of twenty-seven Grand Slam titles, the fourteen of Pete Sampras and the eleven of Rod Laver. They seem calm, but they aren't. That night of January 26, 2014, is special, because Rafael Nadal has the serious potential of winning his second title in Australia, adding his fourteenth Grand Slam, and going after something that no one had achieved since Laver last did it in 1969: with this Grand Slam, conquering all four of the great tennis tournaments in the same season.

It wasn't the first conversation between Laver and Sampras that weekend. They had both seen each other the day before during a reunion of tennis legends. The presence of the Sampras, however, was unusual in Australia. He travels very little since he retired and is almost never seen in the great tournaments. The former number one doesn't indicate any possibility of repeating that memorable photo in which Sampras, Laver, and Björn Borg surround Roger Federer in 2009 after the Swiss player's seventh title at Wimbledon.

Laver and Sampras talk. The Australian has been an older gentleman for a while now, his face somewhat ruddy, but in his tailored suit and wearing a matching tie he maintains the demeanor and elegance of someone who was very good at what he did. Sampras is much younger, and is as awkwardly dressed as he was in his days as a player. He's also wearing a suit, but no tie. Being elegant was never something he worried much about. A few feet away from them, on the wall facing them in the stadium hallway, ten flat-screen television monitors were ready to broadcast the final of that Australian Open, which would end in surprise and drama: Stanislas Wawrinka the champion and Rafael Nadal betrayed by his back. But an hour before the match, anything seemed possible. Even that Australia would become just the first of the four steps on Nadal's way to the Grand Slam. After all, the Spaniard was coming from a very notable 2013.

The Grand Slam is a rarity in tennis, almost impossible to achieve. Donald Budge did it in 1938, Laver in 1962 and 1969. And that was it. Fred Perry, Roy Emerson, Andre Agassi, Federer, and Nadal are the other players who have won each of the four greats at least once, but never in the same season, something which was achieved in the women's circuit by Maureen Connolly, Margaret Court, and Steffi Graf.

Sampras interrupted his conversation with Laver for one moment to listen to the question, *"Everyone talks about the record of seventeen Grand Slams, but, beyond that, do you think Nadal is capable of conquering the Grand Slam this year, the four greats in the same season?"* The former number one answered by entrenching himself in the history. "The stars would have to align, even though he has won on every surface. I understand that he is still a bit vulnerable in Wimbledon. If he measures up against the wrong rival in one of the first rounds, when the courts are faster, it could be hard for him. Anything is possible, but I don't see it as being probable." The following months proved he was right.

Laver, for his part, opted for humor. "Well, one never knows. What is true, though, is that if he wins here, he has a chance." After the laughter, the Australian got a bit more serious, "He's won all of them in the past, why shouldn't he be capable of bringing them all together?

But you have to be in good physical form, you have to have the luck of a favorable draw. That always plays a role. But if you play your best tennis, that's what usually prevails. You can't be injured, that is one thing: I was lucky enough to achieve it and not be injured at all." So, is it possible? Yes and no. "It's possible and it's hard because there're competitors. It's very competitive out there."

History is something that is taken very seriously in tennis, and for those who were there to experience different eras, the debate over who is the best of all time can be irritating. It happened to Gianni Clerici, an Italian journalist born in 1930 who played Wimbledon in 1953. An authorized journalist at more than 170 Grand Slam tournaments, Clerici is one of the glories of tennis journalism. As the owner of a refined sense of humor and the appearance of an old gentleman who meanders through his mansion on Lake Como, Clerici enjoys unsettling anyone who approaches him. And if that person is famous and powerful, all the better.

He did this at the Fiesta del Tenis, an event that is organized every April in the Monte Carlo tournament. The Hall of Fame was honoring the Romanian Năstase, the Frenchman Françoise Dürr, the Italian Nicola Pietrangeli, and Clerici. The person in charge of delivering the rings chosen as awards was prince Alberto of Monaco. When Clerici received his own, he took the microphone and used his strongly Italian-accented English to leave both the leader of the princedom and many of the attendants, including Rafael Nadal, open-mouthed. "I have a ring from a prince. I feel like Cinderella!" But Cleric wasn't always so humorous. The venerable journalist and writer can also go beyond vehemence if he is angered. It happened during that same week, and on the receiving end of the explosion was Björn Borg. The Swede appeared on television saying that Nadal is the greatest player of all time of tennis on clay courts. Clerici exploded and yelled at the television, "What foolishness! I can't go on listening. Have they never seen Bill Tilden play?"

History sometimes arrives to personally defend itself against the inevitable ignorance of the youngest. So it was for the Australian Darren

Cahill with Neale Fraser, the legendary captain of his country's Davis Cup team for twenty-three years. It is often said that tennis was born in France and was made big in England, but there may be no country in which it is more alive than in Australia. There is a combination there of history, passion, and genuine sportsmanship that exists in no other country. Cahill made his countrymen laugh when he recalled his first steps in the Davis Cup as a young tennis player. "They told us that we would be sparring partners, but they didn't tell us we would be slaves," he said in 2015 during a brilliant speech in homage to Fraser, champion of Wimbledon and the United States Open. "Bring me that ball, bring me water, take this bag, return those serves . . . It was exhausting!"

Next to him, Pat Cash, Roy Emerson, John Alexander, Rod Laver, and Fraser himself were laughing. And then Cahill told *the* anecdote of the day. "Both Pat and I have a background in Australian rules football, not in tennis. We knew who Rod Laver, Roy Emerson, and Ken Rosewall were. But really, I had never heard anything about Neale Fraser. So when I arrived on the Davis team and he mentioned Rod Laver, I asked him if he really knew him. He looked at me and . . . 'I played against Rod Laver,' he said. 'Yeah, yeah, *yeah*, sure, ha, ha, ha . . .' I said. A while later I got an invitation to a barbecue at his home. 'I'm here! I made it,' I told myself. 'Fraser invited me to a barbecue at his home, I'm part of the team!' I got there at five in the afternoon and there was no one there. He sat me down in a chair and played a VHS of the Wimbledon final in 1960. 'Wow, that's Rod Laver!' I said. Laver easily won the first game. But the rival won the next. 'Who's that?' I asked him. 'That's me,' he said. 'Naaahhh . . .' I answered. I didn't believe him. He didn't say anything. When the Fraser on the television was about to win the final, the Fraser in front of me knelt down and made the same gesture that would show up on the television. I could not believe it."

The Frenchman Guy Forget, owner of a hit-and-run style of tennis during his years as a player, laughs when he's asked whether he would say that Nadal and Federer are better than Laver was. "It's funny, because some months ago we had that discussion at the Davis Cup with Jo-Wilfried Tsonga. Jo was telling me that Sampras played well, but with his style of playing he wouldn't be able to win many tournaments today. I was trying to explain how good Sampras was on cement and turf when he was playing at his best. But I suppose it's always like that when you're young; you think your players are better than those ten years before."

It's clear that trying to define who was the best tennis player of all time is a question that is as close to impossible to answer as it is fun to debate. The duel between Roger Federer and Rafael Nadal contained every possible contrast: right-handed against left-handed, Swiss-German against Hispanic, offensive game against baseline game, refinement and detail against power and physical deployment. But the question is, how do you decide who was the best? If it's through titles, then by June 2016—with Djokovic pushing hard and already owner of twelve Grand Slams—Federer had seventeen Grand Slams and was greater. Nadal, with fourteen, has an opportunity to catch up and maybe even surpass the Swiss player. But both Federer and Nadal have said time and time again that they do care about all the titles, and every once in a while they remember Laver's two-time achievement of conquering the Grand Slam.

On top of that, Laver was away from the circuit for six years, sanctioned for having turned professional. Nadal has asked the question in public more than once: how many Grand Slam titles would Laver have if he had been able to play during all those years in which he didn't have the option to challenge the greats? History shows that he won eleven, but if he had won just one each season during which he watched the Grand Slams from the outside, he would have seventeen, like Federer. Or more, because thinking that he would only win one per year is to underestimate Laver's game.

The truth is that Laver could have easily been the greatest. And you shouldn't forget Bill Tilden, as Clerici would say, along with several others with enough credentials to be able to fight for a spot on the podium. What there is no doubt of, however, is that Nadal and Federer are motivated by the fight for a place in history, their obvious incentive during the later years of their careers. The Spaniard, whose habitual quips include "I'm not going to lie to you"—although he once proved otherwise at a Roland Garros when he prefaced a statement with, "I'll only lie to you a little bit"—tends to deny that climbing the steps towards the peak of history is on his mind. But it is. "History: I always say that it doesn't matter to me, but of course it matters," he confessed to Juan José Mateo, of the Spanish newspaper *El País*, not long after conquering his tenth Grand Slam event. "The thing is that I also hardly ever have time to explain it, because the next day I'll be playing another competition. Of course history matters to me. Of course I care about having the same number of Grand Slam titles as Borg. Of course I want to be one of the players with the most Grand Slams. Of course it matters to me. I love the sport, and history is what makes the sport. You have to be humble, but you don't have to be foolish as well. With ten titles, are you among the greatest in history? Well, yes. It is a great personal achievement."

The debate over who is the best of all time is not a favorite of the former Spanish tennis player, Àlex Corretja, at one time number two in the world, Masters champion, and two times defeated in the Roland Garros final. "If we only look at the Grand Slams, I'm not sure that makes sense. I feel that there are players who have won a Grand Slam, who I wouldn't trade careers with. Federer has six Masters. Having won six Masters has to be a very valuable achievement for Federer," Corretja explains on a cold and rainy November afternoon in the Sant Cugat Golf Club on the outskirts of Barcelona.

A former Davis Cup captain and television commentator, Corretja is a keen observer of his sport. He's convinced that trying to define the best of all time doesn't make any sense, and doing so by just looking at Grand Slam titles even less so. "What are you measuring? The seventeen Grand Slams and the six Masters, the Davis Cup, the three hundred and something weeks as number one? If we just take the Grand Slams, we're wrong, even though it's true that when they retire they'll be comparing who has won the most Grand Slams, because those are the tournaments with the most weight and power.

"It's absurd to even consider . . . Who was the best, Maradona or Pelé? Why choose one if you've had them both? Enjoy them both. I'm not saying that there should be no debate, but it seems to be a bit more external than internal.

"Being qualified as the best in history is of course personally important. I won't say otherwise, of course anyone would like that. But I don't think the debate is feasible. And if they tie in the number of Grand Slams, then who's better? Do Federer's Masters count for more, or do Nadal's Olympic gold and four Davis Cups? Or the number of weeks as number one?"

Corretja also has a very clear opinion about one of the arguments used by the "Nadalians" to assert that their player is better than Federer: the clear advantage that the Spaniard has over the Swiss player when looking at the numbers from their personal encounters. "I don't think that's true," says Corretja convincingly. "There are different styles of play that can go better or worse. I beat Sampras on turf and at the Masters. Are you going to compare my career against Sampras's? That's a topic about systems of play. Nadal's system of play is the worst that Federer could go up against."

Corretja's explanation is very interesting; it comes from the point of view of someone who knows them both very well, because he faced them on the court and followed them afterward from outside it. "Federer doesn't lose against Nadal because he's worse than Nadal. He loses against Nadal because he does poorly against Nadal's system of play." This brings up the memory of all the times that Federer lamented the fact that Nadal is left-handed. What if Nadal had been right-handed? The decision had been more or less up to his uncle Toni. "It's such a ridiculous argument . . . He's left-handed, period! That's like saying what would have happened if Messi had been right-handed. He's just not right-handed."

Corretja returns to the topic that he wants to clear up: why Nadal's system of play is the worst one that Federer could be up against. First point: "Everything that Federer does to damage his rivals only does half the damage to Rafa." Second point: "The system that Rafa uses to do the most damage to his rivals is the system that most damages Federer. And the system Federer uses to do the most damage to his rivals is the one that does the least damage to Rafa."

Corretja describes several classic situations in Federer's game and why they don't affect Nadal:

- Federer dominates his rivals with his forehand and inverts it, from the inside out, to attack the backhand and get them out of the court. "The shot goes towards Rafa's right, no problem for him."
- Federer attacks his rival's backhand with a slice. "That's to Rafa's right, it barely makes him blink."
- Federer's second serve, which tends to be sharp and high. "It presents no problem for Rafa."
- Federer dominating first with a crosscourt forehand and following up down the line. "The shot goes to of Rafa's forehand, who is a great pusher."

In addition to how much Nadal's game unsettles Federer—and it's not just because he's left-handed but also because he hits the ball with that tremendous top and height that only he can create—there is another factor that Corretja mentions: Nadal has the perfect game for disarming Federer. "If he shoots two or three crosscourt backhands, he knows he's dead. By the third forehand he's been put out of place and forced out of the court. Federer never dominates Rafa." This, though, changed dramatically in the 2017 season, when Federer won the four times he faced Nadal, showing new skills and weapons to make Corretja's analysis partially out of date. Tennis, once again, showed one of its best sides: the unpredictability.

Martina Navrátilová suggested something once at Wimbledon that sounded like a provocation. If Federer had a two-handed backhand, he would win more. The American stood by that during the interview in front of the mirror. "Yes, he would beat Nadal more often. It wouldn't matter with others, but Nadal is who it would really damage. You could also think that if Nadal were right-handed, he wouldn't do so much damage. The fact is that to counter Nadal's forehand, Federer needs to hit the ball with both hands."

Things would be easier for Federer against a right-handed Nadal, and harder for the Spaniard, Navrátilová sums up before adding an aside, "I think that Nadal would still win most of his matches due to his top spin, anyway. The top spin is what most bothers Federer, on top of which is the fact that Nadal is left-handed. It's a combination of the two things."

Goran Ivanišević brings up two names in order to explain why the quantity of Grand Slam titles should not be used to answer the debate about the best in history: Björn Borg and Rod Laver. "Let's go back. Borg retired at the age of twenty-six with eleven Grand Slam titles. He never played the Australian Open, never won the US Open. And think about Laver, six years outside of the circuit, and he won the Grand Slam two times, the only player in history to do that. Six years outside, impossible to know how many more he would have won."

"Laver says that the best tennis player in history doesn't exist. Is he right?" Nadal is clearheaded during that ride in the van on the way to Manhattan, and he doesn't hesitate to answer. You can tell it's a topic he's thought about: "Beyond whether or not they exist, that fact is that it's hard to make an objective assessment or comparison, because every era is completely different. I always say the same thing. To me, Federer is the best in history that I've seen. Because of records and his skills at tennis. It's complicated to talk about who the best in history is, because Laver has obviously conquered the Grand Slam on two occasions and he spent several years without playing."

Laver is the only man to have ever done this, but on that afternoon in Australia when we sat down to chat he talks so modestly that you might think that he won much less than he actually did. "When I completed the Grand Slam in Forest Hills, the old home of the US Open, in 1962, there were ten or twelve journalists there, and no more. And of the things I can clearly remember is that, when I left the court, I was greeted by Donald Budge, who conquered the Grand Slam in 1938 and wanted to shake my hand." Budge's words to Laver were perfect, "You're in an exclusive club now."

Nadal, Corretja, and Ivanišević all agree on my asking the question of Laver what he could have done during those years in which he couldn't play Grand Slam tournaments, keeping in mind that the Australian conquered the Grand Slam twice. "Did he ever think about how many Grand Slam titles he would have won if he hadn't been out between 1963 and 1968? I'm sure he did . . ." Laver's response confirms that he is truly great; he diminishes his own achievement, lowers its importance. "During '62 the best players, Gonzales, Rosewall, Hoad, were professionals, so they couldn't play. That's why the one in 1969 was grandiose. I became professional in 1963."

"How many more would you have won?" "I was out for five years, twenty tournaments that I couldn't play in because I chose to be professional. Nobody made me do that, it was an economic decision, because you don't make money as an amateur. And as a professional you went around the world and might win a thousand dollars. So, when I look back and ask myself if I made myself a professional for the money, the answer is that I wanted to measure up against the best in the world: Rosewall, Gonzales, Buchholz, MacKay, Davies. That whole group. I became a professional to play with them, and also for the money."

Some years before that conversation in Melbourne in 2009, Laver gave a press conference in Wimbledon. He became fully involved in the debate about history and did not do so timidly. "If Roger wins sixteen or seventeen Grand Slams, the media would start to ask if he is the best of all time. Maybe there are people who don't know who Bill Tilden was. Was he the best of all time?"

Tilden, an American, dominated tennis during the '20s and '30s of the last century, while Laver was *the* player of the '60s. "Who's the best of all time at boxing? I don't think anyone knows. What matters is the era. You're the best of your era. To me, that is already high praise."

In the game of guessing, playing the game of "what would have happened if," Laver makes one thing clear: Federer was very close to conquering the Grand Slam. He only ran into one small problem: "Winning three of the four greats was easy for him. But Nadal showed up. Without Rafa, Federer would have conquered the Grand Slam."

If you can't accurately define just who is the best of all time, then maybe it's worth looking at history in a different light. Maybe it makes more sense for the greatest players to dream of the best story of all time. And then share that dream.

The scenario is a bit unusual, but simple enough. Imagine that the end of the world is coming but that you still have the chance to put together one tennis match that has never been played before nor never even considered. You'll decide; you'll give shape to the match of all matches, and then calmly enjoy it while everything else comes to an end.

Unusual or not, Cliff Drysdale likes the idea, and he doesn't select either of the two "R"s for that match. "I would like to see Djokovic against Laver. Djokovic is currently the best player, and Laver was the best during my time."

He also likes the Bulgarian Grigor Dimitrov, who will be called upon as the leader of skillful and refined tennis the day that Federer retires. Dimitrov says he is content to share his era with Federer, Nadal, and Djokovic, but his reaction shows that his interest really doesn't lie in admiring another; he wants to be the participant. "Probably Novak at Wimbledon and Rafa in the Australia 2014 final." *"But then they wouldn't be playing each other, so what kind of match would it be?"* the journalist asks the Bulgarian. "No! It's me. I want to play against them in those two matches."

Another man of the future, the Australian Nick Kyrgios, begs off before the question. "No, man, no, it's too hard! Too hard for me, there are too many options." *"Do you admire Rod Laver?"* The intent was to help him, but Kyrgios had already found his stellar protagonist: the Frenchman Gaël Monfils. "Monfils is my favorite player. If he's in good shape, no matter where he plays it's always the most fun; he puts on the best show. Watching him play against anyone is fun. A Monfils-Federer, for example." Gianni Clerici and Guy Forget might enjoy a conversation with Kyrgios.

The Czech Tomas Berdych is like Dimitrov. If it is an end-of-the-world match, he wants to play. "It might be a little selfish, but I would play against Sampras because he's a player that left tennis when I was just starting out." Carlos Moyá doesn't need to think too much. "I would like to see Kuerten at his best against Nadal. For curiosity's sake. Kuerten, before Nadal showed up, was the best on turf courts for the past ten or fifteen years. I think Rafa would win, but I would like to see how Kuerten would save those high balls. He had one of the best one-handed backhands on clay courts."

Moyá gave his answer on a hot afternoon in January in Australia. Ten months later, on a cold November in 2014 in Catalonia, Corretja said nearly the exact same thing as Moyá, the friend who deprived him of the title at the Roland Garros final in 1998, and whom he beat to reach his greatest achievement at the Masters that same year. "I would love to know what would have happened with Kuerten and Rafa, both of them in their prime at Roland Garros. It would be really dramatic. I do think that Rafa is on top because of what he's achieved, because the mobility of his legs is more explosive and he would have cornered him, Guga, in his prime, had a lot of shots."

The Swiss players suggest different scenarios when it comes to the end-of-the-world concept with just enough time for tennis. "Would Nadal win at Wimbledon on the old turf from fifteen years ago, which was devilishly fast? Would he win if you pitted him against Greg Rusedski, Goran Ivanišević, or Sampras? I'd like to know, I don't think he would win. I would like to know the answer to that."

While he would still be interested, Marco Chiudinelli still would not choose to watch his friend Roger in a match if it were his last afternoon on Earth. "I'd like to see a Nadal-Djokovic. That final they played in 2011 at the US Open, or the one at the Australian Open in 2012, were tremendous. I think that is the sum of everything tennis has to offer." Martina Hingis thinks otherwise. "A Federer-Nadal, it's the best there's ever been."

The Croatian Ivanišević, the same one whom Rosset wanted to see against Nadal at Wimbledon, makes a small snort, "Ufff!" It's not easy for him to decide, that's why he says he would choose between two matches, maybe three. "I would want to see a Djokov-Sampras; I would like to see how Sampras plays against him, without rhythm. And then an Agassi-Nadal, a Sampras-Nadal. On clay, Agassi wouldn't stand a chance. So we'll put him on turf, but the turf of the '90s, not today's," he says in agreement with Rosset. "My turf," adds the 2011 Wimbledon champion.

Guy Forget also thinks the question is a very difficult one. "Could I pick four players?" Granted his request, he goes on to describe an afternoon before the end of the world that wouldn't be too bad at all. "I'd like to see McEnroe against Federer on a hard court, and Rafa Nadal against Pete Sampras on hard court or turf. I'd really enjoy watching the four in the prime of their game."

Another Frenchman, Fabrice Santoro, is excited by the question. "I'd want to see a McEnroe-Federer at the US Open and during a night game." *Why?* "Because McEnroe was the player whose photo I had on my bedroom wall when I was a kid. And Roger, because I have great memories of him. Everyone dreams of playing tennis like him."

Navrátilová also has a clear answer: She wants to see Laver play. "Laver against any of these boys. A Laver-Sampras, for example, would be a great match. And are we talking just about the men or also the women?" When the American confirms that she is indeed free to make use of a female time tunnel, she dives in enthusiastically: "I would like to measure myself against Alice Marble, Suzanne Lenglen, Helen Wills Moody, and Margaret Court with her in her prime and me in mine." "Ah! I would also want to watch Bill Tilden against any of these guys," she adds.

"And if you have to choose just one match, Martina?" "Just one? A Laver-Federer. Laver would win on fast surfaces. Federer would on a slower one." The nine-time Wimbledon champion smiles when she's told that Chris Evert, her historic rival, would spend her last afternoon before the end of the world watching a Navrátilová versus Serena Williams. "How sweet! I'd love to face off against Serena."

Chris Evert had indeed chosen a Serena-Navrátilová as an end-of-the-world match. And what would you be, the chair umpire? "I would be the ball girl," she responded jokingly. "And from the men I would choose a match between the best Federer and the best Sampras." *Why?* "Because I think those four players I chose are the best of all time."

Stan Smith, who was a Wimbledon and US Open champion towards the start of the '70s, has his name on a model of tennis shoes that is still valued by lovers of everything vintage. He doesn't need even two seconds to imagine his perfect end-of-the-world match. "I would want to see a Borg-Nadal in the French Open. They're the best two players on clay courts of all time. And Borg was incredibly fast, Nadal is incredibly fast. Borg would hit with a very good spin. The rackets were different, there's that. If you played with wooden rackets, Borg would win. Nadal would win with modern rackets. And in a Laver-Federer, Federer would win; he has a slightly stronger serve. Although, of course, Laver would respond to Federer's backhand with a slice, which would be like Federer was playing Nadal. It would be a tough match for Federer. A very interesting match, let me tell you."

Mats Wilander doesn't just know what the match would be; he also knows the results he would expect. "I'd like to see Roger Federer defeating Rafa Nadal in the French Open final. There would be my all-time best match." Wilander isn't put off by the comment that that particular match never ended with Federer victorious. "It didn't happen, but it would still be my dream, because that match, in terms of tactics, is the best match I could imagine. It would be because of everything that Federer would have to do to beat Nadal on clay. His choice and execution of shots would have to be perfect. And even if his tactics and execution were perfect, he would barely win, 6–4, in the last set."

Boris Becker doesn't hesitate; if you're talking about a great tennis match before the end of everything, best to have a match that's familiar. "One of my own, of course. What I would really like to see is my second Wimbledon title."

Björn Borg is also clear about what his perfect match before calamity would be. "I never missed a match between Nadal and Federer, maybe just one or two of the ones they played. They each force the other to give their best. That's the kind of tennis that you want to see, not just as a spectator but as a former player. I like to see how they go into it, the tactics, how they can give it their all."

Ken Rosewall asks for permission before answering. "And could I play in that match?" With permission granted, the Australian confesses, "I was always a fan of Federer, so I'd like to see myself playing against him." Rosewall, additionally, would like to win, although he knows it would be difficult. "I would have to choose the day, the surface, and count on a lot of things being in my favor." He thinks about it again and gives up, "I think that he would probably win." *On any surface?* "Yeah, Yeah. I think so."

Rosewall was Laver's great historic rival, and he believes that rivalries are what make tennis great. The Nadal-Federer fascinates Laver, but when it comes to the last match before the end of the world, he opts for a duel of great potential and only one chapter in reality: Sampras versus Federer. "It would be a great challenge," says a dreamy-eyed Laver, who, like everyone else, only saw one clash between those two greats: the 7–6 (9–7), 5–7, 6–4, 6–7 (2–7) and 7–5, in which the Swiss eliminated the American during the fourth round of Wimbledon 2001. That was Federer's launching match, his great card of introduction to the world. "If both of them were at their best, Sampras with that serve and that forehand, and Federer with his well-rounded game, you'd have to ask: *What would happen in that match? Who would win? Could Federer dominate that serve and return it? Could he challenge that forehand?*" Three years before, at Wimbledon, Laver had already answered that question: "Sampras would win. Simply because of his great serve."

Pete Sampras remembers the Borg-McEnroes, and even the clashes against Andre Agassi. But at the end he opts for what many consider to be the best match of all time, "The match between Rafa and Roger at Wimbledon, when it was getting dark. It was passionate."

Novak Djokovic, who in 2016 was already clearly threatening the historic supremacy of the two "R"s, is amused by the question. He laughs, "Just to watch or also to play? If I could choose both options, I would love the idea of a match with a half-clay and half-turf court, like Roger and Rafa already played once. I would make it half clay and half turf, and I would play against Rafa." *And if you were just a spectator?* "I would want to watch a Nadal-Borg. That would be fun."

During that same week, Nadal is asked the same question in Monte Carlo. It's the end of an interview, and the Spaniard's first reaction is uncomfortable. "Uff . . . I have no idea, man." But a second later he changes his mind. "I would choose to play, not watch, because ultimately I love to play and I love the feeling of complicated matches. There are many great champions, but after all we've been through together, I would play against Federer."

The question is presented to Federer in 2014 during the Paris Autumn. His choice is different from Nadal's and Sampras's; he would rather see his trainer (at the time) in a final that never was. "It would be Edberg against someone . . . probably against Sampras at Wimbledon, simply because he was my idol when I was growing up and I would love to see them play again on the Wimbledon central court." Edberg defeated Sampras during two Grand Slam finals, but never measured up against the American on grass, where Federer and Nadal played what was perhaps the most epic final in history.

Federer then hears that, on the last day before the end of the world, Sampras would want to watch a Nadal-Federer, and that the Spaniard would also want him on the other side of the net just before the Armageddon. His reaction, as Navrátilová would say, is notably "Swiss." "Interesting . . . it is maybe because we have a great contrast of style and personalities which make up for great matches."

ACKNOWLEDGMENTS

THIS BOOK GAINED PAGES IN my houses in Madrid and Buenos Aires, but most of all in cafes, bars, and local joints in different cities all over the world.

I took refuge in the HD, La Realidad, and, quite especially, the Federal in Madrid. In Buenos Aires I owe a "thank you" to Helena, as well as Slices, De Clieu, Arcadia, Sonidos, and The Wilde in Melbourne. Thanks to Mariano Andrade's home, several localities in the West Village in New York provided the focus that often can't be found at one's own home, and which I also found at the home of my friend Laura in Hamburg, on a key day during the final stretch of writing.

Thank you to Florencia Cambariere, editor for the original Spanish version, who supplied a good portion of whatever my readers may find attractive in these pages. Big thanks also to Julie Ganz, my patient and sharp editor for this English version.

I must also acknowledge also my then-leaders in DPA, who gave me the ability to travel and write in this book. In addition, and very especially, my friends at the editing table and the correspondents during those years I shared with them. A good part of the statements and interviews described in these pages are a product of my work during all those years in the agency, although, to avoid being redundant, I only mentioned sources as an exception.

Thanks to my many colleagues and friends in Madrid, Buenos Aires, Mallorca, Zúrich, and París, who either read these pages and warned me of necessary corrections, or who supplied ideas, information, or even photographs.

Thanks to the International Tennis Hall of Fame in Newport, Rhode Island, for helping over the course of an entire day to go over material in their library for this book. And a special mention for my editor, Florencia Cambariere, who supplied a good portion of whatever my readers may find attractive in these pages.

Thanks to Javier Martínez, journalist for *El Mundo* and the author of a tennis blog called *Sin Red*. As the original book edition was about to go to press with a title confusingly similar to his blog, and we were alerted by Oscar Fornet of the involuntary coincidence, I asked Javier if he would rather we changed it. Javier reacted like the friend he is.

Stephanie Myles, from Montreal, contributed to the transcription of dozens of interviews with her perfect English and her tennis wisdom.

Also, a thanks from my heart to my mother, Margarita, always an avid reader of my writing, and my two brothers, Dominique and Leandro, and my whole family and so many friends with whom I spoke, probably too much, about this book.

And a sincere thanks to my partners during the years that this project took. No one, not even they, are immune to so many trips and hours of writing.

Madrid and Buenos Aires, May 2016